Other Books from Shuvu Banim International:

One in a Generation Volume 1: From Haifa to Uman
The Official Biography of Rabbi Eliezer Berland

One in a Generation Volume 2: Into Exile
The Official Biography of Rabbi Eliezer Berland

Rabbi Eliezer Berland's Advice

Rabbi Eliezer Berland's Prayers

Rabbi Eliezer Berland's Conversations

Rabbi Berland's Miracles

Rabbi Eliezer Berland's Passover Haggada

Rabbi Eliezer Berland
on the Parsha

"Know: By way of the Torah, all prayers and supplications that we supplicate and pray are accepted, and the favour and prestige of Israel is elevated and exalted before all those [in whose eyes the Jewish people's favour and prestige are] needed, both in spiritual and material matters."

- Rebbe Nachman of Breslov, 1:1 Likutei Moharan

CONTENTS

ACKNOWLEDGMENTS

We would like to thank the authors of the Tzama Nafshi newsletter; and *Eish Moharan*; and the Shuvubonim.org website for their help and contributions in putting this volume of Rabbi Eliezer Berland's teachings on the Parshah together.

On a technical note, you can find all the italicized Hebrew terms in the glossary of terms at the back of the book.

Completed in Jerusalem with Hashem's help on Marcheshvan 19, 5780 (November 17, 2019).

Bereshit

LUMINARIES OF FIRE

The Gemara in Tractate Zevachim teaches that the sacrifices of lesser holiness, such as the peace offering, the offering of the firstborn and the thanksgiving offering, can only be sacrificed and eaten at a time when the altar in the Temple is in existence, even when there is no longer a *Mishkan (sanctuary)*.

In other words, the altar alone is sufficient to enable these sacrifices to be brought. The fact that there was a *Mishkan* is enough to permit the eating of *kadoshim kalim* - the sacrifices of lesser holiness. According to one opinion, even the most holy offerings, the *kodshei kodashim,* are permitted to be eaten, as long as the altar exists.

The gravesite of Rabbi Nachman of Breslov has the status of the altar. Even though we have no *Mishkan*, still, the altar we do have. It even has the status of the *Kadosh Kadoshim* - the Holy of Holies - the chamber in the Temple where the *Aron Hakodesh* was kept, which only the *Kohen Gadol* was allowed to enter once a year, on Yom Kippur.

Whenever someone visits the gravesite of Rabbenu, it is as if he is entering the *Kadosh Kadoshim*. Rav Natan brings in *Likutey Halachos*, that wearing a white *kittel* on *Rosh Hashanah* is from the aspect of the *Kohen Gadol* entering the Holy of Holies on Yom Kippur, when he also had to wear white garments. The Temple has the same numerical value as *Rosh Hashanah*. Here we are, already meriting to enter the Holy of Holies on Rosh Hashanah, ten days before Yom Kippur!

The gravesite of Rabbenu is from the aspect of *"aish tamid tukad al haMizbeach, lo tichbe"* (a fire which is kept burning eternally on the altar, never to go out). The fire of Rabbenu has not been extinguished now for over two hundred years since his passing. The *Tzaddik* is such a powerful fire that it cancels out all other fires. It even outshines the light of the sun. The heat of the sun is a few million watts, but the gravesite of Rabbenu is such a fire that even billions of kilowatts would be insignificant beside it.

The *Midrash Rabbah* teaches that the light that shone from the heel of Adam canceled out the light of the sun. As the Zohar in *Parshas Kedoshim* states, Adam had no connection to this world whatsoever, so much so, that a unity took place in the Upper Worlds and produced a body whose light was brighter than all the angels and the heavenly bodies.

Adam and Chava (Eve) were created through a unification of *Zer anpin* and *Nukva* in the world of *Briah*. Their birth was in the world of *Yetzira*, and they had no connection to this world, the world of *Asiyah*. The Garden of Eden was in the world of *Yetzira*. Adam and Chava were two luminaries in the world of *Yetzira*, Adam the sun and Chava the moon, and at their creation they blotted out the light of the sun and the moon in the world of *Asiyah*. The sun and the moon were ashamed before the light of Adam and Chava, similar to a candle in the daylight that is indiscernible against the light of the sun, so it was as if no light shone from the sun and the moon at all.

After this, the snake came and fooled Adam and Chava with all kinds of cunning teachings: "*If you eat from the tree you will be just like Hashem! You'll be able to create just as He did, and you know how all creators hate their rivals...*" The snake told them that they would be able to create worlds, and they listened to him and ate. If only they had waited another three hours until Shabbos came in, they would have been able to eat safely, for then everything would have been allowed. But they fell into temptation, and their light became darkened.

Every Jew is a flame, but a person has to be so careful not to allow his light to turn into a flame of desire - of chasing after the pleasures of this world, instead of filling his life with serving Hashem by performing the *mitzvos* and earning his place in the world to come.

The truth is that all the desires and lusts of this world are just foolishness. If a person would stop and think about what exactly it is that he's devoting so much time to chasing after, he would abandon it completely and not give it another thought. It happens sometimes that a person gets tested. The Kotsker Rebbe said that all such tests only last for five minutes. All you have to do is to be strong, and hold on for five minutes, and the test is over. A person gives up because he does not know his own strength.

When a person comes to the gravesite of Rabbenu, who is the flame that forever burns on the altar, all his flames of desire are canceled out by the flame of Rabbenu. In fact, all the *Tzaddikim* are fire, they all shine like the sun. The *Zohar Chadash* in *Parshat Bereshit* explains that the verse, "*veyiten autam elokim berakia hashamayim lehair al haaretz,*" (and Hashem placed them in the heavens to shine on the earth) is referring to Moshe, Aharon and Miriam. Meaning that Hashem hung their souls in the heavens, so that they would be able to light up the world.

They see everything that is happening in the world and they are able to exert their influence as they see fit. The *Baal HaTurim* says on *Parshat Chaye Sarah*, "*vehayu chaye sarah meah shanah*" (the life of Sarah was a hundred years) that the initial letters of each word spell out the word *shemesh*, the sun, meaning that Sarah shone as brightly as the sun.

The *Midrash Rabbah* on *Parshat Lech Lecha* relates that when Avraham came down to Egypt, he hid Sarah in a chest because he was scared that the Egyptians would kidnap her. When he came to the customs, the officers asked him to open the box. He told them that he didn't want to open it, and that he was willing to pay them whatever they asked for, by way of taxes, not to be forced to have to open it.

They said, "Perhaps it's filled with silver?" He told them, "I will pay you as much silver as you want." They said, "Maybe, it's filled with gold?" He told them, "I will pay you as much gold as you want." They said, "Maybe, it's filled with diamonds?" He said, "I will give you as many diamonds as you want."

By this time, the Egyptians were totally suspicious and forced him to open the box. The Midrash relates that when he opened the chest, a light shone out from it, from Sarah, and lit up the whole of Egypt. They had arrived in Egypt at midnight, and the light from her shone out as though it was the middle of the day.

The Zohar says on *Parshat Chayei Sarah* that when Avraham brought Sarah to bury her in the cave at Machpela, Chava jumped up out of her grave, and started to run away out of embarrassment, because of Sarah's light. So then Sarah had to run after her and convince her to return, by telling her that this light would also shine from her. The whole cave of Machpela is a fire, Adam and Chava, Avraham and Sarah, Yitzchak and Rivka, Yaakov and Leah, they are all fire.

ADVICE ON SHALOM BAYIS

A man needs to tell his wife: *"You are my Neshama, you are my 'kaparah' (my forgiveness), I am your 'kaparah' (your forgiveness)."*

A person needs to always speak words of praise to his wife. The Zohar says that each person should tell his wife that all women are like monkeys in comparison to her. He should never say to her that some other woman is better than her for some reason, because right away it will lead to a divorce. It's better that a man gives his wife a divorce, rather than telling her that another woman is better than her.

Every woman has something unique about her. That's why the Zohar in Bereshit says that every person should say to his wife, *"you are the best woman in the world, you are the most wonderful woman in the world, there's no other woman like you."* This is what a man needs to say to his wife day and night, to say this a hundred times a day, every time he comes home. If he comes home in the afternoon, or in the evening, or when he comes back after *Shacharis*, right away to tell her, *"you are the most wonderful woman, the best woman, your food is the tastiest food in the world, only you know how to cook, there is no such food like this in the world."*

A man always needs to give his wife praise. If not, he shouldn't come home at all, he should just divorce her right now! If he doesn't know how to say a good word, then he should just get divorced. He should give her a *get* (*divorce document*) and she can then go find another husband who will speak to her with kind words.

If you don't know how to say a kind word you should just get divorced. You have to always know how to tell your wife kind words, only words of encouragement.

It says in the Parsha, *"and the man said, this time, this is the bones of my bones and the flesh of my flesh"* (Bereshit 2:23). You are my flesh, you are my soul, you are part of me, we are one *Shidduch*. This is the best *Shidduch* in the world. Always to tell her that this was the best *Shidduch*. Sometimes, a woman says that maybe you made a mistake. You should respond to her, 'I made no mistake, I got the best *Shidduch* that could be'.

"You are a bone from my bones, you are flesh from my flesh." Where in the world do we find such words of praise? All the writers and libraries and books that people write about *Shalom Bayis*, about love between a man and his wife, there is no such book which writes such words of praise.

The Zohar says, there are no such words of praise like what the Torah writes about a wife, "*this time, this is the bones of my bones and the flesh of my flesh*". You are my own self, you are my soul, it's impossible to separate between us, we will never separate. This is what you have to say a hundred times a day, *you are the bones of my bones and the flesh of my flesh.*

Even if the wife says something, some negative word, you should just ignore it, don't take it to heart, and don't answer back. A woman always wants to say whatever she feels like, but for a husband it is forbidden. Only words of praise.

'You are the only woman in the world', this what you always have to tell to your wife.

It is forbidden to say that there are better women, more successful women, 'look, have you seen how successful this one is etc.' You simply have to always say, '*You are the most successful, you are the most wonderful, you are the most unique, what you do, no one else can do, the food that you make no one else can make, you are the best cook in the whole world.*'

The verse says, "*and this he called a wife*" (Bereshit 2:23). A man should tell his wife, '*the term 'wife' was created only for you, only you, there is none like you, there's no other like you to be found, there was never like you and there will never be like you, you are the most precious to me, there is no person in the world who is precious to me like you, you are the most precious of all women.*'

And this is what we said at the beginning, '*all women are like monkeys compared to you*', this is what you have to tell her, '*you should know that all women in my eyes are like monkeys, I don't see a woman at all, I don't see any other woman other than you. All women are like monkeys in my eyes, really, like monkeys, and you are the epitome of perfection.*'

You should never tell her, '*you're not perfect, you are like 'this' or like 'that', you need to perfect yourself a bit more, you need to get a bit more advice.*'

6

You should tell her, *'you are the most perfect woman, everyone should come to get counselling from you, you are the best counsellor, you don't need any counselling.'*

A woman doesn't need any counselling, she knows what she needs to do. It's just from time to time, when her husband angers her, he has to suffer the consequences. You angered her, so you have to pay for it, you don't even know at all that you angered her, you forgot, and because of that you're confused and you don't even know at all how all this started.

So you should always tell her, *"You are 'perfection', you don't need any counselling, you can be the one who counsels others, you're the most successful woman in the world, besides you there is no other successful woman, there isn't, there just isn't, you are the 'perfection of all women'. You are the perfection and no other.* To express this clearly, *'only you and no other',* so she shouldn't think that maybe there's another perfect woman, maybe there are two perfect women in the world, perhaps three perfect women?

No! There aren't three perfect, and there aren't two perfect women. There is only one perfect woman! Only my wife. There is only one perfect woman!

It all depends on the husband. If he will be gentle, and speak nicely, and he doesn't come home stressed. You should always come home with a present, with some pizza, with something, falafel… He should come home with something.

He should come with a sweet or a delicacy. They should sit together. He should always come with something. One time he should come with ice cream, one time with pizza, and they should sit together and speak a bit. They should tell a few stories, with patience, not with nervousness, not with *'I'm in a rush'*.

When a person comes home, he shouldn't be in a rush. He shouldn't have anything other than his wife in his mind. The moment he comes home there isn't anything in the world other than his wife. Nothing. Nothing else exists. The world is dead, the world stopped, the world stopped running, suddenly time stopped, *'you are the perfection of everything! Only you! Only you, there is no other!'*

NOACH

NOACH COULD HAVE BROUGHT MOSHIACH

In the story by Rabbi Nachman, "The Prince of Gems", the king, who had no children, issued a decree that the Jews should pray that he should have children. In the time of the Turkish rule in Israel, whenever the rain didn't come soon enough, the Turks used to make all the Jews go to the graves of the *Tzaddikim* to pray for rain.

Similarly, throughout the ages the nations always knew that there was a very good chance to make something happen by making the Jews pray for it. The story of the Prince of Gems continues that the Jews searched for, and found, a hidden *Tzaddik*, who the King then ordered to pray for him. The *Tzaddik* promised him that he would have a child. The Queen then gave birth to a daughter.

The child was exceptionally beautiful and by the age of four she knew all types of wisdom. She could play musical instruments and she knew different languages. The daughter represents the forces of evil. The force of evil always precedes the power of good. As we see, the husk grows before the fruit, *Eretz Canaan* before *Eretz Israel*, '*Tohu veVohu*' before the creation of the world, etc.

The story continues that still, the King yearned for a son. So, he told the Jews to pray for him again. They searched for the *Tzaddik* that had succeeded last time but they could not find him because he had died. A *Tzaddik* who is supposed to be hidden, but who then becomes revealed, is placed in great danger. He has to remain completely hidden.

When the *Tzaddikim* perform miracles, either they have to pray very much that they will be forgotten, or that someone will come and argue against them, and sweeten the harsh judgments against them.

9

The story continues how the Jews found another *Tzaddik* to pray for the King, who then went on to have a son who later turned out to be made completely of precious gems.

We have up until Chanukah to pray to sweeten the judgments passed on Rosh Hashanah. Chanukah is the final sealing of the judgment. The word Chanukah contains within it the letters of the name Chana. Also, the number of days between the end of *Succ*ot and Chanukah is the numerical value of the name Chana.

Chana prayed very much, until she was worthy of giving birth to the prophet Shmuel. He was on such a level that he merited to anoint two Kings. King Shaul was the aspect of Moshiach ben Yosef, and King David was the aspect of Moshiach ben David. If King Shaul had only waited, and not performed the sacrifices too early, he would have been Moshiach ben Yosef, and David HaMelech would then have been able to remain completely hidden, as Moshiach ben David, and that would have been the situation up until the Revival of the Dead.

David HaMelech had no connection at all to this word, he really should have remained hidden, as he said about himself, "*Libi chalal bekirbi*" (my heart is an empty void inside me).

The final redemption could also have come at the time of Noach. Hashem originally wanted to give Noach the privilege of bringing the Moshiach ben David, after he had suffered so much in the Ark. The Zohar explains that the olive branch bought by the dove came directly from Gan Eden and carried with it the soul of Moshiach ben David.

But, Noach also failed the test. He had been given a vine shoot, also from Gan Eden. He should have planted pear trees and apple trees, grains, etc., first when he came out of the Ark. However, instead, he first planted the vine and drink its wine. He shouldn't have planted the vine first, which is only for pleasure. This should have been left till last.

The Vilna Gaon was asked why he never slept on Shabbos; surely it is one of the Shabbos pleasures! The Gaon answered that he tried to distance himself from all the pleasures of this world, even when it was a *mitzvah*, even from Gan Eden. Noach, because he fell into desire, lost the opportunity to bring Moshiach ben David, who would have been born as his fourth son.

And if one has to be careful to distance oneself from pleasures that are permitted, how much more must one distance oneself from those which are forbidden! And to guard the eyes, not to see forbidden sights, i.e. that which is indecent and immodest. When the 'breaking of the vessels' occurred, the holy sparks exploded out and were scattered throughout the world, especially in the streets and all the filthy places, and became covered in terrible *klipos* (evil husks.)

One who seals his eyes hermetically and does not look at the *klipos*, through this, he rescues the holy sparks and they return in repentance. These sparks beg a person not to look at them and thereby to free them. One who does look at them, adds even more *klipos* to them, and to himself also. But, when he manages not to look, he merits to see the *Or HaGanuz*, the hidden light with which Hashem created the world.

MAKE A LIGHT FOR THE ARK

In *Likutey Moharan* (I:9), the Rebbe said on *Parshat Noach*, "*When a person sees that he can't pray and he can't learn, and the darkness and the klipos surround him...*" he should "*make a light for the Ark*". Start to be an honest person! The speech should emerge from your mouth with truth. "*Through this, Hashem will be a light, as in 'Hashem is my light and my salvation'.*"

A person has to escape from his sleep. A person sees that his mind is blocked up, so he goes to sleep. Your mind is sleeping? You should go out to the fields! Scream to Hashem that He should open your mind!

Therefore, David said, "*I called out to You from the depths Hashem*" (*Tehillim* 130). Everyone is caught in the depths. The Rebbe said, 'It was also hard for me to pray. It was also hard for me to learn. I cried and screamed to Hashem.'

A person can study mathematics and physics, but finds that he just can't learn Gemara. He can still learn; after all the mind is a physical mind, it's an animal mind. But when it comes to something spiritual- -the Gemara is spiritual--then it's the very opposite (of the physical mind). So, it's this (learning Gemara) that overturns the control by the body.

If a person sees that he can't learn and he can't pray, then he should pray about that fact itself. He should scream about that fact itself. He should cry out to Hashem in truth, from the depths of his heart. True cries from the depths of his heart. This saves him from the darkness, which is an aspect of, "*And you shall place an opening in the side of the Ark.*"

Place an opening in the side of the Ark. When you are in the darkness, break through it. Doing this will make millions and millions of people come and repent. For people only repent through the letters of the prayers and the letters of the Torah. "*I called out to You from the depths, Hashem.*" Meaning, because of the intensity of the forces surrounding a person on all sides, he turns to truth and calls out to Hashem--in truth, from the depths of his heart.

A person needs to know first of all, that the foundation of the Rebbe's teachings is truth. The main point of the Rebbe's teachings is the point of truth. It isn't eating, and it isn't drinking. All that the Rebbe wants is this point of truth! He doesn't want politics, nor anything else.

When a person doesn't feel good, he starts to cry out to Hashem. This saves them from the darkness, as it says, *"You shall put an opening in the side of the Ark."* And when a person cries to Hashem, then millions of other people repent too. With every letter of prayer, people repent and call out to Hashem in truth from the depths of their heart.

LECH-LECHA

THE SOURCE OF TRUE WISDOM

"Go forth from your land, from your birthplace and from the house of your fathers, to the land that I will show you... and your name will be glorified."

*"And **your name** will be glorified"* – this hints to the study of *Shas*, because the words *"your name"* have a numerical value of 360, and *Shas* also has the numerical value of 360.

We need to know that if a man doesn't study Shas, he has nothing. He doesn't have a *tzelem elokim* (*the image of God*). We're not even talking about being a human being. A man's whole name, his whole essence, is built from the study of Shas. The whole person – it comes only from the Shas he's studied!

And this is what Hashem promised to Avraham Avinu, *"and **your name** will be glorified"*, meaning that his descendants should be busy learning Torah and studying Shas, and should only be called 'simple', as it's written: *"Praiseworthy are the simple [ones], who go in the way of Hashem's Torah"* (Psalm 119).

Simplicity occurs only when a person learns Shas. The Rebbe brought down in Lesson 1 of Likutey Moharan: *"know, that by way of the Torah, all the prayers and requests are accepted. When we make requests and pray, then the grace and the importance of Israel will rise up and be revealed...both spiritually and materially."*

Our prayers and requests are only accepted by way of Torah. Whenever a person sees that his prayers aren't being answered, it's because he's not learning enough Shas. All the grace and the importance of Israel depends upon the study of Shas, because the Torah is called a 'beloved woman, gracious woman', that gives grace to its study.

The Torah really gives grace to a person. When he goes home after meriting to learn Torah, he's full of grace. His wife will see that he has grace and charm and that the Shechina dwells on him and there will be happiness in that home.

But, if he goes home without any Torah and without any grace, he goes home broken or aggravated. Then, there's no happiness in a home like that.

And now, because of our many sins, the grace and the importance of Israel has fallen. Today, the essence of importance is found by the nations of the world, and by the evildoers, and this is only because of one reason--that we aren't studying enough Shas!

"For a Jewish man always needs to study the intelligence contained in everything, and to connect himself to the wisdom and the intelligence that exists within everything, in order to be enlightened by the intelligence that is contained in every thing, because intelligence is a huge light that will illuminate his every path." (*Likutey Moharan* 1:1)

True intelligence is only to be found in the study of Shas. Besides this, there is no other intelligence in the whole world. Intelligence is the only thing that illuminates a person and directs him. A person needs to make sure that his intelligence lights him up and goes with him.

A person's whole work is only to expand his intelligence. According to how much he expands his intelligence and his study of Shas, that's how much he builds the *Beis HaMikdash*. If we want to rebuild the *Beis HaMikdash*, and to hasten the redemption, we need to expand our intelligence and to expand our *da'at* (spiritual knowledge). As our Sages taught, *"everyone who possesses da'at, it's as though the Beis Hamikdash was built in his days."*

According to how much a person expands his *da'at* and intelligence, that's how much he builds the *Beis HaMikdash*. The *Beis HaMikdash* hasn't yet been rebuilt, only because we aren't learning Shas with proper concentration and plumbing its depths.

Today, if we want to build our own *Bayit* (home/Temple), the only way this is going to happen is by learning Shas. The moment someone learns Shas, the *Sitra Achra* (dark side) falls. The *Chesed L'Avraham* says that there are ten masks covering the mind, ten *husks* over the mind, and that each of us needs to remove these *husks*, to clean them away. This only occurs by way of studying Shas with the proper concentration and plumbing its depths.

A person has *apikorsus*, heresy in his heart; he doesn't believe that Hashem is really standing in front of him at every second. Whenever a person can't concentrate on his prayers, and doesn't feel that Hashem is standing before him, this is because he has heresy in his heart, and he doesn't believe that Hashem really exists.

Hashem is *chai v'kiyam!* (alive and exists). He's present here, in front of us, and we don't feel Him. This shows us that we don't have an intellect, we don't have a mind. When a person can't feel Hashem and can't concentrate on his prayers, it's only because he lacks an intellect. It's like those illnesses when people lose their intellect and can't even recognize their own parents. This is also how it is for a person who doesn't have an intellect.

He doesn't have any Torah, so he can't recognize his own father. If a person could somehow arrange an 'intellect' transplant for himself... but they still don't know how to do a brain transplant.

Rabbenu tells us that we only receive an intellect, we only get a brain, by way of studying Shas in depth, and learning Torah. When we learn Torah, we merit to nullify the heresy that's in our hearts and to really feel Hashem. Then we also merit to have importance and that our prayers and requests should be accepted.

VAYEIRA

LIKE THE LIGHT OF THE SUN

The Zohar asks, it's written in verse 14 of Parshat Vayeira "*and the Egyptians saw the woman*". And in verse 15, it's written again, "*and Pharaoh's ministers saw her*". Why are there two mentions of the word "*vayeira*" (they saw)? Why do we need such a long discussion about this? They saw, and then another time, they saw again.

But the Zohar tells us something awesome: when Avraham Avinu came to Egypt, the Egyptians told him to open the chest that Sarah was hidden in. We want to see what you've really got in there; we want to see what you're hiding.

When Avraham opened the chest, a huge light shone out of it, a light akin to the sun at midday. Twelve midnight suddenly became twelve noon. Hashem '*took the sun out of its sheath*'.

Sarah Imenu looked like the sun. All the Egyptians were suddenly set ablaze by Sarah's light, there was light throughout the whole of Egypt. The Egyptians thought that the Avraham had some sort of patented device in the chest, some type of electronics, some sort of spell, some sort of hidden lazer beams, some sort of diamond that was giving out all that light.

They didn't want to believe that Sarah was the one who was giving off all that light. They said, '*What? A person can shine so brightly?!*' They didn't want to believe that this sort of light could shine out of a person. The chest shone with a different light. They thought that there was some sort of different light inside the chest. It was impossible to believe this light was coming from Sarah. '*Maybe, there's some sort of hidden lazer beam here, that's shining out?*'

And so, they decided to properly examine the chest. They took Sarah out of it, and they started to check with all of their gadgets, to see where the light was really coming from; where were the hidden lazer beams that were lighting up the whole of Egypt?

It's written that 'the Egyptians' saw the woman. Why isn't it written that 'Pharaoh's ministers' saw the woman? Rather, we can learn from here that her light shone throughout the whole of Egypt.

They realized then that the light wasn't coming from the chest. They saw that it was coming from Sarah. That's why it's written *'vayeira'* (they saw) twice. They took Sarah out the chest, then put her back in a few times, and checked around the chest to see where the light was coming from.

'Maybe, there's some sort of diamond, some sort of hidden lazer beam, that's lighting everything up?'

After they'd thoroughly checked out the chest a few times, they saw that this massive light really was shining out of Sarah. Sarah merited to remove her spiritually-impure body, to take off the skin of the snake, and so she shone like the sun!

The *Baal HaTurim* comments on Parshas Chaye Sarah, on the verse, "*vayihu chaya Sarah meah shana*" (and the years of Sarah were 100 years), that the first letters spell out the word 'SheMeSh' (sun)! Sarah was truly a sun. If a person wants to remove the garments of their body, and to get out of all their evil illusions, to transform this body, this body of 'leprous skin' to a pure body from *Gan Eden*, and to merit to shine like the sun, this can only be accomplished by way of learning Torah.

The Rebbe [Rebbe Nachman] tells us in *Likutey Moharan*, Lesson 101: a person is governed by 70 bad character traits and only by learning Torah, and learning the Gemara, is it possible for him to escape from these bad traits. Only this is what's called 'taking upon oneself the yoke of Torah'.

Only the Torah can transform a person's body.... It's full of jealousy, full of hatred, full of *ayin hara* (the evil eye), forbidden sights, forbidden thoughts. It's only learning Gemara, learning the Torah in depth, that can transform a person's body. Only when he merits to get a 'shining face' [a kabbalistic term] will he be able to destroy all the bad traits and lusts.

A person is fighting against his bad traits and his lusts all the time. He doesn't realize that he can only escape from them if he learns Torah.

IN THE HEAT OF THE DAY

On that day, when Avraham Avinu went out to look for guests, Hashem took the sun out of its sheath, which meant it was so hot that no one was able to leave their home. It was the fire of *Gehinnom*! No one went outside. The only person who went out was Avraham Avinu. It was virtual suicide. He was the only one who ran outside looking for guests that day.

The Torah is telling us about Avraham Avinu's fulfilment of the *mitzvah* of welcoming guests for a specific reason. After all, what actually happened here? Avraham Avinu just gave them some bread and water? What's so special about that? Hospitality exists everywhere in the world. Any house in the desert welcomes guests. But Avraham Avinu is another matter altogether. By him, it was a matter of *mesirus nefesh* (self sacrifice)!

It's not for nothing that the Torah relates that it was the third day after Avraham's *bris* milah. Not only was he feeling weak, but Hashem had even taken the sun out of its sheath. The Torah is telling us that Avraham Avinu preformed the *mitzvah* of hospitality with complete *mesirus nefesh*, under the most difficult possible conditions.

Rabbenu said, *"the love of Hashem needs to drive a person to do crazy things in order to perform His mitzvos and do His will. One must be willing to get covered in mud and muck in order to serve Hashem and to do His mitzvos"* (*Likutei Moharan* 2:5). The Rebbe is teaching us that we need to have *mesirus nefesh* for each and every *mitzvah*, even if it means rolling around in mud and filth. We are required to fulfill each and every *mitzvah* with *mesirus nefesh* – even for the crown of the letter yud.

A person needs to sacrifice his soul to do each thing that is the will of Hashem Yisborach. One is forbidden to pass up any *mitzvah*, unless someone is literally standing there threatening you with a gun to your head. The Rebbe himself lay down in the muck and mire for every *mitzvah*.

When Yosef Ha*Tzaddik* went to look for his brothers, he did so with *mesirus nefesh*: "It is my brothers whom I am seeking" (Bereshit 37:16). He knew that they intended to kill him. He knew that he had nothing to protect him. He knew that they were going to throw him into the pit. He knew everything! Nothing was hidden from him. He simply said, "I need to have *mesirus nefesh* for each and every *mitzvah*."

During the time when the Greeks ruled over the land of Israel, the Jews had *mesirus nefesh* for each and every *mitzvah*, even the rabbinic *mitzvos*. They gave their sons a *bris*, waved lulavim, and kept *Shabbos* even though, because of the circumstances, they were actually exempt! They had *mesirus nefesh* for each and every *mitzvah*. In parshas Vayishlach, the Midrash HaGadol comments on the verse, *"the generation of those who seek Him, those who strive for Your presence [the nation of] Yaakov, Selah"* (Tehillim 24:6) and asks, 'who counts as *"the generation of those who seek Him"*?' Who is seeking Hashem? Who wants Hashem? Who is willing to have *mesirus nefesh* for Hashem? Are we this generation that seeks Him? All we do is spend our whole day eating and drinking, almost without pause! We don't stop eating and drinking for a minute. Can this be described as *"seeking Him"*? Rather, the Midrash HaGadol says, only people who have *mesirus nefesh* for each and every *mitzvah* are called, *"the generation of those who seek Him, those who strive for Your presence [the nation of] Yaakov, Selah."*

Tzaddikim cried over each and every *mitzvah*. How many tears did the Kloisenberger Rebbe shed over every *mitzvah*? He cried so much that he shouldn't fail to keep any *mitzvah*, even while he was in the death camps! He literally shed rivers of tears that he shouldn't have to desecrate *Shabbos* or eat non-kosher food. There is a story about him that one day he arrived back at the camp and it was almost empty. From 6,000 people, there remained only 2,000. Just as he arrived at the camp, the announcement was made that they would be distributing food. He didn't take any of the food. Instead, he immediately went into a shack at the edge of the camp and started shedding rivers of tears. He burst out in a bitter cry and said, "I don't want to be defiled by their food!" Suddenly, someone called him and said, "There is someone calling you to come outside." He went out and saw an elderly Jew standing there holding out to him a loaf of bread and a saucer of jam, and he said to him, "Here, you can eat from this." The Kloisenberger Rebbe said, "I immediately realized it was a miracle. It was then that I understood that Hashem was watching over me, that Hashem was with me." Also by Rabbenu HaKadosh, everything only came to him after tremendous effort and suffering.

Every person needs to have *mesirus nefesh*, to struggle and to overcome the obstacles. If your Torah study wasn't successful, don't just say 'that's it' and walk away. 'I'll go and drink a cup of tea, or go take a nap'. On the contrary, if your *chevruta* didn't show up, then go to his house and drag him out! If a person doesn't have *mesirus nefesh* to go and learn Torah, then this is not *Chassidus*! It's not Breslov! It's nothing more than laziness! Are you greater than the Rebbe? You think you should have it easier than he did? There is no such thing as someone having an easy life! If it's easy, then it's from the *Sitra Achra*. Therefore, each of us needs to have *mesirus nefesh* for each and every *mitzvah*, and in fact, for everything which is holy.

LIKE A LAMB TO THE SLAUGHTER

The moment Avraham took Yitzhak to the *Akeida*, the *Satan* didn't know what to do. How could he cancel this *Akeida*? Yitzhak went happily to the *Akeida*, for the sake of heaven. The *Satan* knew that the moment Yitzhak was placed on the altar, he (the *Satan*) would have to surrender control for all the generations. So, he tried all kinds of tricks to prevent the *Akeida*. He changed himself into a river, etc., as explained in the Midrash. But, he was totally unsuccessful.

So, the *Satan* said to Yitzhak, 'I heard from behind the *Curtain* that the lamb is destined to be the sacrifice, not you. It's only a big show that you appear to be going to let yourself be slaughtered. They may be taking you to the *Akeida*, but it won't happen in the end. I'm telling you, there will be no *Akeida*! Rather, a lamb will be the offering.' And then Yitzhak screamed, 'Father, what are we doing? Where is the lamb for the offering? Am I being offered to Hashem? Will I be a complete offering for Hashem, or will I only be the *shelamim*[1]? How will you sacrifice me?'

Yitzhak was afraid the whole time that Avraham would find

---

[1] A *shelamim* offering is one which is partly offered up to G-d, and partly eaten by the owner and the *Kohanim*. Here, Yitztchak is saying he wanted to be completely offered up to Hashem (like an *'olah'* offering).

22

some lamb on the way and he would sacrifice the lamb as an 'olah' (an elevation) offering, and he would simply be offered as the *shelamim*--a lesser offering. Because, if he was already going to be sacrificed, he wanted to be the holiest offering. Then Avraham Avinu said to him, "*Hashem will seek out for himself the lamb for the offering, my son.*" [The Midrash teaches that Yitzhak understood from this reply that he himself would be the sacrificial lamb.]

Forget about the *Satan*! Don't pay attention to anything that he told you! We're going to the *Akeida* to sanctify His name - literally! Go with simple and straightforward thoughts, that you're truly going to be the *Akeida*. You have nothing to worry about. You will always be the holiest of the sacrifices, the elevation offering to Hashem. You are completely G-dly.

So, that's why when a person starts the prayer service, he must say the portion of the *Akeida*. It is forbidden to ever skip the section of the *Akeida*. As it says in *Seder HaYom*, whoever merits saying the *parshah* of the *Akeida*, merits being saved from all suffering on that day. Because through the *Akeidas* Yitzhak, all the judgments are sweetened until the end of all the generations. One must read the *Akeida* every day! Since there are new judgments every day, we need to sweeten them afresh every day. This can only be done through reading out loud the portion of the *Akeida*. A person absolutely must say the *Akeida* without skipping it, ever! For whoever says the *Akeida*, it's promised that he will not suffer any damage on that day, and he will merit sweetening all the harsh judgments.

CHAYEI SARAH

THE HIDDEN TREASURE WITHIN YOU

"Avraham bowed to the people of the land and said, 'please give me the cave which is at the end of Efron's field, for full value I will purchase it, so that I may bury my dead'. Efron answered, 'no, my Master, listen, may the field be yours, and the cave which is in it, take it! Bury your dead!' Avraham bowed and said, 'please, take this money, so I may bury my dead there'..." (Bereshit 23).

Efron had a wondrous treasure in his backyard, *Me'arat HaMachpela (the Cave of Machpela)*. He had Adam and Chava (Eve) whose dazzling light shone from one end of the world to the other. But to him, *Me'arat HaMachpela* was just darkness and gloom, an utterly pitch black darkness. Since Adam and Chava were buried in this cave, Hashem made sure that the people would have a terrible fear of the cave, including all kinds of illusions that it harbored demons and ghosts. People were full of dread at the thought of even drawing near to the place. It was in such a remote spot on the slope of a mountain that no one dared to want to buy it, so clearly Efron knew he was cheating Avraham Avinu when he sold him the cave.

Rav Natan explains that the holiest place, the holiest *Tzaddik*, or anywhere where there is holiness, always seems like a place of darkness and gloom, surrounded by demons and evil spirits. As it's written, *"the more holy a person is than his friend, the emptier he seems"*.

'Efron' has the numerical value of 400, which is the same numerical value as the 'evil eye'--the opposite of a 'good eye'. So, Efron saw only darkness and gloom in the *Me'arat HaMachpela*, but David HaMelech had a good eye, about whom it is written, *"beautiful eyes and lovely to behold"*. He saw only the light in every Jew, only the good points in every Jew, the holy spark in every Jew.

A person usually sees his own light, but he doesn't see the light of others, neither his friends nor even his family at home. Sometimes, a person sees the light of his wife, but she doesn't see the light of her husband. Or it could be the reverse: a woman sees the light of her husband and he doesn't see her light. But in truth, each person needs to see the light of others, because it's very bad for a person to see the other's weaknesses, the other's flaws. The essence of a bad eye is when a person can't stand seeing that his friend is succeeding more than he is, or when he feels that he is better than his friend.

A person is quick to notice if his friend learns more or prays more than he does. But why should he care if his friend is praying better than he is or learning better than he is? Everyone has a bad eye and no one is ready to accept that someone else is better. If a person was able to accept that someone was better, he would be able to live forever; he would be able to fix the entire world!

A good eye is something altogether different. If a person wouldn't be jealous of others, would love others, would be happy with the success of others, then he would have the eyes of the true *Tzaddik*, who has a completely good eye. This is David HaMelech who has *"beautiful eyes and is lovely to behold"*. He is completely focused on the good and doesn't wish bad on anyone.

Each person has countless treasures. He only needs to remove the materialism that covers them - to escape from the *spiritual husk* of Efron, from the bad eye. In every man, in every woman, in every Jewish soul there are unlimited treasures. The Jewish soul is blazing and burning for Hashem. Every Jewish soul wants to do *teshuva*! Every Jew has a heart that is on fire for Hashem, a blazing heart that could burn up the entire world. Every Jew has a fiery flame inside, *"the everlasting fire shall burn on the altar, it shall never be extinguished."*

Every single Jew can bring the whole world back in *teshuva*, even the greatest sinner can make *teshuva*, because to the extent that he can be bad, so too does he have the power to be good – it just means that he has a bigger soul.

This is what is related in the Midrash about Yosi Misita, who was a heretic. He denied everything and went and joined the Romans. Whoever kept *Shabbos*, whoever gave his child a *bris* at that time was crucified. He saw that the nation of Israel was lost, about to be erased from the earth, and so he gave up and said, "Why do I need to be a Jew? I'll be a Roman instead." So he went along with them to burn the Beis *HaMikdash*, threw torches with them, and before the Beis HaMikdash had finished burning the Romans said to him, "Wait one minute! Who will go into the sanctuary to get the menorah?" So, they told him to go inside and take something from there. Everyone knew that anyone who would go into the sanctuary would be burned alive. Whoever would go into the *Kadosh Kadoshim* would be burned alive. Everyone was afraid to enter, so they told him, "Whatever you bring out first is yours to keep."

Yosi Misita went in grabbed the golden menorah and came out with it, and they said to him, "Give us that menorah! You can't take it, it's too valuable. Take some goblet, some spoon, but not the menorah!" At that moment his Jewish spark ignited. Suddenly, his spark was awakened. The menorah lit up his inner spark, and he saw that the menorah was completely made up of light. So he held on to the menorah and said, "This menorah you are not going to get. You are not going to get the menorah." They said to him, "What do you mean we're not going to get the menorah? It's not yours! It's the king's! We need to bring Titus the menorah." He told them, "You will not get this menorah under any circumstances, I will die together with it!"

And then he was completely aflame, completely on fire for Hashem. "I am returning to Judaism! I will start being a Jew." Cut me into bits!" They said, "OK", and grabbed him and put him on a carpenter's table which was used for cutting wood and began cutting into him, chopping him up. The minute they began cutting him up, he felt pleasure. Each time they sawed into him he felt such pleasure, he was full of joy and exhilaration, and he said, "I take upon myself all this suffering with love! Master of the world! It is good that they are chopping me apart, it's good that they are cutting me. Forgive me for all my sins! How did I join the Romans who killed millions of Jews? How can it be that I didn't realize that the nation of Israel is eternal? Baruch Hashem, they're sawing into these rotten bones, these poisoned bones that led me astray. They led me to where they led me, and Yosi Mesita is now a dedicated servant of Hashem, completely happy while they are cutting me apart, and he is still singing and doesn't feel any pain--a servant singing, 'my soul is sick with love for You.' They are chopping him apart and he is sick with love for Hashem. He only feels Hashem, he feels nothing but Hashem!"

TOLDOT

THE SECRET HIDDEN IN THE HEEL OF ESAV

The work of the *Tzaddikim* is to extract the sparks that have been swallowed up by the *Sitra Achra*, and that are now hidden within the *klipos* and the evildoers. This is what was written about Yaakov Avinu, *"and his hand was grasping the heel of* Esav*"* – even whilst he was in his mother's womb, he'd started trying to draw out the soul of Rabbi Akiva which had been swallowed up into Esav's heel.

This is also why Esav asked Yitzhak 'how do we tithe straw?' and 'how do we tithe salt?' (Rashi 26:27). Since when would we expect an Esav to ask 'how do we tithe straw?' Or 'how do we tithe salt?'

The Baal Shem Tov says that this hints to the soul of Rabbi Akiva that was hidden in Esav's heel, and that this is what caused Esav to start asking all these questions about Jewish law.

Every time a wicked person says something good, it's only because the soul of a *Tzaddik* has somehow been aroused inside of him. It's written (in Tractate Nedarim 50a) about Rabbi Akiva and his wife that they didn't have any pillows or bedding, and that they used to sleep on straw.

When Eliyahu Hanavi came to them disguised as a poor person, Rabbi Akiva gave him some straw…We see from here that Esav only asked about how to tithe straw because the soul of Rabbi Akiva became aroused within him, and that's what caused him to ask these questions.

Because Rabbi Akiva was the only one who tithed [i.e. donated] straw.

Yaakov's work was to extract the souls from Esav's heel. The souls of converts had been swallowed into there, the biggest souls, and the greatest time to raise these souls up is at *chatzos* (halachic midnight). As Rebbe Pinchas of Koretz said, "There are such big souls, the biggest souls in the world, who have fallen from *Igra Rama* to *Bira Amikta;* they've fallen into the deepest depths of the *klipos.* And when the time comes around to say the *Tikkun chatzos,* then we raise up the biggest souls that have descended to these places, and with each and every letter, we raise up another soul and another soul."

This is like King David, who was the biggest soul, and who was *dafka* 'extracted' from Sdom [1], and rescued from the most awful things.

The *Tikkun chatzos* (midnight lamentation) is the hardest thing to do, because it's in the middle of the night. Some people want to be learning at that time; 'if I woke up already, let me at least learn some Gemara! What?! I should always just repeat the same chapters?! The same verses?! The same sections of *Tehillim*?!'

People think that the daily prayers they recite today are exactly the same ones they said yesterday, and that's why they don't have any strength for them. They want to say something new! But really, getting up for *chatzos* is what builds the new day. This is what renews a person!

The more a person can begin his day at an early hour, and can start with *Tikkun chatzos* and then continue on from there, filling his morning with prayers that he recites word by word, and letter by letter, with *niggunim* and songs – this is how he'll build a new stage of life for himself, and how he'll rescue *Am Yisrael* from all the difficult decrees.

This is what Rebbe Pinchas of Koretz taught, "only if a person recites the *Tikkun chatzos* word by word, and letter by letter, will he raise up all the souls throughout the whole world. By way of reciting the *Tikkun chatzos,* every single soul will be rectified, and the biggest souls – the very biggest souls – that fell into the deepest depths of the *klipos* (husks of evil) will be extracted."

Every single soul that made *teshuva*, this is only in the merit of those people who recite the *Tikkun chatzos*, and who weep in the night. These are the people who are rescuing souls from the deepest pits of purgatory.

If a person really knew what the *Beis HaMikdash* really was, he would cry and mourn every single night at *chatzos*. But hardly anyone misses the Temple, hardly anyone needs to have the Temple back, because everyone has their piece of cake at home, and their food, and their drinks. They don't need the Temple. Baruch Hashem, everyone feels great, right up until their 120th birthday.

But there are still a few people who do miss the Temple. Reb Nachman Shuster was a simple Jew who spent some time in Uman and saw how the people there prayed with such enthusiasm, and how they used to weep when they recited *Tikkun chatzos*. When he returned home, he also started to recite the *Tikkun chatzos*, and to weep over the *Beis HaMikdash*.

Everyone started laughing at him, because they could see that he didn't know how to say the words properly, and that he'd only say half the words. They came over to him and said to him, 'why are you saying the *Tikkun chatzos*?! First, go and learn your aleph-bet!' Reb Nachman replied, 'you don't miss the Temple. You're Torah scholars and geniuses and *Tzaddikim*. You don't need to say any lamentations or *Tikkun chatzos*. But me? I'm a simple cobbler and I miss the Temple.'

After this happened, Rabbi Mordechai Sokolov and Rabbi Shlomo Gavriel came over to him – two of the biggest Torah geniuses – and asked him, 'where did you get a heart like that?' Reb Nachman told them, 'I got it in Uman.' They responded, 'if that's so, then we're also going to go there!' And that's how they merited to draw closer to

Breslov, by way of a simple Jew who used to weep while reciting *Tikkun chatzos.*..."

[1] King David descended from Ruth the Moabitess, and the people of Moab in turn descended from Lot's forbidden relationship with his daughter that occurred after Sdom and Gomorrah had been destroyed.

VAYETZE

A LITTLE MORE AND THERE WILL BE NO MORE WICKED PEOPLE

The Torah tells us: *"Vayetze Yaakov"* (and Yaakov left). When Yaakov left Beersheba, he'd already completed the seven levels of holiness, the seven Sefirot, namely: *Malchut, Yesod, Hod, Netzach, Tiferet, Gevurah* and *Chessed*. These are called the seven *'Gevurot'*.

"Vayelech Charana" (and he went to Charan). Yaakov went to Charan, to the place where the roots of *din*, or judgment, were found because he wanted to draw down *chessed*, or kindness, into the world, and to bring *shefa* (bounty) into the world, because the work of the *Tzaddikim* is to bring *chessed* and *shefa* into the world.

From the moment that Rebbe Nachman of Breslov came into the world, he sweetened all of the judgements in the world until the end of all generations. He drew down *shefa* into the world, he drew down *chessed* into the world and he announced that there are no more wicked people, that the age of wickedness in the world had come to an end! From the moment that Rebbe Nachman was born, the age of wickedness finished. There were no more wicked people in *Am Yisrael*, as he himself revealed in Lesson 282 of *Likutei Moharan* (popularly known as 'Azamra').

In that lesson, Rebbe Nachman explains: *"Od me'at v'ain rasha"* (a little more, and there will no longer be a wicked person). Just a little more – today, tomorrow, the day after tomorrow – and we'll already see that there won't be any more wicked people in *Am Yisrael*, because everyone will be on the path of *teshuva*.

This verse, *"Od me'at v'ain rasha"*, comes from Tehillim (the book of *Tehillim*), and Rabbenu explained its simple meaning: 'just a little more!

32

A little more, and there will be no more wicked people, and everyone will be *Tzaddikim*, and everyone will reach the level of *"your entire nation are Tzaddikim"* (*Yeshaya* 60:21).'

One Jew will become a *Tzaddik* today, another one will become a *Tzaddik* tomorrow and yet another one the day after. And the one who will become a *Tzaddik* after a few more days will fulfil the verse: *"the smallest one will be like a thousand and the youngest will be like a vast nation"* (*Yeshaya* 60:22).

This 'small' one will rise up and up, as the greater the soul that a person possesses, and the more refined their soul, the more difficulties and obstacles they have to overcome when they want to make *teshuva*.

Rabbenu teaches us in Lesson 282 that there is no such thing as a wicked person in Am Yisrael! There is no such reality. Even if you see a completely wicked person, from his head to his feet, you can't see any *Yiddishkeit* in him at all, he is completely anti-Torah, anti-observance, G-d forbid, even if it seems to you that there was never a more wicked person than this since the creation of the world, you should know that the main problem is that this person simply lacks *da'at*, or spiritual awareness.

But a huge fire of holiness still burns inside of them! A raging fire of holiness and yearning for *Hashem Yisborach* burns inside of every Jew. It's just that it's covered over by mountains of dust. Their soul is on fire for G-d, but it's covered in a layer of dirt. These Jewish souls are like spiritual volcanoes. From the outside, a huge mountain covers the heat and the lava flowing just beneath the surface, but the moment the fire and the lava burst forth it consumes the entire mountain. The mountain explodes!

A spiritual mountain of dirt and rocks is currently resting on every Jewish soul, but the day will come when the fire will burst forth and consume all of these mountains of sand and dirt.

In Lesson 282, Rebbe Nachman writes: "And you need to search and find in him a small amount of good. And in that small place, he is not a wicked person." Rabbenu is teaching us that here is no such thing as a wicked Jewish person, from his head to his toes. It's just that it currently seems that way to you. But it's only your imagination! You imagine that he's a completely wicked person, but if you train yourself to look for some little bit of good that he has done or some kindness that he did to help someone else, you'll always find even in the most worst wicked person lots and lots of good. And the very act of you finding some good in this person, and judging him favorably, through this very act you raise him up to the side of good, and you can cause him to make *teshuva*.

We need to look at every Jew with a 'good eye', and stop thinking to ourselves, 'well, I made *teshuva* and I keep *Shabbos*, and I learn Torah, so why doesn't he make *teshuva* like me?! Why doesn't he keep *Shabbos* like me?! He should be doing the same! I went through what he went through and more, so why doesn't he also make *teshuva*!?'

It's exactly about this that Rabbenu said: "*Od me'at v'ain rasha*". A little more! He is going to do it eventually, tomorrow or the day after. You can't interfere with Hashem's order for the world, and the order of the *teshuva* process. The order of *teshuva*, when each person will make *teshuva*, how he will make *teshuva* - this process is hidden from all of His creations. But it's a process that needs to happen to every single Jew. Every single Jew will one day make *teshuva*!

Now, it's possible to speed this process up, but only if we start looking with a 'good eye'. Only if a person merits to look at every Jew with a 'good eye' then, "*he will consider his place and he [the wicked person] won't be there anymore*", [ie, in the place of being wicked]. If people would realize this and internalize that if they started to judge others favorably, and to stop looking at them with a 'bad eye', then there wouldn't be any more wicked people in *Am Yisrael*. Because it is possible to bring all of them back to make *teshuva*, in the blink of an eye.

Even when a Jew appears to be the most wicked person, know that he really has the most righteous soul. It's the opposite of how it appears to be externally, the 'worse' the soul appears to be, the more righteous it actually is. It's only because it's so full of righteousness that it's scared. It has a hidden, internal fear about keeping *mitzvos*, because it knows if it starts the process of *teshuva*, it will go 'to the end'!

There are many Jews who are far away from *Yiddishkeit* who say, 'if I start to fulfil *mitzvos*, then I will go to the end... not like you! I will go to the end, I will learn Torah day and night. I will become holy, I will purify myself, to the end!' But to go 'to the end' seems very difficult for them. So, we try to say to them, 'go at least halfway, and keep half the laws'. But they tell us no, they are not prepared to do that, because by them, they want everything – or nothing. And in truth, if you were to show them and to explain to them how to reach the entire way, and how to become holy, and how it's really not as difficult as they think, they would all make *teshuva*!

Every Jew is a part of Hashem, and every person has G-dliness in him. "Man is beloved that he was created in the image of G-d" (Avot 3:14). The heart of every Jew, even the most wicked, burns for *Hashem Yisbarach*. There is no Jew whose heart does not burn for *Hashem Yisbarach*. Because a Jew is not a cow or a sheep; every Jew is a holy *neshama*, that was carved out from the Throne of Glory. Every Jew, in the place where he is, even if the burning coals of his soul and heart are currently covered over by mountains of sand, billions of grains of sand, nonetheless, the coals continue to burn. We need to blow away the dirt covering his heart, the mountains of sand covering his heart, and this is what Rabbenu said: 'come, let's blow away the mountains of sand from his heart, because there is no such thing as a wicked person in *Am Yisrael*.' There is no such thing as '*chilonim*' [secular Jews]; there is no such thing!

There are people who succeed in fulfilling the Torah's commandments 80% of the time, 70%, 20% and 10%. Every Jew fasts on Yom Kippur and eats Matza on Pesach. There is no such thing as a 'secular Jew'! Every one of them fulfils some aspect of the Torah. Every Jew is a holy Jew, a pure Jew.

This is the foundation of what Rebbe Nachman taught us, that there are no wicked people in *Am Yisrael*. It's forbidden to call any Jew 'wicked'. It is forbidden to say, 'this one is wicked'. We need to fix this way of speaking, because there's no such thing.

How can you believe that so-and-so is wicked? Were you in his place? Do you know where he was born? Do you know who his parents were? What he went through? How can you decide to call a Jew wicked? How can you decide to call a Jew '*chiloni*' (secular)? How can you say things like this? Do you think you can decide who is righteous and who is wicked? Do you think that you can really know? You need to know that everyone is righteous, because "*your nation is entirely righteous*", and there are no wicked people in *Am Yisrael*.

VAYISHLACH

WHEN YAAKOV ARRIVED IN
THE CITY OF SHECHEM

When Yaakov arrived at the city of Shechem, where the worst murderers resided, he came with *he'arat panim*, with such a shining face that there was an immediate awakening in the town. Everyone wanted to make *teshuva*--to keep *Shabbos*, to throw away all their idols, to stop running after money and to start serving Hashem. Yaakov Avinu soon made them Shabbos boundaries, fixed a currency and established bathhouses. Everything he told them to do was holy in their eyes.

This is what Rabbi Nachman means when he explains in Lesson 27 of *Likutey Moharan*, "*when he [Yaakov] came [to Shechem], he established faith*". 'Fixing a currency' means that he rectified the desire for money and when he rectified the desire for money, the flaw of idolatry was also rectified. And this is the meaning of 'he made bathhouses for them'. As it's written, "*and the daughter of Pharaoh went down to bathe*" which *Chazal* explain (Megillah 13, Sotah 12) as cleansing herself from the idolatry of her father's home (*Likutei Moharan* 23). The Ramban explains that this is what was bothering Yaakov when he said to Shimon and Levi [after they had killed the people of Shechem], "*you have achartem/ embarrassed me*" (Bereshit 34:30).

In truth, the inhabitants of Shechem were ready to make complete *teshuva*. They had started making *teshuva* and they saw Yaakov and his sons as angels, like heavenly beings. All the people of Shechem nullified themselves before them. It pained Yaakov because they had already accepted upon themselves the Shabbos boundaries and they had already established a currency, which meant that they had already started to break their desire for money. They had also established bathhouses, which meant that they had started to distance themselves from idolatry. *"You have achartem/embarrassed me"* --I wanted to bring everyone back in *teshuva* and by wiping out the city, you destroyed everything I wanted to do, all my hopes.

All the hope of the redemption depends on converting the whole world, on bringing the whole world back in *teshuva*. This is the ultimate embarrassment! Any generation that doesn't bring the whole world back in *teshuva* – it's as if they themselves caused them to sin! The greatest thing is to bring people back in *teshuva*. The Rebbe wanted people to go all over the country, all over the world, and to bring people back in *teshuva*, as is written in the holy Zohar, *"fortunate is the person who takes wrongdoers by the hand..."* The holy Zohar says that whoever brings people back in *teshuva* has no gate closed before him. All the doors are open for him. All the paths are open to him. He is given all the keys. A person who goes out and works to bring people back in *teshuva* is the greatest honor for Hashem. He is glorified in all the worlds, 'see what a person I have here, one who goes out and brings people back in *teshuva*.'

Truly, the greatest thing is to bring people back in *teshuva*, but how does one do this? How does one merit this? Only if a person has *hadrat panim*, a majestic countenance, will he have *panim me'irot*, a shining face. Then, he will have a holy face, so that just looking at his face will cause people to return in *teshuva*.

On the gravestone of Rebbe Aharon from Karlin, it is written that 80,000 people made *teshuva* because of him. How did they make *teshuva*? Did he go and give classes and lectures? What happened was that people saw his shining face, his *hadrat panim*, and everyone returned in *teshuva*. To merit *hadrat panim*, *he'arat panim*, Rabbenu says in Lesson 27 of *Likutey Moharan*, comes only through learning the holy Gemara, because you can't get people to make *teshuva* if you have no intelligence, if you have no understanding. A person needs to have great intelligence, just as the Rebbe said, *"I wanted that you would have such intelligence that there hasn't been for several generations already."*

Why shouldn't we take the Rebbe's advice and do what he wanted us to do? Let's do what the Rebbe wanted. The Rebbe didn't want us to run around aimlessly, dancing around for no reason. The moment that a person learns Gemara and *poskim*, he receives such a light, the 360,000 *holy lights* (*nehorin*). Everyone will run after him, everyone will abandon all their heretical thoughts. All their questions will be answered. He'll come with such a light, such a *he'arat panim*, emitting such rays of light-- *"the wisdom of the man enlightens his face"*. People see such a light, such wealth, such joy on the face and they return in *teshuva*. What do people want? People want to be happy; that's what they want. The minute they see that true joy is found by someone who learns Torah, who learns *poskim*, and whose face is shining like the sun, then everyone returns in *teshuva*.

The main point of learning Torah is in order to teach it to others. As it's written [in the blessings before Shema], *"put it into our hearts... to learn and to teach"*. Once a person is knowledgeable in Torah, he is obligated to teach it to others. The Torah that a person learns is measured according to how much kindness and how much self-sacrifice he is prepared to give in order to teach others. After a person learns eight or ten hours, he must show that he has the strength, the light, the influence, to bring people back in *teshuva*. This is the primary action that comes from learning. Each person can bring thousands and thousands of people back in *teshuva*. A group of 100 people can bring a thousand back in *teshuva*, and within a few years all of *Am Yisrael* will do *teshuva*. If we start bringing people back in *teshuva*, then the nations of the world will also return in *teshuva*.

Our purpose is to bring the whole world back in *teshuva*, even the non-Jews. This is what Hashem loves. Hashem is waiting for us to bring all of *Am Yisrael* in *teshuva* and all the nations of the world in *teshuva*.

"All flesh will call Your name, and all the evildoers will turn to You, and every being in the universe will recognize and know You..." Why do we say this? Why do we say these verses? We need to draw the farthest people close so that everyone should call out in the name of Hashem, even the non-Jews. But first we need to draw the Jews back. If we start with the Jews we can then bring the non-Jews back. Everyone will do *teshuva* and will come close to the faith of Israel and will serve Hashem together.

"And he graced the countenance of the city"-- for six days you studied, worked, and traveled to bring people back in *teshuva*. Now *Shabbos* has come; do nothing but sing to Hashem. This is *"and he graced."* Yaakov made them take a break; he taught them not to go out on *Shabbos* from their homes. 'Stay at home on *Shabbos* – sing on *Shabbos.*' One day a week is given to man to sing to Hashem. *Shabbos* has arrived - sit with your children, sing with your children, learn with them, so that they will see what *oneg Shabbos* (delighting in the *Shabbos*) is all about. This will make such a *kiddush Hashem* in the world, in all the worlds, in all the *sefirot*. When a person sings the *Shabbos* songs, the whole world hears it; it's heard in every country. This is what awakens all the souls to return in *teshuva*. A person sings in the privacy of his own home and sings songs to Hashem and all the souls hear his songs and his melodies.

"And He rested" - sit at home and sing the *Shabbos* songs. You will see the whole world return in *teshuva*, simply from the *Shabbos* songs, the *Shabbos* tunes. When one sits at home on *Shabbos* and sings the *Shabbos* songs, this gives his children *yiras shamayim*, fear of heaven. When they see their father sitting peacefully and singing tunes, they will have such a good feeling in their hearts, such peace of mind. This becomes their whole life force. This is their whole joy. From this alone, they will lose all interest in what is going on in the street. They won't be interested in the futility of the street. This is all that a child needs--to see his father smiling and happy, calm and singing, sitting for at least two hours at

the *Shabbos* table and singing. This gives vital energy to the child for the whole week.

Start to be a simple Jew. The minimum one needs to be a Jew is to sing the *Shabbos* songs. Without this, one hasn't even started being a Jew. If a child sees that his father doesn't sing the *Shabbos* songs and he doesn't learn with him, then he won't have any reason to stay at home. In the end he will fall into bad behavior, G-d forbid. He won't comprehend holiness. He won't comprehend purity. A person doesn't realize the greatness of the *Shabbos* songs. One can resuscitate the dead with the *Shabbos* songs.

Just as it's told about Rebbe Mordechai who wrote the song, "*mah yafit, umah na'umt ahava b'ta'anugim*" (*such beauty and such pleasure are in loving Your delights*): His son passed away on Friday night after candle lighting and he asked that they put the child in the living room on the couch to hear the *Shabbos* songs. He started singing, "*chai zekof mach*" (*Hashem stands erect the one in need*) and the child revived!

Shabbos arrives. A person sings all the *Shabbos* songs and he enlivens everyone. Everyone comes alive. Everyone is happy, everyone is content, because the *Shabbos* songs give the joy and life force to the whole week.

41

VAYESHEV

RELEASING THE HOLY SPARKS

Yosef Ha*Tzaddik* guarded his eyes, he never opened his eyes. Through this, he sanctified all the 'emptiness' of the world. He experienced terrible torment and such difficult hardships; he had to spend a year in the house of Potiphar and then another 12 years in prison.

The *Midrash* tells us that three times a day, the wife of Potiphar used to come to try to entice him and to tempt him with all sorts of invitations. Three times a day, she used to change her clothes in the morning, at lunchtime and in the evening. Every day, she'd come and poke him with all sorts of needles and barbs, with iron combs-- "*iron entered his soul*" (*Tehillim* 105:18).

She'd say to him, 'I'm going to blind your eyes! I'm going to remove your eyes!' He'd reply, 'Hashem will open the eyes of the blind. I'm going to continue to walk with my eyes closed and Hashem will open my eyes.' She'd come and stick pins in his neck, but he never opened his eyes.

She'd tell him, 'I'm going to break you! I'm going to humiliate you!' He'd reply, 'Hashem straightens the bent.' She'd say, 'you're going be under arrest in prison and you'll never get out again'. He'd tell her, 'Hashem frees the captives'.

The holiness of Yosef sanctified the whole world. When Yosef was alive, even the earth itself was sanctified. The *Midrash* says that Yosef was sold for a pair of sandals. What is the meaning of 'a pair of sandals'? No one sells their brother for a pair of sandals! Who ever heard of something like this, that you'd sell your brother for a pair of sandals? What, they didn't have sandals?!

42

The *Pelech HaRimon* explains that Yosef Ha*Tzaddik* guarded his eyes perfectly and that he never opened his eyes in his life. By way of this, he sanctified the emptiness of the world, and the entire land of Israel. The whole land of Israel was sanctified with the holiness of the *Beis HaMikdash*. So, everyone could walk around the whole country without wearing sandals. As in the *Beis HaMikdash*, people walked around without shoes, on account of the tremendous holiness there.

And so it was at the time of Yosef; you could go everywhere without shoes. They could feel so much holiness with each and every step taken that they didn't even notice the thorns pricking them, or the sharp stones stabbing them. For as long as they believed in Yosef, and didn't think about selling him, nothing could stab them at all. The thorns were holy; everything was holy.

The brothers didn't know who the *Tzaddik* really was, or that in his merit the whole country was full of holiness. Each of them thought to themselves that maybe it was thanks to his own merit. They didn't believe that it was in the merit of Yosef. The moment they sold Yosef, everything stopped. They didn't feel the holiness of the land anymore; the earth was just *stam*, regular earth, and suddenly they felt how everything was pricking them and stabbing them. Immediately, they needed 'sandals'!

The *Talmud Yerushalmi* says that Yosef rebuked the brothers for looking at the country's womenfolk. He said to them, 'what are you looking at?' They replied, 'this doesn't harm us!' But Yosef argued that even if a man is holy and pure, and looking [at women] doesn't harm him, it's still forbidden to look! Because the very act of looking itself harms him. Rav Natan explains that such an enormous spiritual light comes from the eyes, such a wondrous light. All of a person's vitality passes through his eyes. A person transfers all his vitality, all of his *neshama*, all his *nefesh* – everything! – to the person he looks at.

43

Essentially, the act of looking itself, the vision itself, transfers energy and transfers the life force. Because a person is full of Torah, full of prayer and full of G-dliness. When we look at the *klipos* (husks of evil), at the evildoers, at the non-Jews, we give them our vitality and energy.

This is what Yosef rebuked the brothers about: 'yes, it's true that looking doesn't harm you; you're the 12 holy tribes. But the act of looking itself is transferring all this strength to the *sitra achra* (the dark side), and the forces of *tumah* (spiritual impurity). So, it's forbidden for you to look!'

The *Tur* (Orach Chaim 1:1) says, "*swift as an eagle*" – this refers to guarding the eyes, that you should close your eyes as swiftly as an eagle. This is how the *Tur* begins his commentary. When a person opens his eyes, and walks around with his eyes open, all the Torah he learned goes over to the *klipos*, to our enemies, to the evildoers – everything goes to them!

He gives them strength; he gives them their energy. Because their energy comes from you. Their strength, their vitality, it comes from the Torah you just learned. If you learned for 10 hours and spoke out 60 measures of holy words, through this (that you looked at forbidden sights), you just energized all the forces of evil. All 60 measures just went straight over to them! If we wouldn't look at them, they wouldn't have any strength or power.

If a man walks in the street while guarding his eyes, he raises up all the holy sparks that are to be found amongst the *klipos*. When a man closes his eyes, he burns up all the *klipos*-- and within every *klipa* is a spark of holiness. When a man walks in the street, guarding his eyes, he frees that holy spark.

The *Heichal HaBracha* tells us that, when the world was created, holy sparks were buried in the streets and in the marketplaces. These sparks are waiting for someone to raise them up and to rectify them. Only someone who closes his eyes can do this.

These Divine sparks can be found in every place, but we don't see them. They're hidden, because looking at them is forbidden. So, we see only the *klipa* (the husk) and by looking we only create more and more *klipos*.

So, don't look! If you look then more and more *klipos* will be created. The holy spark that's imprisoned inside that woman, it's crying out to you, 'don't look! My brother, have mercy on me and please don't look at me. Free me! If you look, you're going to bury me even deeper; you're going to cover me with even more chains.'

This holy spark is begging us, 'my brother, have mercy on me! Free me from prison. If you don't look, you'll bring the redemption. Until now, no one has redeemed me, and no one has rectified me. Have mercy on me! Help me get out of prison; don't look! That one time that you don't look at me, you'll cause all the innumerable walls and *klipos* that are surrounding me to to fall!'

We have to know that if an angel walked around the streets, he couldn't make any *tikkun* (spiritual rectification), and he couldn't raise up any holy spark, because he doesn't have the same *yetzer hara* to look. He doesn't have a *yetzer hara* attracting him to spiritual impurity. But a human being, a man made of flesh and blood, he needs to set out a tremendous amount of self-sacrifice in order to guard his eyes.

At that moment, when you're walking in the streets and when you're going to the marketplaces, you're experiencing an enormous test. Guarding your eyes will raise up and rectify all the holy sparks to be found in those places.

MIKETZ

HOW TO PERFORM MIRACLES

Every Jew comes to the world in order to do miracles and wonders. Hashem created the world only in order that there would be miracles and wonders. This is the only reason He created the world! What's more, these miracles and wonders are not just for when there's other choice, or no other way.

In Lesson 1:97 of Likutey Moharan, Rabbenu tells us that, "*before creation, G-d adorned and embellished Himself with the prayers and good deeds of the Tzaddikim.*" Hashem saw that there would be *Tzaddikim* who would perform whatever deeds were required, who would change the course of nature and all the laws of nature by their prayers. This is what motivated *HaKadosh Baruch Hu* to create the world, for the enjoyment that He would derive from the *Tzaddikim* who busy themselves with their prayers and who change the course of nature.

Even before the creation of the world, Hashem entertained Himself with the miracles and wonders that each person would perform with their prayers. This was His enjoyment and pleasure and the reason why He created the world.

Rabbenu continues, "*and this is the explanation of: 'Mine is Gilad' (Tehillim 60:9). Namely, that G-d's pleasure was revealed (Hebrew: 'giluy') before the creation when He adorned and embellished Himself with the prayers of the Tzaddikim.*" 'Gilad' (from the same root as the word 'giluy') is the revelation of G-d's pleasure and enjoyment, because "*Hashem has no greater pleasure than when he sees a person pray and succeed in making something that he wants happen - this brings miracles and kindness down into the world.*"

If a person wants to change nature, and to perform miracles, he needs to pray from a place of humility and lowliness, with submission. He needs to know that 'I'm a very minor person, lesser than any other Jew in the world'. Then, he can make anything happen with his prayers. This is the secret of why Yosef called his son 'Menashe', because "*G-d caused me to forget (Hebrew: nashni) all my suffering and the house of my father*" (Bereshit 41:51).

How can we understand Yosef? How is it possible to give a name like this, 'Menashe', to his son, whose meaning is that 'I forgot about my father, and I forgot my brothers, and all the Matriarchs. I forgot everyone; I forgot my father's house?'

However, according to what Rabbenu is teaching us in Lesson 97, we can understand this secret. Yosef merited to attain the aspect of 'Menashe', which is humility and lowliness. This is the explanation of the verse, "*for G-d has caused me to forget the house of my father*". This is a reference to Yosef's ancestry. The verse, "*and all my suffering*" is a reference to the suffering he endured in his *avodat Hashem* (spiritual endeavors).

A person may strengthen himself in prayer and in his *avodat Hashem*, by saying he's got an important father, and an illustrious mother, and a well-known grandfather. But Yosef Ha*Tzaddik* says, 'I'm only serving Hashem! I'm not praying just because I have an important father, or an illustrious grandfather, I'm praying for Hashem! My strength comes from the fact that Hashem created me and from the fact that Hashem exists in the world. Hashem is alive and here. I see him alive and here, that's why I'm serving Hashem.'

Yosef Ha*Tzaddik* lives for Hashem. He doesn't live for his father or for his mother. Rather, only for Hashem. This is how he reached his lofty spiritual level and this is why he called his son 'Menashe' – from the language meaning 'to forget' – in order 'to forget all my suffering and the house of my father'.

A person needs to forget about all his *yichus* and about all the effort he's put into his *avodat Hashem* In order to merit being able to govern the creation through his prayers and in order to be able to perform wonders in the world.

VAYIGASH

SEARCHING FOR THE TRUE TZADDIK

The first thing that a Jew needs to search for in his life is who is this *"Tzaddik yesod ha'olam"*? - the *Tzaddik* in whose merit the world is sustained. He needs to search for the *Tzaddikim* who are the foundations of the world, the *Tzaddikim* who are protecting us.

In all three of the *parshiot Vayeshev*, *Mikeitz* and *Vayigash* the *'Tzaddik yesod ha'olam'* (the *Tzaddik*, who is the foundation of the world), the true *Tzaddik*, is being sought for. In *Parsha Vayigash*, the *Tzaddik* cries out, *"I am Yosef!"* – and the true *Tzaddik* is revealed.

The brothers were all true *Tzaddikim* of the utmost holiness, but they didn't believe that Yosef was the *'Tzaddik yesod ha'olam'*. The brothers mistakenly thought that Yosef Ha*Tzaddik* was just like them, perhaps he just served Hashem a bit more than they did, learned a bit more than them and guarded his eyes more. Each of the brothers was certain that he, himself, was a true *Tzaddik*, but they didn't know that the *Tzaddik yesod ha'olam* is something else entirely.

In his commentary on the Torah, "Heichal HaBracha," the Kamarna Rebbe says that the light of Yosef Ha*Tzaddik* shone in all the worlds, and in throughout all the *sefirot*. He shone like the sun and the brothers had absolutely no idea what a big light they had here. It's written in the holy Zohar, on *Parshat Vayayshev*, that Yosef was everything, the root of everything. All the *shefa* (abundance) was drawn down into the world only through him.

Yosef was able to hide his light and his power at all times. The verse says, *"Yosef was beautiful of form and beautiful of appearance"* – the initial letters spell out "yatom" (orphan). The true*Tzaddik* is an orphan and he is completely hidden. He is totally concealed, and no one knows anything about him.

This is what Rabbenu brings in Lesson 67 in part 2 of Likutey Moharan, *"because there is a Tzaddik who is the beauty and the glory and the grace of the entire world, and his whole being is from the aspect of: "and Yosef was beautiful of form and beautiful of appearance." (Bereshit 39:6) and from the aspect of: "a beautiful landscape, the joy of the entire earth." (Tehillim 48:3)*

"For this true Tzaddik represented by Yosef is the glory and beauty of the entire world, and when this beauty and splendor is revealed to the world, that is, when this Tzaddik who is the beauty of the entire world becomes renowned and famous in the world, the eyes of the entire world are then opened. Whoever is encompassed within this true beauty of this Tzaddik who is the grace and beauty of the world. That is, whoever becomes his follower and becomes 'part' of him – his eyes are opened and he becomes able to see…. One becomes able to look into oneself regarding all the character traits, where one is holding in them… One also becomes able to see and behold G-d's greatness." (*Likutey Moharan* 2:67)

For the true *Tzaddik* only comes to the world for one thing-- to reveal Hashem. The true *Tzaddik* comes to reveal that there is Hashem in the world, and that a person shouldn't think that he's making things happen under his own steam, that he can walk by himself or do things by himself or run around by himself or make things happen by himself, without Hashem. Here, he'll get a blow on his hand, there he'll hurt his leg, every second he'll get another blow, but he still continues to think '*I'm* walking, *I'm* running around, *I'm* doing things'...

A person thinks that he's the ruler of the world, he walks around, he breathes. But he can be shown in a split-second that even if just something tiny moves in his body, just a thousandth of a millimeter – he's finished! He immediately needs surgery, medical tests, x-rays and then he already comes to understand that he's not G-d, he's not an angel and he doesn't rule the world.

Slowly, slowly, life teaches us that a man is built with *"all manner of openings, and all manner of cavities. It is revealed and known before the throne of Your glory that if even one of them would be ruptured or blocked, it would be impossible to survive and to stand before You, for even for a single moment."* (From the *'Asher Yatzar'* blessing).

Once a person gets to 60, already one of his vertebrae starts to move around here, and over there some nerve starts to move around. At age 60, the limbs start to wither, the sinews start to dry out. Up to the age of 60, a person can fool himself that he's something, that he can do everything. But by this age, he already starts to see plainly that he's really not something. 'See, here I fell over. I can no longer walk so well over there.'

So, who can open our eyes and show us while we're still healthy, strong and robust that everything is really only Hashem? Our health comes from Hashem, our strength comes from Hashem – everything's from Hashem! Only the *Tzaddik* who comes from the aspect of Yosef can show us that there's Hashem in the world.

The entire reason we come down to the world is just to know that we aren't doing anything. We came here to know that Hashem is running the world. All we need to do is see Hashem's Divine providence, to see Hashem everywhere, to see Hashem in every movement, to see Hashem in every thought and word.

A person moves his hand or moves his leg – everything is Hashem! Hashem is moving his hand; Hashem is moving his leg. A person lives in the world as though he's 'cool', he's constructing buildings, he's building yeshivas. If he doesn't know that really Hashem is doing everything, then everything is really just a Tower of Babel. As King Shlomo said, *"I surely built a fertile house."* Hashem said: *"You* built it?! If so, the house (i.e. Temple) has been decreed for destruction. You should say 'Hashem built it! Hashem did it!'

The Maggid of Mezeritch forbade himself from saying the word 'I'. The *Tzaddikim* are very careful not to say the word 'I'. If a person says the word 'I' – *oy vavoy!* All the Torah, all the *Gemara*, all the *Shulchan Aruch*, all the *Yoreh Deah*, all the prayers, everything, is only so that we'll know that Hashem is doing everything, and that there is Hashem in the world.

We're not doing anything. We're not even moving our hand or moving our leg. We aren't breathing ourselves – *"every breath will praise Hashem, halleluyah"* (*Tehillim* 150:6). Every single breath we take is from Hashem. The entire work of a person over his 120 years is to know who this *Tzaddik* is, who is enlivening the whole world and in whose merit the *shefa* is coming to the world.

As the Gemara recounts about Rabbi Chanina Ben Dosa: *"the whole world is sustained in the merit of Chanina ben Dosa, but he is sustained with just a measure of carobs."*

The first thing that a Jew needs to know about is on what foundation the world rests and in whose merit the world is sustained. We have to search for this *Tzaddik* who is truly sustaining the world with his merit and to seek out the *Tzaddikim* who are saving the world. Who are these *Tzaddikim*, who are protecting us?

And each person who comes close to this *Tzaddik* and who is encompassed within this *Tzaddik* for the sake of truth, he'll be able to see where he's really holding in relation to rectifying his *middos* (character traits). The concept here is that when a person comes to the *Tzaddik*, he starts to detest the bad that's within him and to detest his *yetzer hara*. He starts to hate all the materialistic stuff that's surrounding him and he starts to hate his corporality and all the bad things and all his lusts. He no longer makes everything he wants 'the ideal' and he no longer boasts about all these things.

The moment a person comes close to the true *Tzaddik*, he only starts seeking out good things. He only sees the good in other people and he starts to love *Am Yisrael* with a deep love that causes him to sacrifice himself for others. He only wants to escape from all of his bad *middos* and all his lusts, and to make complete *teshuva* and return to Hashem *Yisborach*.

This is the power the true *Tzaddik* has to rectify the world, because this *Tzaddik* can bring the whole world back to its Creator. If people would draw close to him and believe in him, they would escape from all their evil, and become completely purified, because this *Tzaddik* has already broken away from the four elements. He has purified the four elements and he is already free from any base desires. So, he can purify any person from any of their bad desires.

This is what the *Gaon*, Rebbe Meir Simcha HaCohen from Dvinsk (author of the *Ohr Same'ach* on the Rambam) said on the Gemara (Sotah 13a), *"And there they held a great and imposing eulogy"* (Bereshit 50:10). "It was taught, even horses and even donkeys." Rebbe Meir Simcha HaCohen says *"a great and imposing eulogy"*-- even the horses eulogized Yaakov Avinu! There was such a great and imposing eulogy that even the horses cried, the donkeys cried, everyone cried for the *Tzaddik*!

Even the horses knew that the *Tzaddik* had gone. Even the donkeys knew that the *Tzaddik* was gone. *"The ox recognizes its owner, the donkey the trough of its master. But the Children of Israel do not recognize [Me], My nation doesn't consider."* The horses acknowledge the true *Tzaddik*. The donkeys acknowledge the true *Tzaddik*. This is a complete and total embarrassment, that people don't recognize the *Tzaddik*. How can people be so blind? They run around the world not even knowing who the true *Tzaddik* is.

A person, with all his pride and with all his evil inclinations, doesn't want to believe in the *Tzaddik*. He doesn't want to know who the *Tzaddik* is. But the horses and the donkeys felt that they were lost without the *Tzaddik*. Who would sustain the world? Who would protect them? Who will watch over the horses? Who would guard the donkeys? Who will protect the world? They knew in whose merit they are alive. If the *Tzaddik* isn't around then there will be a famine; there will be a holocaust in the world, there will be wars. This is what Rabbi Meir Simcha HaCohen says - search for the *Tzaddikim*, follow the *Tzaddikim*, open your eyes and search for the *Tzaddik* in whose merit you are alive.

VAYECHI

WE ARE RESPONSIBLE FOR ALL OF CREATION

Yissachar was the only, unique soul from amongst all the tribes that had absolutely no connection to this world. Yissachar was the soul that possessed nothing in this world other than Torah learning. This was the soul that everyone else needed to serve. Every one of the other tribes did something.

Zevulun engaged in business dealings, "*happy is Zevulun when you go out*". Yehuda went to war, Levi served in the *Beis HaMikdash*, but Yissachar's soul had absolutely nothing to do with this world, other than to learn Torah. Yissachar was only Torah, for Torah learning is greater than serving in the *Beis HaMikdash*, as it's written, "*more precious than pearls*" (Proverbs 3:15). It's greater than the *Kohen HaGadol* who used to enter the Holy of Holies.

Our sages teach that a Torah scholar who is a *mamzer* (born as a result of a union forbidden by the Torah) is greater than a *Kohen Gadol* who's an *am ha'aretz* (unlearned man). If he's learning Torah day and night, then he's greater than the *Kohen Gadol*, because it's impossible to escape from the *yetzer hara* except by in-depth Torah learning. And this *dafka* only occurs when a person toils in his Torah until the point of death, to the point where he feels like he wants to die.

We have to toil in Torah and to kill ourselves on its behalf, not to learn Torah in a lax fashion or in a relaxed fashion. The completeness of learning Torah doesn't happen when we're relaxed! A person has all kinds of lusts and he also has a lust for 'relaxation'. All of our lusts and desires hint to the chiefs of Esav - one of these chiefs was the 'Chief of Relaxation'.

A person likes to pass his life in a relaxed way, to feel relaxed, and so he also learns in a relaxed way too. But, in truth, the true 'relaxation', the true repose, only comes from the Torah – *"And he saw the rest, that it was good..."* (*Rashi*). True relaxation is the rest of the soul. Learning Torah polishes the soul and cleans it, scrubbing off all the dirt. It sends all the spiritual grime outside, and then we merit to have a peaceful soul.

A person needs to know that he's responsible for all of creation. Every day, we need to create the world anew. The world is managed by those who learn Torah. By way of the Torah learning, the world is created. *"The entire renewal of creation that Hashem Yisborach always does on each day, so on this day there will be rain and on that day it will be dry, and so that one time it will be cold and moist, etc, and similarly for all the other changes – everything comes by way of the Torah."* (*Likutey Halachos, Yibum 3).*

Rav Natan (in *Likutey Halachos*) is explaining that you are creating the world. If you start to neglect your learning and spend your time sleeping, a disaster will happen. If you're daydreaming or talking to someone during the time you're meant to be learning, a disaster will happen. A person needs to know that he doesn't need to read any newspapers and he doesn't need to know what's happening in the world. If you take an interest in the world for even a split-second, there will be a disaster.

A person needs to believe that the moment he neglects the Torah, a disaster will happen! You need to know that all the changes in the world, they are occurring because of your Torah learning. When a Jew learns Torah, the whole world starts to love us. By all the nations, one time they love us and one time they hate us. If you study history you see that one year they love us and one year they hate us and want to destroy all the Jews, because everything depends on our Torah learning – and not on politics, and not on any other thing.

When a person learns Torah in-depth and he really puts his brains into learning Torah, he's creating new worlds! He's creating a new reality! Suddenly, they create new laws of nature for him! Now he has the money to travel to Uman! And suddenly, he enjoys spiritual and material abundance.

Why? Because he built a new world. Before, he was in a world where he didn't have any money and now he's in a world where he does have money. It's a completely new world, because every moment, a person can build new worlds. If a person learns Torah in-depth, then each second new worlds are being built.

The Rebbe brings down in Lesson 101 (*Likutey Moharan*) that, "*when a person does a sin, G-d forbid, the transgression is engraved on his bones, as it's written: "and your sins will be on your bones.*" (Ezekiel 32). The Rebbe says, you want to atone for your sins? You want to erase your sins? It's really hard to do this! Your sins are engraved on your bones, the sins fracture your bones – all the bones of a person are broken. It hurts him here; it hurts him there. All of this is sins, each and every sin is engraved on a bone: "*and your sins will be on your bones.*"

The bones are hollow, they've already been engraved on, they're broken from all the engraving. If a person wants to recompose his bones from scratch and rebuild them anew and to escape from the 'sins on his bones' this can only be done by learning Torah in-depth, by reviewing the material and being tested on it, to learn Torah in-depth.

When someone is already blemished or damaged, *teshuva* alone doesn't really help him, because his bones are already fractured and engraved upon, so how is *teshuva* going to help? Now, we need to inject some new 'brains' into the bone, to renew the bone. This occurs by way of learning Torah in-depth.

By learning Torah, you can affect every cell that was damaged or weakened or was already starting to decay. Torah learning renews them and affects them and gives them brains. The Torah rebuilds you and recreates you anew.

A person searches for all sorts of advice about how he can escape from his bad character traits. So, he has *hitbodedut* and *chatzos*, and all this is wonderful and fine, but if he doesn't also have in-depth Torah learning, nothing else is going to help him. If a person isn't also learning Torah in-depth, then he's missing the crucial ingredient.

If that's the case, then he has no *moach* (brain, intellect), because we only get our intellect from learning Torah in-depth. If a person does *hitbodedut*, but he simply has no brains, when Hashem wants to give him things, He doesn't have anywhere to put the *shefa* (bounty)! If a person prays with deep concentration, but then after prayers he runs off to eat or he runs off to speak with his friend... While we're still saying *'Alenu'*, he's already taking off his tefillin, he's already talking to his friend... So, Hashem says to him, 'I want to give you things after the prayers, just say a verse of Torah, just say two or three *halachos*, learn a few lines of *Gemara* and you'll have a wondrous intellect and you'll understand everything.

In his prayers, a person requests from Hashem to, "put understanding into our hearts, so we can understand and become wise, and so that we can listen to, learn, teach and guard your *mitzvos* and perform them". And Hashem wants to give him – right now! – all the mental capacity, but he immediately starts talking with his friend and sometimes he even runs away before *'Alenu'*, and this one's already taken his tefillin off, and this one's already outside, and that one's arguing with someone, or already eating... And Hashem says, 'I wanted to give you some amazing *moach*, where did you run off to?'

So, the Rebbe says that without learning Torah in-depth, there's no *moach*, and the crucial ingredient will be missing from everything that person is trying to do. The Rebbe says that in-depth Torah learning is the *ikker* (the main thing), and so the Rebbe brings down in *Sefer HaMiddos* (in the section on 'Learning', point 33), that 'a person who is used to learning will be able to perform all the *mitzvos*'.

We have to become habituated to learning Torah, which is why we request in the morning prayers, *"Habituate us to Your Torah"*, that we should be used to learning Torah. And the Rebbe says, regularly learning Torah isn't enough! If a person recites his *Gemara* like he's reading *Tehillim*, that's not enough, we need to be *habituated*. 'Habituated' means 'learning Torah in-depth'.

We need to study commentators like the *Rashba*, the *Ramban* and the *Ritva* and the other commentators, like the *Rosh*, the *Rif* and the *Ran*, and the *Nimuki Yosef*, everything there is, also the *Maharam Shif* and the *Maharsha* and the *Bach*, and everything else possible. If the *Maharsha* is hard for you, so take an easier commentator. But this is how your brain has to be, all the time engaged with in-depth learning. Learn in-depth!

If a person learns in-depth, it means that he immerses himself in it and he understands the wisdom of the Torah. Then he merits that they remove the yoke of government from him and also the yoke of making a living. We only understand the wisdom of the Torah by learning in-depth. Then, we merit to reach the level of *Anpin Nahirin*.

When all of a person's thoughts revolve around in-depth Torah and understanding the *Gemara* really well, and understanding the *sugya* really well, and understanding the *Rishonim*, and the *Achronim*, and summarizing them, and writing them, and coming up with new *chiddushim* (original ideas), then, at that moment, he merits to reach such a level of *Anpin Nahirin* that the whole world can make *teshuva*. The whole world can make *teshuva* simply from seeing his face. A person's wisdom lights up his face, 'and then they remove the yoke of government from him and also the yoke of making a living'.

And then, there are no yokes of government in the world - there are no Russians, there are no Arabs, there is nothing; there is no yoke of government. And all because of one man who put his head deeply into learning Torah.

Hashem is ready to remove the yoke of the world's governments, of all the governments in the world. Hashem is ready to cancel all the governments, so that only *Am Yisrael* and the Torah will rule.

Shemot

SEARCHING FOR THE RIGHT DESERT

There's a diamond, and the diamond is inside a box. There is a man who spends his entire day renovating the box, polishing the box and taking caring of the box. But what about the diamond? The main thing is the diamond! The main thing is the soul!

The Torah says that Moshe Rabbenu used to herd his sheep *after* the desert. What does this mean, "after the desert?" What does it mean, "he went after the desert"? What, Moshe went to look for better grass for the sheep to graze? Rabbi Avraham, son of the Rambam says, "Moshe went in search for a desert beyond the desert." He was not satisfied with just any desert; he was seeking a desert far from all other deserts, one that no one ever travels through, one that no foot ever tread upon. Only there could he come to his *shleimus* (completeness), to truly cling to Hashem, to know that *"ein od milvado"* – there is none other than Him, to know that he has no ties to this world, to anything materialistic. He wanted to reach self-nullification before Hashem.

A person must strip himself from all *gashmius* (materialism), and know that there is no *gashmius*, there is no world. This world is a dream; it is no more than imagination. The holy Zohar (in *Parshat Shlach*) says that in the future, there will be nothing left of this world, nothing at all! Not one hair will remain! No houses, no assets, no troubles, nothing will remain of this world! As long as a person has even one memory left of this world, he cannot complete his *tikkun* (rectification). Unless he is given troubles and sufferings to purify him from the lusts of this world, from the hallucinations of this world, until he forgets it all, until he has not one memory left of this world.

A person cannot enter the World to Come if he has anything left from his body or from this world at all. In the World to Come there are no houses, there is no food, nothing! Everything is going to be completely different. The body will turn into a soul and nothing else will remain of this world.

A story was told about 'Rabbi Shimshon of the forest', a *Breslover chassid* who served Hashem day and night with such passion and strength to the point that he suddenly fell and passed away. One night, he came to Reb Avraham Berenyu, a grandson of Rabbenu, in a dream and told him the story of his passing. "Reb Natan came and took me to Rabenu Hakadosh. The Rebbe said to me, 'who says you are a Breslover Chassid? You were in Uman, you went to my gravesite, you acted with *mesirut nefesh* (self sacrifice), it's all true! But to be a *Breslover chassid* is not so simple, it doesn't come so easily. I have a notepad here; let's look into it and see.' The Rebbe looked into his notepad and said, 'it's okay, you're in my notepad, so you are a *Breslover chassid*. But you still smell of this world!'

So long as a person has something left from this world, some point that binds him to this world, a smell of *gashmius*, of the lusts of this world, he cannot come to his place in Heaven. Two angels then came and took me to the river *'Dinor'*, a river of fire, and immersed me in it. What can I say? How can I describe the extent of the suffering and pain I experienced in that river? Unimaginable and unthinkable. There is no such pain in this world. However, the extent of the pleasure one feels after being cleansed in that river is also beyond description. After immersing in the river, Reb Natan took me back to Rabbenu. The Rebbe replied, "You still have a smell of this world. Go immerse once more!

One must have no faith at all in this world, no connection whatsoever to this world! Until the person rids himself from all the impurities and contaminations of this world, he cannot enter the World to Come.

Reb Natan took me to immerse once again in the river of fire. Upon returning to Rabbenu, he declared, "indeed, now you are purified!"

We all want a life of eternity. The body is just a box. The body is a box for the soul. Why did Hashem create for us a body? This is only to prevent the soul from going back up to Heaven before its time. The soul has no desire at all to be in this world, it always wants to return to Heaven, to its source. It has no connection to this world at all. Once again, it is forced to eat, once again it is forced to drink – it is fed up! A person must eat because if he doesn't, his soul will escape and return back to its source.

Really, the soul has no desire at all to be down here! A hundred and twenty years is all too much, as far as the soul is concerned. It can't take anymore down here; it wants to leave. It will last until 120 years but only through eating. This is why we must look after the needs of our body. Yet the body is really just a box for the soul. It's like a diamond inside of a box and there's a person who spends his days looking after the box, fixing it up, caring for it, that's all very nice, but what will be with the diamond?! The most important thing is the diamond! The main thing is the soul! Fix up the diamond! Polish it! You are a G-dly creation! Why are you polishing up the box? Why? So that it will shine? You waste your life polishing it; in the end it won't shine anymore because you'll have polished it too much. Nothing will remain from the body – from the box. That box serves as a cover, it's the cover for the diamond!

You must seek out that diamond. Every person has two ways to go, as it says in the Torah, "*See, I have given to you life and good, death and evil... and you shall choose life.*" Does man really need to be told not to choose death?! Who chooses death?! Rather, this is to show us that here in this world, everything is confused, everything is upside down. Death appears to be life. Materialism and lusts appear to a person to be the good life, whereas real life – prayer and the holy Torah appear to people as death! This is why the Torah warns us to beware. What you may think is life is actually death – beware! You could die! *"And you shall choose life"* – choose the Torah, holiness and purity.

Every person is fighting long and difficult battles. So many people have entered holiness and are serving G-d and many could not withstand the tests. They couldn't hold on. As soon as the evil thoughts and desires enter the person's mind, the person breaks, and thinks, 'perhaps this way is not really for me after all?'

What, you have another way?! *"And you shall choose life"*- there is good and there is bad, there is no middle ground. There is no such thing as, 'this is not right for me.' If you're not choosing life then you are choosing death! You might fall and leave the Torah path, you might see forbidden sights, etc. But, that is why you must keep choosing life.

In truth, if a person wants to come close to Hashem, if he would just *want* this, then nothing stands in the way of true desire. Nothing can stand in the way of a G-dly desire. Whatever the person desires, he will achieve. As Reb Natan says in *Likutei Halachos*, *'People who want to get rich travel to diamond mines. They travel long distances, through jungles, facing Indians, across deserts… most of these people were killed along the way. They gave their lives to travel far in order to earn a kilo of gold or a kilo of diamonds. So, why won't a person go through such self-sacrifice for the sake of Hashem? For the sake of holiness?'*

We can learn a lesson from the *Sitra Achra* (the side of evil). Look how hard people work for the *Sitra Achra*! University students sit day and night learning, barely sleeping for the sake of nonsense, for a temporary world. So, why can't we sit and learn Torah for the sake of Hakadosh Baruch Hu? Can't we also make some effort?

VA'EIRA

LEARNING FROM THE FROGS

The moment that Moshe Rabbenu arrived in Egypt, he brought the plagues; he brought the plague of blood and then after this he brought the frogs, as it's written, "*The frogs came out of the river and they went up and came into your houses…and into your ovens*" (Shemot 7:28).

The Egyptians closed all the doors and all of the windows. They closed every door and window that they had, until everything was hermetically sealed. No frog and no insect was able to get in, but the frogs pushed on, they split the marble. The marble split from above and from below and the frogs were able to enter.

There were even frogs that jumped into fire. They sought out the most dangerous places and they entered them. These frogs said, 'we need to sacrifice ourselves as a *kiddush Hashem*. After all, Hashem said, "*and they went up into your houses… and into your ovens.*" So where is the most dangerous place, and which place requires the greatest self-sacrifice? That's the ovens. Tons of frogs *mamash* jumped into the ovens, and *mamash* jumped into the fire.

The moment that they heard the words, "*into your ovens*" they jumped into the ovens; they ran to get burned up. They agreed to get burned up, because the main thing is to fulfill the words of Hashem and the will of Hashem with self-sacrifice.

But, in truth, the frogs that jumped into the fire didn't die, but the rest of the frogs did die, because it's written in verse 9, "*And the frogs from the houses and from the courtyards and the fields died.*" It's not written that those who were in the ovens died. So, it's written in the *Midrash* that the frogs that jumped into the ovens and into the fires continued to live. There's a *Midrash* that says that they live forever and that they're still alive even today.

The holy Zohar says that Hashem only created the world for those who sacrifice themselves on *kiddush Hashem* (to sanctify Hashem's name). The world was created only for those who are prepared to sacrifice themselves and to jump into the ovens and fires like Chananya, Mishael and Azaria--who learned, *kal ve'chomer* (all the more so), from the frogs that jumped into the fires.

They said if the frogs, which are only vermin which lack *da'at* and intelligence, jumped into the ovens and the flames to do G-d's will, all the more so we should jump into the fire!

At every moment, a person needs to agree to jump into the fire. Today, to jump into the flames means to pray with concentration. This is called jumping into the fire.

In Lesson 80 of *Likutey Moharan* the Rebbe says, *"When a person sees that he can't pray at all, and that he can't connect his thoughts to his words, then he should remind himself that he would certainly still wish to die to sanctify G-d's name."*

A person sees that he can't pray with concentration or that he can only pray very slowly. He gets up from sleeping and he can't concentrate at all. He gets to the *Shemoneh Esrei* prayer and he still can't pray, or perhaps his mind is still stuck in the middle of his *sugya*, in the middle of his learning or in the middle of his business, in the middle of that argument he just had…. So he's thinking about his business throughout the whole *Shemoneh Esrei* or about that argument or about his learning.

The whole time, a person is thinking about his money, his house, his kids or what he's going to be doing in an hour's time, where he's going to go. He doesn't stop thinking. His mind is busy processing a million thoughts a minute. So how can he cut himself off from all of these thoughts?

Rabbenu tells us a wonderful piece of advice about this: *"When a person sees that he can't pray at all, and that he can't connect his thoughts to his words, then he should remind himself that he would certainly still wish to die to sanctify G-d's name."*

If a person agrees to lay down his life before every letter and every word of prayer, then he'll have peace [from all the extraneous thoughts]. Suddenly, his mind will open and the light will turn on. The Rebbe says that this is something that's very simple to do, that everyone can do very easily, to sacrifice his life *for kiddush Hashem.*

Our whole work is only to create vessels to constrain our negative traits. Each one of us is full of negative traits, full of negative thoughts and full of worries. Our mind runs at 600,000 kms a second and it's making plans all the time. Here it's trying to make a million dollars, there's it's trying to open a *kollel*, here it's trying to start a *gemach*. The mind runs at the speed of light.

Even *Tzaddikim* find it difficult to stop their minds. The Rogachover Rebbe wasn't able to stop his brilliant mind. Rav Natan also said, *"I was unable to stop my mind, it was difficult for me to pray with concentration. Until I came to Rabbenu... only Rabbenu, only Rabbenu. Only Rabbenu taught me to take all of the negative traits and all of the negative thoughts and to put them into the letters. The Rebbe taught me this and he also gave me all of the strength required to do this."*

The Rebbe said that when anyone prays *Shemoneh Esrei* slowly and with concentration, this is *mamash* self-sacrifice, this is the greatest suffering that there is. This is called jumping into the fire. Every *Shemoneh Esrei* is a completely new beginning. A person needs to nullify everything that happened to them up until now before every *Shemoneh Esrei*.

67

A person says, behold! I made a mess and blemished things the whole last 24 hours! I stumbled into forbidden sights, forbidden thoughts, and so on and so on, until it's impossible to even list all of them or tell them over – and now I need to pray?! How can I possibly pray at this point? So, then he opens the prayer book and then closes it again after five minutes. And he says, 'look, I've been doing all those terrible things the whole day!'

This is what the Rebbe was talking about when he said that we should know that these things aren't connected to each other. Even a thief needs to pray. Even a thief needs to say thank you Hashem that you didn't make me a non-Jew. He can't say, 'I stole something, so now I'm exempt from praying.'

So, the Rebbe says sacrifice your life in your prayers, for each and every letter. You got to the stage of praying, so pray with concentration. Even if you just did the greatest, worst sin beforehand. Make *teshuva* and go into your prayers renewed, as though you had just now been born.

All the success that we achieved throughout all the generations, all of it was only in the merit of those who sacrificed their lives to sanctify G-d's name, who jumped into the flames with happiness and dancing. When we pray with concentration, letter by letter, very slowly, then this is exactly the same thing. It's as if we'd also jumped into the flames and into the ovens.

THE PATH TO REDEMPTION

When Moshe Rabbenu arrived in Egypt, he said to them, 'Holy friends! Hashem revealed himself to me! The redemption is going happen soon! Start being happy, start to sing, start to play melodies; the time to dance and sing has arrived; bring a band, bring a violin, bring a flute; start to sing about the wonderful news that the redemption is near...' But, *"they did not hear Moshe from their shortness of breath and back-breaking work."*

Rebbe Nachman of Breslov says, in Lesson 86 of *Lekutey Moharan*, *"They were in a state of shortness of breath due their lack in emunah and, because of this, it was necessary to place upon them back-breaking work and fasts."* Those who are in a state of lacking *emunah*, since they do not have complete *emunah* they turn to penance and fasts.

The Noam Elimelach says this was the argument between Moshe and the *Tzaddikim* of his generation. Moshe said, "Stop with the fasts and the penance, stop doing the back breaking work. Start being happy, start singing and dancing." Because, when the Jews began to be enslaved by the Egyptians, *Am Yisrael* was not silent, the *Tzaddikim* were not quiet, the *Tzaddikim* fasted and cried, they sat on the floor.

They saw that every day Jewish children are being thrown into the Nile, every day the Egyptians were slaughtering Jewish children and placing them into the walls of the buildings. Pharaoh was bathing himself in babies' blood. No one was silent, everyone was fasting and crying. They fasted to try to bring the redemption. So, Moshe came to them and said, "Holy friends, this is not the way! This is a mistake! If you want to fast, so you can fast, but this is not going to bring the redemption. With fasts and penance, we are not bringing the redemption."

They said to him (the *Tzaddikim* of the generation said to Moshe), "What!? You're trying to place before us a new way of serving G-d!? You want to take away our fasting and penance, after we have already been fasting for years, fasts and penance year after year". As a result, *"they did not hear Moshe from their shortness of breath and back-breaking work."*

Due to their hopelessness, from their shortness of breath and from all their back breaking work, they weren't able to shake off their despair or to believe that there really was hope. They weren't able to believe in the redemption. Moshe said to them, "The time has come to serve G-d from a place of happiness, from a place of tremendous happiness. Only happiness is going to conquer the evil forces (the *klipos*). Only happiness is going to bring the redemption."

The Noam Elimelach says that the *Tzaddikim* search for back breaking work and fasts since they have precious souls, and not regular souls. However, nonetheless, they do not see what the *Tzaddikim* possessing the essence of Moshe see, because the True *Tzaddik* (meaning the *Tzaddik* possesing the essence of Moshe) is able to nullify all the harsh judgments and decrees with complete ease. He doesn't need to exert any effort. He doesn't need any penance or fasts, since he is able to nullify all the harsh judgments through happiness, through playing melodies, and through singing.

The world is mistaken, since a person thinks that in order to merit salvation and to mitigate harsh judgments one needs back-breaking work and fasts. Practically speaking, the Baal Shem Tov already completely nullified the concept of fasts and back-breaking work. This, too, is what Rabbenu is saying-- if only the Jews of world would also know and believe that through *happiness* it is possible to merit salvation and to mitigate all the harsh judgments that ever have been and that ever will be.

BO

A PERSON'S GREATNESS IS HIS HUMILITY

The essence of a person's greatness is only his lowliness and humility, because only someone who dwells in the dust is going to rise at *techiyas hameitim* (the revival of the dead), and will merit eternal life. As we say in the *Shemoneh Esreh* prayers, *"He establishes His emunah for those who sleep in the dust."*

The more a person feels their own lowliness, and is humble, that's how much he'll merit to be revived in *techiyas hameitim*, and to have eternal life. The more he gathers all these points of lowliness every day, that's how much he'll merit to eternal life, and to the pleasures of the World to Come. As it's written, *"Rise up and rejoice, those who are asleep in the dust"* (Isaiah 26).

Every time a person is insulted, he collects another spark of lowliness. So, the more he's humiliated and the more he's put to shame, the happier he should be! If you know that someone is going to shame you on the street, you should go and immerse in a *mikvahh* first, because you will receive such an enormous (spiritual) light as a result of being humiliated, that's it's worth immersing first in order to give yourself the vessels to receive this huge light.

Being humiliated brings such a tremendous light down to a person, which can't be achieved by doing any other *mitzvah* in the world. Humiliation turns a person into 'nothing'. He then merits such great light, the infinite light, a light which is above all the worlds and which includes and surrounds all the worlds. The more you collect these sparks of lowliness, the more of this Divine light, this infinite light, you'll merit to have.

King David says in *Tehillim*, "*Cleanse me with hyssop[2] and I will be purified*." Cleanse me with hyssop! I want to be like the hyssop, I want to be humiliated, that everyone should degrade me, that everyone should laugh at me, and take me down a few pegs." Only this is true *teshuva*.

I need to know that I am the worst of the lot and that I did more sins than anyone else, that I caused more destruction than anyone else. All I ask is please, 'cleanse me with hyssop, and I will be purified'. I want to be hyssop, like the moss growing in the cracks, the moss that everyone walks on, so that I will be humiliated. Every day of my life, I want to be like the hyssop.

There are two levels to making *teshuva*. There's a level where a person is insulted and he stays quiet. This is called, "*He's insulted but doesn't respond to his insult; he hears his disgrace but doesn't respond.*" He's humiliated, but he stays silent, he doesn't answer back. Like it says in the verse, "*And Aharon was silent*".

But there's a level of "*brought about from love, and being happy with suffering*", when we merit to reach an even higher level. A person is humiliated, he's degraded, but he's happy the whole day long! He's singing and dancing, he accepts all the insults happily, with love, with songs.

Every humiliation is a healing salve for his injuries; it heals his wounds. When you insult him, he feels as though you're spreading a healing salve on his injuries. His whole body is full of wounds and lesions. "*From the sole of the foot to the crown of the head, nothing is whole.*" He feels as though every humiliation is healing his illnesses, every humiliation is 'purifying waters'; "*and I threw on you pure waters, and you were purified*".

---

[2] Hyssop was used in Temple times to sprinkle the blood of purification on the Israelites to purify them from their sins. The word for hyssop, אזוב, also means moss.

Lowliness and humiliation have no measure. When a person is humiliated, he's transformed into the *'ein sof'* (the infinite), he's transformed into something which has 'no measure' – into nothing. Now that he has no measure or boundary, now he can feel the Divine light.

People may say about him, "This person is nothing, he's worthless, he's a liar, he's a hypocrite." But everything they say just makes him even more of a 'nothing', and thus he achieves every success and abudance. When a person is humiliated just once, it's really a million successes! After he gets humiliated, his successes won't stop and his bounty won't cease. He'll be the provider for everyone in the land. He'll merit to have infinite bounty, just like it was said about Yosef, *"And Yosef provided for all the people in the land."*

Yosef provided for the whole country, because after he was sold and humiliated, he was nothing. So, all the bounty came down to the world through him. The more shame a person receives, the more success and abundance he'll attain.

Sometimes when a person is humiliated, he may say, "You're humiliating me, because I'm a *Tzaddik*! And because I'm a servant of Hashem." This is arrogance. We shouldn't get arrogant about being humiliated. Rather, we should think that we're being shamed because in fact we actually deserve it - because I am really not a *Tzaddik* and I'm not a *chassid*. I don't learn Torah the way I should, I don't guard my eyes; in truth, I'm a *rasha* (evil-doer)! We have to acknowledge the truth. If someone tells you you're a *rasha*, then you have to think, 'Baruch Hashem, he's telling me the truth.'

A person is obligated to acknowledge the truth. When someone comes and reminds me who I really am, I should give him a kiss, I should kiss his feet, that he's telling me the truth. We have to repeat to ourselves the verse, *"Hate the one who loves you, and love the one who hates you"*.

You need to love the people who hate you. A person needs people to speak badly about him, and to humiliate him, as much as possible. When people like you, it counts for nothing. You need to hate the people who like you. That person who likes you, they are really only flattering you and covering things up.

He's just dragging you into delusions that you're a *Tzaddik*, that you're doing fine. So, hate the one who loves you, but love the one who hates you! This is the person who's rebuking you and humiliating you. *This* is the person you need to love. This is the person you need to carry round on your shoulders.

FROM THE SMALLEST SPARK

From one tiny miniscule speck it's possible to sanctify a person and bring him to the greatest holiness. The secret of *"This month for you all is the head of the months"* is that *"when the moon is a small sliver in the sky like 'this', you will see it and you will sanctify it."*

Any small point or tiny speck, *"like this, you will see it and you will sanctify it"*. It is almost impossible to see this speck at all, but already it is possible to sanctify it: *"like this, you will see it and you will sanctify it"*. If there is still any tiny, miniscule, Jewish speck within a person the *Tzaddikim* can still bring out the holiness from that speck. Any speck or any spark of Judaism, *"like this, you will see it and you will sanctify it"*. This is the reason why our Sages said that we should have started the Torah from the verse, *"This month for you all is the head of the months"*.

We should have started the Torah from this point, from the tiniest most miniscule point.

If there remains in a person any speck of Judaism, even if there remains the smallest, most miniscule speck in the world, it's possible to bring that person back to Judaism and to teach him the whole Torah.

The Rebbe (Rebbe Nachman of Breslov) says in Lesson 12 of *Likutey Moharan*, about the verse, *"Where is G-d's Honor?"* that even if a person fell to the most impure places, even if he fell into the *10 crowns of the side of evil*, if there remains within him any speck [of hope], he can call out from there, "Where are You G-d!? Master of the world, where are You!?"

He is not yelling out like a heretic. Rather, he's calling out, "Master of the world, where are you? I want to see the Master of the World!" If a person is able to call out and scream, "I want to see the Master of the World! Where is G-d's glory?", then Hashem is able to reveal himself to that person.

Therefore, after the Parsha of the Red Heifer comes the Parsha of 'Ha Chodesh' (this month shall be to you...). This is because, what is the Red Heifer? After a person was already turned into dust and ashes, when he's already been completely burned, he's been completely turned into dust and ashes so there is not even a speck left in him, only ash--yet, this remaining ash still has within it the tiniest, most miniscule aspect of Judaism; Moshe Rabbenu is able to detect this speck of holiness (and bring this person atonement and return him in *teshuva*).

We cannot see any speck of Judaism in a person like this, but a *Tzaddik* like Moshe is able to detect this speck of holiness.

Hashem showed Moshe Rabbenu that from this miniscule speck, one's revival begins, from here a person is reborn. *Am Yisrael* suffered for the generation of the Tower of Bavel and for the generation of the Flood.

Am Yisrael were all reincarnated souls and through the back-breaking servitude in Egypt they brought out from Egypt the sparks that were within *Adam HaRishon,* since there were sparks within him that got lost. *Am Yisrael* came from these sparks, and *Am Yisrael* had to break the evil forces (*klipos*) that surrounded these sparks.

If *Am Yisrael* knew the secret that when *"they groaned"* and when *"they cried out"*-- that from one tiny, miniscule speck it is possible to sanctify a person and bring him to his greatest holiness, they would have brought the redemption speedily by calling out to Hashem. But they didn't know the secret of calling out to Hashem. Only when Moshe Rabbenu arrived in Egypt, he revealed to them the secret of crying out to Hashem. He then placed within them the *emunah* that from the tiniest, most minuscule speck a person can be raised up to the greatest holiness.

BESHALACH

BELIEVING IN THE TZADDIK

When the Children of Israel left Egypt, Datan and Aviram didn't follow along with Moshe Rabbenu. In fact, the sea split for Datan and Aviram a second time, in their own merit. The author of the book, *Ma'ayanah Shel Torah*, asks a question in *Parshat Beshalach* on the verse, "*The water was like a wall for them on their right and on their left*". He asks, 'how was it that Datan and Aviram didn't die in the plague of darkness?'

The *Midrash* says that no one told Datan and Aviram that *Am Yisrael* were leaving Egypt, or going to the Land of Israel. No one told them this secret. They thought that everyone was just going to Mount Horev and then returning back to Egypt. They said that just going to Mount Horev and back again wasn't worth all the effort. So, no one told them that they were leaving completely. If they'd have been told that they were going for good, and not coming back, then they too would have left at the same time as the rest of the nation.

So, why weren't they told? The answer is because every little thing they heard they passed on to Pharaoh. If Pharaoh would have been told that the Children of Israel had no intention of returning, he wouldn't have chased after them-- and then the *Yam Suf* (Sea of Reeds) wouldn't have split.

If Pharaoh would have known that they were leaving forever, he would have agreed for them to leave completely. But, instead, he was told: "*[We will go] for three days' journey into the desert.*" They didn't tell him that they weren't coming back.

Moshe didn't lie to Pharaoh. He said, "*[We will go] for three days' journey into the desert, to sacrifice to Hashem, our G-d.*" Pharaoh understood that they would be returning. However, Moshe had requested that Pharaoh should give them three days, but he didn't say that they were going to come back after those three days. Pharaoh simply inferred that they were going for three days now, and that they would return afterwards. Hashem only said three days; Moshe only said three days, so Datan and Aviram thought that they were only going temporarily, to Mount Horev, for the giving of the Torah, and this wasn't worthwhile enough for them. *'What's the big deal, the Torah will be given… We could also experience the giving of the Torah in Egypt; we could just as well have 'matan Torah' here in Egypt too…!'*

A person can listen to a tape or a recording of the *Tzaddik* speaking, but the *ikker*, the essence, is to see the *Tzaddik*, and to see the movements the *Tzaddik* makes. The *ikker* is these movements, which speak volumes. A person may listen to a recording, but he can also listen to that recording while he's still lying under his duvet too.

Datan and Aviram said, 'we'll listen to *matan Torah* in Egypt. We'll hear it; there's going to be sounds that will travel from one end of the world to the other, and it'll be translated into all 70 languages, so we'll also hear it.' Datan and Aviram really didn't want to leave Egypt. Suddenly, however, they hear that everyone's going to *Eretz Yisrael*! Pharaoh's messengers came back with the message that the Children of Israel don't intend to come back at all. So, Datan and Aviram started running.

They already saw that the sea had split, that there was no sea, and then the sea came back and covered over the Egyptians. So, that's why it's written a second time in the Torah, *"the sea was like a wall for them on the right and on the left."* The second time the sea split, it did so only for Datan and Aviram.

So, how did they suddenly develop the *emunah* to believe in and run after Moshe Rabbenu? After all, even the people who left Egypt didn't automatically follow Moshe because they believed he was the *Tzaddik* of the generation. They just believed that he was a good leader. They believed that he knew how to make use of Hashem's holy names and that he knew how to bring down the plague of wild animals and the plague of the death of the firstborn by using these names. They said it was possible that Moshe also knew how to curse, but Bilaam too knew how to do that.

As Balak said, "*If you bless they will be blessed, and if you curse they will be cursed.*" Bilaam also knew how to curse. If Bilaam cursed someone, then they died. So, who says that Moshe was any better than Bilaam?!

It's written in the *Midrash HaGadol* that Bilaam was certain that when *Am Yisrael* left Egypt they would call him. Bilaam was sure that if Israel left Egypt they would call him. In the *Midrash* there are different opinions; one says that Bilaam was Lavan himself. The Ari says that Bilaam was a reincarnation of Lavan.

Another opinion says that he was the son of Lavan. And yet another says that he was his grandson. So, if he was the son of Lavan, that would mean that he was the brother of Rachel and Leah. And, if he was the grandson of Lavan, then would make him the nephew of Rachel and Leah.

If so, he was around 400 years old now, so it was fitting to call him (to take the Children of Israel out of Egypt). Instead of some youngster, aged 80 years old; they should have called Bilaam. So, Bilaam said, "*The wicked man will see this and be angered. He will gnash his teeth and melt away*" (*Tehillim* 112). Bilaam said, 'I'm going to take vengeance against Moshe Rabbenu for this. I'm not going to forgive Moshe Rabbenu, that he was so brazen to take my place. What, Moshe Rabbenu, that small kid, aged 80… He's 300 years younger than me! Why should he take my place?!'

So, the people who went out with Moshe Rabbenu, they didn't

really believe that he was the *Tzaddik* of the generation. They thought that he had some sort of power to curse and some sort of power to bless, but that Bilaam also had the power to curse and to bless. So, after all, what's the difference between Moshe and Bilaam?! We still haven't seen any difference between Moshe and Bilaam. Bilaam also curses, Bilaam also blesses, and he also curses and blesses.

So, the fact that they were following after Moshe Rabbenu, still didn't mean that they believed in him, or that they thought he was the *Tzaddik* of the generation or the messenger of G-d. Rather, they thought he was a good leader and that he could give blessings. So they left anyway. It wasn't until they saw the sea split that it says, *"and they believed in Hashem and in Moshe, his servant"*.

YITRO

RETURN TO YOUR WIVES!

One of my security guards in the prison, Yitzhak, only used to talk to me about *divrei Torah* and didn't let me sleep at night because he was saying words of Torah 24 hours a day. He asked me, "Explain to me how it's possible that Yitro, the biggest *rasha* (evil-doer) in the world, the biggest 'Pope' of them all, married into the descendant of Amram?"

The holy Zohar says that Yitro was the biggest 'Pope' of them all; there was no *avoda zara*, idol worship, that he hadn't worshipped. He knew the *segula* (spiritual attribute) for every form of idol worship, because every idol worship has its own *segula*. 'If you're sick with this disease, go to this particular *avoda zara*; if you're ill with that disease, then go to that *avoda zara*' – because every form of idol worship was given the merit of 'working' for one day a year, and he knew which day to tell people to go to them.

And Yitro took all of his idols and smashed them! He had a house full of idols – 365 idols, one for every day of the year. He took a gigantic staff, a big iron bar, and smashed and shattered all of the idols in front of everyone. He told everyone, 'come and see me, the Pope, shatter 365 idols!'

In the morning, they grabbed his daughters and threw them into the Nile; they threw them into a well, into a pit of water. Each pit was 50 meters deep. We're not talking about some pit in the desert; each pit was 50-100 meters deep. It was impossible to get them out. Then Moshe came along and said the ineffable name of Hashem and rescued them. This happened because Yitro threw everything into the sea; he smashed all of the idols.

So, Yitzhak said to me, 'what's the connection between Yitro and Amram?' 'Why is it that Yitro suddenly became related through marriage to Amram?' He answered by saying that Yitro got up one day and broke all 365 idols, plus a few hundred others, smashing them all in front of everyone.

The next day, they caught his daughters and asked them, "Who are you? You're the daughters of that *meshuggeh* (crazy person), of that lunatic who broke all the idols!" and they threw them into the Nile. So, Moshe came and said the ineffable name of Hashem and rescued them.

The same thing with Amram. What did Amram do? Everything is written in Rashi. If you read the Rashi, it says that 'Amram separated from Yocheved.' What does it mean 'Amram separated from Yocheved?' We're not talking about some random Jew in the background, some Jew in Eilat or in some basement or cave. Amram was the *Gadol HaDor*! Amram who kept the whole Torah! Amram who was going to be the father of Moshe Rabbenu.

When Amram divorced his wife, everyone else also divorced their wives. 'What is this?! Every male newborn is going to be taken to the Nile?!' 'What?! We're going to have children just to throw them into the Nile?!'

But then, Miriam came. A girl aged 5 ½, she was six years and six months older than Moshe, calculated from the time that she returned Yocheved to her husband. She said, '*Abba*, you're sinning to Hashem! Pharaoh doesn't exist, he never did and never will exist. There is no Pharaoh, there are no terrorists, there is no ISIS, these things simply don't exist!'

'The *sitra achra* (dark side) doesn't exist. Pharaoh is the dark side, he doesn't exist! And what's more, you should know that Pharaoh only decrees in this world, while your decree is affecting the World to Come!' Because these souls need to come down into the world. A person thinks to himself. 'I'm not going to bring any more children into the world, and it'll be easier for me that way.' Those children that should have been born through that person may have been destined to become the *Tzaddikim* of the generation. Now, maybe they'll be dropped into some *rasha's* (evil-doer's) lap; who knows where these souls will end up?

And that person will be held responsible for whatever happens to them, because he was meant to bring another 10 souls down into the world, and he didn't. So now, they got reincarnated who knows where, maybe by non-Jews, maybe they need to convert now... So, everything that now happens to them, that person is responsible for it, because he was given the job of bringing down another 10 souls, and he didn't do it. He abstained.

He thought maybe he wouldn't have enough food for them. He didn't know that the souls bring their own food with them. Children bring their own sustenance with them. The moment a person brings another child into the world, they bring another room along with them. You'll see how the apartment's rooms expand with each and every child and you can sit there comfortably with each and every child.

Those children that you were meant to bring into the world and you didn't, their blood is on your head. And Amram was also held responsible. He was 120 years old, maybe even 130 years old, already, and a little girl aged 5 ½ came and said, '*Abba*, you're sinning to Hashem! Pharaoh never was and never will be. It's just our sins, it's the darkness of our sins, and what's more, these souls need to come down to this lowly world, no matter what!'

She also told him, 'Pharaoh only decreed against the males, while you are also decreeing against the females. What's going on here?!' So, there'll be a girl. If a man has 10 girls, they'll have 100 children. What's the worst that can happen, let's be sensible! You can't prevent the future generations from being born.'

And so, Amram got up, after three months when the whole of *Am Yisrael* had got divorced, and all the children were crying, and all the mothers were crying and everyone was crying, 'Ima and *Abba* have split up, who is going to help us to grow up? We're going to end up being criminals, we're going to end up becoming *chilonim* (secular Jews)!' 'What's going on here?!'

So, Amram got up, banged on the table and said, '*Rabotai (gentlemen)! There's been a terrible mistake; I erred. For the last three months, we've all been divorced, but now return to your wives! Because I've made the biggest mistake of my life!*'

MOSHE PREPARED THE WOMEN FIRST

Before the giving of the Torah, Hashem said to Moshe, "*At this time, tell Am Yisrael in these words and in this order; you will speak softly to the women (Beis Yaakov) and you will speak firmly to the sons of Israel*" (Shemot 18:3).

Hashem said to Moshe, 'this time we are not going to make the same mistake as what happened during the time of the creation, when I initially said the first commandment to Adam and then Adam said it over to Eve and she didn't understand Adam's words. This misunderstanding caused death to be decreed for all the generations. So, this time I (G-d) am going to do the opposite.' As it is written, "*In these words and in this order; you will speak softly to the women (Beis Yaakov).*"

First, assemble all the women, call out to all the women of Israel and speak before them fiery words and explain to them about the giving of the Torah. Explain to them that now, with the giving of the Torah, *Am Yisrael* is leaving the physical world, leaving their vices behind and

84

their bodies are changing – everything is changing. First, prepare the women, before the men.

A woman's simplicity is much greater than a man's simplicity, and a woman's *emunah* is much greater than a man's *emunah*. Therefore, first, "*you will speak softly to the women*". First, Moshe assembled all the women of Israel, and spoke with them fiery words on the greatness of the giving of the Torah, explaining to the women what someone merits by receiving the Torah-- through Torah the possibility exists of becoming a glowing, shining sun which shines forth from one end of the universe to the other. This is possible through the Torah, since the Torah allows someone to rid himself of his lusts, his bad character traits and all his nonsensical behavior.

After Moshe spoke with Beis Yaakov, "*in these words and in this order; you will speak softly to the women (Beis Yaakov)*", Moshe then assembled the men, "*and you will speak firmly to the sons of Israel.*"

In truth, since Moshe assembled the women before he assembled the men, not a single woman sinned during the sin of the Golden Calf. These words, "*In these words and in this order; you will speak softly to the women (Beis Yaakov)*" burned deep down into the women's hearts. Moshe's instructions through his fiery words penetrated down into the women's bones and nothing could disrupt these women's service of Hashem during the times when the rest of *Am Yisrael* began to get confused.

Like when Moshe didn't come down from Mount Sinai and everyone got worried, since Moshe didn't come down on time. 'Even if they had made the correct calculation, what does it matter if Moshe arrives a day late?' 'So, Moshe wants another day to learn Torah in Heaven with Hashem, what's the big deal?'

The truth is that *Am Yisrael* miscalculated the days, but even if they hadn't, 'if Moshe doesn't arrive on the fortieth day, so he'll arrive on the forty-first day, the forty-second day; there's no need to be worried, we'll wait patiently for Moshe's arrival.'

King Shaul lost his whole kingdom and the merit of ruling over the whole world because he didn't wait for Shmuel. If Shaul had waited for Shmuel another twenty minutes, Shaul would have become the king of the entire world. Any person that can wait patiently just another twenty minutes will become the king over the entire world. So, wait patiently another hour, or even just one more day-- since a person that can wait patiently can merit ruling over the entire world.

Yet, while Moshe was up on Mount Sinai, *Am Yisrael* was short of breath-- just like during the Exodus from Egypt, *"And they did not hear Moshe from their shortness of breath and back-breaking work"*, where Rabbenu (Rebbe Nachman of Breslov) says, that 'shortness of breath' is a reference to a lack of *emunah*.

"In these words and in this order; you will speak softly to the women (Beis Yaakov) and you will speak firmly to the sons of Israel." It's from this verse that it's said the redemption will come in the merit of the righteous women. The women in the Exodus from Egypt were the only ones that truly had *emunah* in Moshe. Their emunah in Moshe was so strong they took drums with them out of Egypt and danced after crossing the Red Sea. Because of this, the women did not sin at all.

The men only sang after crossing the Red Sea, but the women had much more joy and *emunah*, so they went out and danced too, as it's written, *"And all the women went out with drums and dancing"*. The men stood solemnly and sang, without drums and without dancing.

According to one's happiness and one's enthusiasm for holy things, so too this is what protects him during the difficult times. The women were joyously enthusiastic for the splitting of the sea and for the giving of the Torah. And it was this joyous enthusiasm that stood for them and guarded them from transgressing any sin. The women didn't sin during the Golden Calf and didn't sin during the Spies excursion into Eretz Yisrael. The women didn't fall or even stumble, but rather it was the men who fell and tripped up in all sorts of ways. The woman, she is the unshakeable one! She is the foundation of the home! She keeps the home, she guards the home and she merits the true giving of the Torah within the home.

All the Jewish souls were present when the Torah was received, yet specifically the women merited to receive the Torah more so than the men, and the proof is that the women didn't fall into any sins after receiving the Torah. The women didn't take part in the sin of the Golden Calf and not in the sin of the Spies, and not in any of the sins mentioned in the book of *Bamidbar,* since the women didn't fall into any sin or transgression after receiving the Torah.

This is the merit of this verse, *"In these words and in this order, you will speak softly to the women (Beis Yaakov)"*. The righteous women of each generation preserve *Am Yisrael* to this day. The woman to this day guards her husband and her home. She keeps the *Shabbos* and she reminds her husband to sing the holy songs of *Shabbos*. She guards the holiness of the *Shabbos* table! Only in the merit of the righteous women did the nation of Israel merit the redemption, and now too in their merit we should merit to be redeemed in our generation and to see the coming of the *Moshiach* speedily in our days, Amen.

ONE NATION WITH ONE SOUL

Why is *"encamped"* written in this verse in the Hebrew singular form? Rashi explains: *"As one person, with one heart"*, i.e. they went together, united as one. In *Parshat Beshalach*, when referring to the Egyptians it says, *"and Egypt followed them in pursuit"* (again using the singular form). Rashi says a similar explanation, only in the reverse order: *"With one heart, as one person."* Why is it that when referring to the the Egyptians, Rashi chooses to state first the heart and then the body, whereas in the case of *Am Yisrael*, he chose to state first the body and only then the heart?

Is this in order to suggest that we're so connected to our bodies? Are the people of Israel tied to materialism? Are the other nations people of heart and spirit? On the contrary! *We* are a nation of 'heart' and *they* are nations of the 'body'!

The author of the book, *Ma'ayanah Shel Torah*, answers this perplexity and explains that the meaning of *"one heart"* in the verse regarding the Egyptians, refers to their 'special desire', the desire that unites together all of the nations of the world, which is the desire to kill and annihilate *Am Yisrael*. This is the one thing that unites them! That is the meaning of *"one heart"*.

It doesn't mean they have a heart-- they have no heart at all! They are completely heartless! However, they share a common desire – one desire, one purpose. There are no disputes or differences of opinions when it comes to this mutual purpose. They all look forward to the return of Auschwitz. All of the nations are just waiting to see who will succeed in killing off the Jewish people. This is the *"one heart"* of all of the nations of the world, without any exceptions whatsoever.

With regard to *Am Yisrael*, however, the meaning is entirely different. *Am Yisrael* are one! They are one body! All of the Jews are one person! This is the reality! We are all one! *Am Yisrael* is one person containing 248 limbs and 365 sinews! Every person is a part of that one body. One person can be part of the head, while another is part of the arm; one is part of the foot while another can be a finger, a vein or the skin, etc. They are all a part of that one body.

Am Yisrael is the living meaning of 'unity'. The Jews are one body, one soul! No person in the world would willingly part with any limb of his body, not a finger nor even the nail of his pinkie! Nothing at all! If a person were to approach his friend and ask, 'How bad could it be if we cut off just a small part of your finger? It wouldn't be so terrible to lose say a third of your finger, would it? What do you need it for, anyway?" The reply would unquestionably be, "No way! I'm not prepared for you to cut off even a speck of my finger!" The same applies to *Am Yisrael*. No Jew is dispensable. We must all love every single Jew with all our heart and all our soul.

The Rebbe of Vorkin comments on the verse, *"and Israel encamped there"* and explains that the Jews who came out of Egypt had an immense love for each other. They recognized the beauty and grace in each other [in Hebrew both the words for grace (*chen*) and the word for "and they camped" (*vayachon*) share the same root] and conceded to one another. They saw and acknowledged the uniqueness in each other – their virtues, their greatness and righteousness. Each person felt that the holiness and righteousness of every other Jew had by far exceeded his own. This is the meaning of *"and they encamped there"*.

"As one man"-- every Jew cared deeply for the other and truly wanted the others to be happy and successful. They wanted only the best for each other! The love and special feelings they had towards each other was what enabled them to receive the Holy Torah.

Our purpose in this world is to observe the commandment of 'loving our fellow Jew', to love each other and be united as one. We need to nullify ourselves to that reality. Every person must feel the suffering of his brethren and try to sense what is causing them pain. We must make sure not to do anything that can hurt people or cause them any type of grief. We should love every Jew with all our hearts and all our souls and never speak against anyone. Even if a Jew is causing you the most terrible suffering and troubles and even if he beats you, you must not fail [in your responsibility to love him]. Don't respond. Don't say a word. *Am Yisrael* is one body - so you and they are just one person.

If you accidentally hurt yourself, G-d forbid, would you then hate the limb of your body that wounded the other limb? Of course not! You must realize that the other Jew (who hurt you) is also a diamond in the crown of *Hashem Yisborach*! After all, that Jew also dons *Tefillin* every morning, keeps *Shabbos*, learns Torah and wakes up to learn at *chatzos*. You should know that the purpose of the slander that he speaks about you is only to sweeten the Heavenly judgment against you. It atones for all your sins and it molds you into a vessel with which to receive the Torah.

When a person lacks love for his fellow Jews, he cannot grow to any higher spiritual levels. The Torah itself spiritually burns the person because the only vessel with which one can accept the Torah is *'ahavat chinam'* – unconditional love. You must understand that the first priority of a person who is truly connected to the way of Rebbe Nachman of Breslov is that he has love of his fellow Jew. Only once he loves every Jew with his heart and soul, can he merit understanding the Rebbe! Only then, will he merit drawing the greatness and the essence of the Rebbe's teachings down into this world.

People have plenty of strength to go out and work for 24 hours a day in order to sustain their family. This proves that they have enough strength to give their very lives for the sake of another Jew. A person becomes an existing reality only in so far as he is absorbed in the Jewish people as a collective!

The expression "I" doesn't exist at all! *I* am only a reality if *I* am able to nullify myself for the sake of another. Everyone is a single existence, one soul, so there is no such a thing as being 'alone'. There is no 'one'. If a person becomes 'one', it means he has cut himself off from the rest, in which case, he is nullified - it's as though he doesn't exist at all!

When does a person become a reality? Only when he is capable of sacrificing his own life for the sake of others, for the only reality is that of the Jewish people collectively and of *Hashem Yisborach*. There are no individuals! Anything that is individual is nullified and non-existent. It is just a figment of imagination. The essence of the Torah and the *mitzvos* and the essence of a Jew is giving--giving to other people, giving to everyone.

When a person separates himself from the *klal* (the Jewish people collectively) and is only concerned with himself, he becomes a non-reality. He has wiped himself off the face of the planet! A person becomes existent, he becomes a reality, only according to the way he includes himself within the *klal* and within Hashem. The only reality is to be included within the *klal* and Hashem. This is the only reality! Every person must know that whenever he thinks only about himself and has no concern for others, he is simply non-existent! On the other hand, when he forgets about his own needs in his concern about others, he loves everyone and doesn't speak against any other Jew and only thinks about the *klal* and about Hashem – then he truly exists.

MISHPATIM

GUARD THE SHABBOS AND IT WILL GUARD YOU

When a child sees his father sitting calmly and happily and singing at the *Shabbos* table, it soothes the child's heart and makes him feel good. A beautiful *Shabbos* table is a child's whole life and all his happiness.

Rabbenu said, *Shabbos* is like a great big wedding, like a great big wedding with many people being happy together and dancing. Yet there's a person in his finest most honorable clothing, he's running fast and wants to get into the wedding and to be a part of the happiness, but it is not so easy to get in. One needs merits even to see the wedding through a hole in the wall, through a tiny crack.

When the holy *Shabbos* arrives there is a wedding in Heaven. This is a wedding of 26 hours from *Kabbalat Shabbos* until *Havdalah*. Every Jew has to join this wedding; he has to join the melodies and the dancing of this wedding in Heaven.

During *Kabbalat Shabbos* when we pray the words, *"L'cha Dodee"*, Hashem immediately enters the Garden of Eden to dance with the *Tzaddikim*. The whole *Shabbos* is as if Hashem dances with all the *Tzaddikim* and all the angels in the Garden of Eden. All of them are dancing in a circle around Hashem saying, *"This is Hashem that we have been longing for, we will rejoice and be happy in his salvation."*

While dancing around Hashem, everyone sees Hashem face to face and, during this dancing, everyone receives his nourishment from the light of the '*aspeklariyah hameira*' (the shining mirror). All the goodness we have in this physical world comes from the happiness drawn down on *Shabbos* from the dancing and the melodies of Hashem with the *Tzaddikim* in the Garden of Eden.

The Rebbe says, *Shabbos* is just like a wedding. This means *Shabbos* is literally a wedding. *Shabbos* is like a big and important wedding that everyone attends, but the problem is that not everyone successfully gets into the wedding hall, since the wedding hall does not have space for everyone. Similarly, to the weddings of the *Chassidic Masters* where 30,000, 40,000, and 50,000 Chassidim all want to attend, yet there is not enough room for everyone.

Some *Chassidim* try to climb up to the window and some stand on the roof in order to get a glimpse of the *Chupah*, to see the great happiness of the wedding, and to see the groom dancing. Perhaps there is a small crack in the wall or maybe from a nearby rooftop where one can catch a glimpse of the happiness of this wedding, maybe one can see the dancing...

The Rebbe says, "*Shabbos* is like a wedding", but how does one merit to see the happiness of *Shabbos*? How does one get into the wedding hall? To see this happiness of *Shabbos* is not a simple thing. The Rebbe explains, "*One requires great merit just to be able look through a hole in the wall.*"

Singing the *Shabbos* songs with complete devotion and in complete happiness - this is how one joins the wedding. *Shabbos* is only for dancing, for singing, for melodies. Once *Shabbos* arrives, a person needs to be happy and to sing and to dance.

Shabbos is happiness without end, a happiness that never finishes. On *Shabbos*, it is forbidden to have any thoughts of sadness, any worries or any feelings of anxiety. One's Judaism totally depends on this. The more a person is happy on *Shabbos*, and the more he dances, the more he merits receiving the light of Hashem throughout the whole week, since the light of Hashem shines for a person according to how happy he is on *Shabbos*. There is no permission for anyone to have any sorrow or any complaints on the holy *Shabbos*; a person needs to feel "*as if all of his work is completed*" and no tasks await him.

When the father of the Great Chassidic Master Dovid of Lelov was asked, 'how did you merit a son like this?' He replied that when he would sing the *Shabbos* melody '*Baruch Ado-nai Yom Yom*' and when he would arrive at the words, "*and may you all merit to see children and grandchildren toiling in Torah and in Mitzvos*," he would say these words with tears. He would cry out these words with complete devotion to Hashem for at least a half hour with the intent that he should merit to have children and grandchildren that are true *Tzaddikim*.

A person wants his son to keep his *peyot*, but why should he keep his *peyot* since he sees his father on *Shabbos* only sleeps and eats, and sleeps and eats repeatedly, G-d forbid! If his son would see his father singing with excitement and dancing with his children and making his children excited over the holy *Shabbos,* then no child would cut off his *peyot.* No child would become obsessed with his lusts, because children want to serve Hashem--but children do not know how if they do not see their father and mother serving Hashem.

For a child, serving Hashem begins with happiness and singing at the *Shabbos* table. Therefore, if a father sings with happiness and devotion the *Shabbos* song, "*and may you all merit to see children and grandchildren toiling in Torah and in Mitzvos*", then all the fathers and sons will keep their *peyot* and merit to live a life of Torah and *Mitzvos*.

TERUMAH

DONATING FOR THE SAKE OF G-D

In the time of the Chofetz Chaim, there was an emissary who used to go by foot, from village to village. He used to do this to collect money for the Chofetz Chaim's yeshiva. There was one villager who would give him 50 zloty, which was a very large sum in those days, the days of the Chofetz Chaim. Every time the emissary came to him, he'd give him 50 zloty.

One time he'd go by wagon, and one time by foot. Then, one day, the emissary said to the Chofetz Chaim: "Listen, I think that if I had my own horse and cart, and my own wagon-driver, I'd be able to collect a lot more money. Now, I have to tramp through all the mud, and through all the snow, just to get to some village. And when I get there, the people aren't always home… If I had a horse and cart, I could collect many times more funds."

The Chofetz Chaim agreed with him. So, he came to that particular village with his horse and his cart and his driver – but this time, the villager didn't want to give him anything. So, the Chofetz Chaim asked the emissary, "What happened with that villager?"

The emissary replied, "He said he didn't want to give me anything. He saw me come with a horse and cart, and he said, 'You've already become wealthy, you've got a horse. I don't give money for horses and wagons. I give money for yeshiva students, not for horses and wagon drivers.'

So, the Chofetz Chaim, in his humility, decided to go and visit this villager himself. The villager told him, 'I'm not prepared to give money for people to start lording it around, and to have horses and wagons. I won't give *tzedaka* for that.'

So, then the Chofetz Chaim explained to him that it was written about Betzalel, "*And he was filled with the spirit of G-d, with wisdom and with knowledge*", and that afterwards it's written, "*He had thoughts about silver, gold, iron and copper.*" What's the connection?

Everyone was giving *tzedaka* in some way. One person was giving charity wholeheartedly, so that it really would get to the orphans and the widows and to the poor. And then, there was the Holy of Holies. There were those who were giving charity for its own sake, and who were praying that the silver that they were giving would be used for the *cherubim* and for the *ark*.

Other people weren't really paying so much attention to this, because the main point was just to give. Their intention was to give a good amount, so they made plinths from this. Then, there were people who gave with less *kavana* (holy intentions), so they made the tendons and the pegs from those donations. And after this, the princes of each tribe donated the bullocks and the wagons [to transport it all].

So, the Chofetz Chaim explained that Betzalel knew exactly what the intention of every single person was. This is what it means when it says, "*he was filled with the spirit of G-d, with wisdom and with knowledge*", and then that after it states, "*He had thoughts about silver, gold, iron and copper.*"

Betzalel knew the intention behind every single cent, every penny, every single golden coin. He knew what the donor intended when he gave it. He knew if someone was donating in order to glorify himself, or whether it was truly donated for the sake of Heaven. And according to his understanding, he knew what to do with it.

And for the Holy of Holies, he only used that which had been donated truly for the sake of Heaven. If that wasn't the case, then he didn't use it for that. Even if there would be a lack, he was prepared to wait for someone to come along and donate solely for the sake of Heaven.

The Chofetz Chaim told the villager that if he was really giving for the sake of Heaven, then his money would find its way to support Torah learning, as everything had already been apportioned from Above.

When a person truly does something for the sake of Heaven, when he really thinks about doing it for the right reasons only, when he's concerned to give his money for *Hashem Yisborach*, then he can merit that through his Torah learning the Temple will be rebuilt.

FINDING A TRUE CONNECTION

When *Hashem Yisborach* chose to create the world, He did so for the purpose of showering His creations with goodness and so that all will recognize His greatness and merit clinging to Him. However, before any of that took place, before the creation, He delegated a certain point, a point of light and vitality. All of the souls were drawn down from that point and each and every person was created from that point.

The verse says, *"And I will speak to you from between the two Cherubs."* Man was created from *"between the two Cherubs"*. That point was drawn down from between the two Cherubs. Every person must find his way back to that point. Every person must return to his root and include himself within that point. The whole purpose of our current lifetime as well as our previous lifetimes is to elevate us to that wondrous point, which is the letter '*Yud*'. That is why we are called, '*Yehudim*' (Jews). We were named after that *Yud*. The essence of a Jew – a *'Yid'*, is that little point.

Every person must see to it that his entire being, his very essence, turns back into that little point, that simple point-- into the letter *Yud*. Rebbe Pinchas of Koritz said, 'What is the purpose of the point on a crown? Who can merit attaining a crown? Who can merit attaining that point? Only one who is humble.'

How can a person become humble? Through Torah and acts of kindness. Like it says in the Gemara (*Avodah Zara*, 17:2): *"Rav Huna said, 'Whoever spends all of his time just learning Torah is likened to one who has no G-d, as it says (Divrei Hayamim 2:15): 'And Israel will have many days without a true G-d.'"* The Gemara is stating that if a person learns Torah but does not do kindnesses for others and doesn't help his fellow Jew, he is considered as one who has no G-d!

During the time when King Asa reigned over Israel, everyone learned Torah. There was not one man who did not study Torah. Asa burned all of the statues of *Avodah Zara* and opened up many yeshivas. Yet, it's written in Divrei Hayamim [that Israel were at that time]: "*Without a true G-d*". Why? The reason is that Asa taught all of the Jews to study Torah, but he didn't teach them to do acts of kindness! He didn't teach them to help the weak, to learn with study partners who needed help in their learning! *That*, he didn't teach them! That's why the verse says they were "*without a true G-d*."

If a person studies the Torah but doesn't do acts of kindness, such as helping his friends, helping the weak, etc., it's as though he learned nothing at all. When he studies on his own, learning with no one but himself, he starts imagining himself as the greatest Torah scholar of the generation! He lives an illusion that he's really the greatest Rabbi of the generation! And slowly, slowly, he loses Hashem.

A person who only learns Torah for his own sake becomes

ego-centric! He says to himself, 'soon, I'll become a great teacher, a big Rabbi, maybe even a big *Rosh Yeshiva*!' This person's so full of arrogance, he simply can't find the time to help others - he's 'too busy'! He thinks that every second he spends helping another is purely a waste of his 'precious' time! *'What a waste of time it is to speak to others and be kind to them...'* He needs to focus on becoming a great Rabbi!

When one does nothing else besides study Torah, he becomes arrogant. Like it says, *"Whoever is arrogant – he and I cannot live together in the same world"* (Sotah 5:1). Whoever is arrogant drives away the *Shechina* (the Divine Presence). He is literally pushing the Shechina away. He is removing the Shechina from the world! And when the *Shechina* leaves the world, terrible things happen-- murder, all sorts of disasters, accidents, etc., may we never know of such things. Every little thought of pride causes the *Shechina* to leave the world.

On the other hand, learning Torah together with acts of kindness nullifies self-pride. If a person studies the Torah and also helps other people, he discovers that there are people who are better than he is. If a man begins studying together with another, one who is weaker than he is, he'll soon discover that his study partner actually has better character traits, better qualities, more holiness and more humbleness and so on. All this humbles him.

The same rule applies to one who only does acts of kindness but does not learn Torah. He, too, will be full of arrogance. A person may start a big *chessed* organization; perhaps he'll give out tons of food to the poor and needy. This will surely drive him to arrogance. This guy starts thinking that he is the world's biggest *chessed*-doer! If a person does *chessed* without learning Torah, he'll start to think that he's the most charitable man in the world. After all, he's the one supporting thousands of families – who can be compared to him?!

Moreover, now that he has already become full of arrogance, due to all of his acts of kindness, the result is inevitable-- even if he starts to tire of doing kindness for others, he'll continue anyway because of his lust for pride and honor. He'll desperately seek out poor families to help, even if that means searching basements and the like-- anything to find poor families who don't have food for *Shabbos*. He'll rescue thousands of families and do things that no one else does because acts of *chessed* build his ego. He thinks that he is saving people. He's the so-called 'redeemer'. He thinks he's the greatest person in the world. He has broken the world-record of haughtiness.

However, if he also learns Torah he will lose his arrogance. He'll discover that one guy knows how to learn better than he does, another guy knows the *Tosfot* better, and yet another guy knows *halacha* better than he does, etc. He'll see that there are people much better than him out there. There are men who are greater than he is!

Now, his balloon has popped. Now, he can become humble. The bottom line is that Torah without *chessed* leads to arrogance, as does *chessed* without Torah. Only a person who learns Torah and also does kindnesses for others can be humble.

This is the meaning of *"I will speak to you from between the two Cherubs"*. Only from that essential point of humbleness can a person have a true connection to his creator. That point of humbleness is only found between the two Cherubs – which represent Torah and Chessed.

SERVING HASHEM LIKE A CHILD

The *Tanna D'vei Eliahu* says that the Cherubim predated the world, the Cherubim came before the act of creation. Just as there were Cherubim in the *Beis HaMikdash*, so too there are Cherubim in heaven that were created before the act of creation. The *Eitz HaChaim* says that the Cherubim are the root of the creation. This is why it says, *"from between the two Cherubim"*, because the whole world, the entire Torah and all of the universe, everything was created from the two Cherubim. Everything came from the two Cherubim.

Every child is an aspect of the Cherubim. The Cherubim were actually children, as Rashi says, 'the Cherubim had faces like children'. Children, who have never sinned or fallen into forbidden sights or thoughts, are like the Cherubim. The world exists in the merit of these children. They are higher than angels. Even the angels have no conception of the greatness of a child.

A child has never sinned in his life. He hasn't done any damage to the world, which is why he is higher even than the *sefirah* of *Keter*. His very breath is the holiest thing in the world. 'The breath in which there is no sin,' which is drawn down from the spiritual world of *Atzilut*, from the Cherubim that are from the world of *Atzilut*. All the abundance that flows down to the world comes through these children.

The world exists because of the breath of the children of *Beis Rabban (the study house)*. The Zohar says in *Vayikra* that when a child says the letter *aleph*, at the same time the whole firmament is shaken up and all the angels and all the *Seraphim* become fire in all the worlds. None of the *Seraph*im, none of the angels, and none of the *Tzaddikim* can even look at this light that comes down and enlightens all the worlds. When a child says the letter *aleph*, it's impossible to imagine in any form or fashion the lights that come down and are revealed at that time. When a child says aleph, 360,000 lights descend. The hidden light descends, and so the entire world and all the spiritual worlds and the whole generation depend on the breath of the children of *Beis Rabban*.

The Rebbe brings in Lesson 37 of *Likutey Moharan*, *"and through giving charity to the Land of Israel, a person includes himself in the air of the*

Land of Israel, which is an aspect of holy breath in which there is no sin… *which is the aspect of the breath of the children of Beis Rabban."* The Rebbe says that one can reach the level of the breath of these children only by giving charity to the Land of Israel. If he merits giving charity, he reaches the level of *"the breath that has no sin,"* which is the aspect of a child. This means that at any moment a person can go back to being seven years old. The whole point is to return to be a seven-year-old child. One's entire life, one should be seven years old. You can even be 70 or 100, but you need the breath that has no sin! You need to be a child of seven years old. If you give charity, then each time you give charity you receive that breath that has no sin and you become the aspect of the Cherubim - you become part of the Cherubim.

"The righteous blossoms are seen in the land" (*Shir HaShirim* 2:12). The righteous blossoms are the children of *Beis Rabban*. When children come into the world they are holy and pure. They don't want to dirty themselves with the filth of this world. A child doesn't see what is going on in the streets. He knows that everything in the street is impurity. The child knows that the whole world is a sewer. It is already clear to him at age three-- it's all clear to him. Everyone can achieve that aspect of a child.

Everyone has to try and remain a child. Hashem wants that a person should remain a child his whole life long. How can we ensure that we will remain children? By not wanting to be big shots, by not wanting to see what's going on in the street. We must have no interest in anything impure. When you see an open sewer you walk the other way! You don't say, 'well, maybe I'll go the shorter way through the sewer.' No, you run away from the sewer! As long as you possess a soul, you aren't prepared to get filthy-- you're not willing to spend even a second in the sewer. A person needs to know that everything that happens here in this world is taking place in a gigantic sewage pit.

After the sin of *Adam HaRishon*, the whole world became a sewage pit, a giant sewage ditch. When you pass through the street, you need to make sure that no impure thing will attract your attention. Don't look at any impure thing. Nothing. Flee from everything bad, from every forbidden sight, from every forbidden thought. Don't try to get involved with any matters regarding this world. The world passes like the blink of an eye. You have to realize that this world is a giant sewer-- there is nothing here worth looking at. There is nothing to see or to listen to.

Think about how you can be a child your whole life long. I want to be a child. I want the breath that has no sin. I don't want any sin to cling to me. I don't want any [worldly] desires to interest me, other than Torah and prayer. Nothing should interest me. Know that the street is full of impurity. Any person who has a drop of intelligence will quickly run through the streets when he has to go out, without looking around. He knows that he needs to skip over a few sewage ditches on the way. He runs to shul, to the yeshiva, from the *Kotel* to Meron. He runs as long as his soul is inside him. He just flees, for he knows that the entire street, any public place, the whole world, is really just a giant sewage ditch.

The Rebbe is the true child. He is a nursing infant. He said, *"I haven't even begun to exist at all"*[3], because the Rebbe never saw the world, he never heard the world, he never looked at anything in this world even for a second. He never talked in this world. He never breathed in this world. He never released even so much as a breath into this world. The Rebbe is the Blind Beggar who, from the day he was born until the day he died, never opened his eyes and saw this world. The Rebbe was a flaming fire, a flaming fire for *Hashem Yisborach*, with infinite attachment to *Hashem Yisborach*. This was our holy Rebbe - totally a flaming fire for *Hashem Yisborach*.

If you know a true *Tzaddik* like *Rabbenu HaKadosh*, then you can always be on the level of the breath that has no sin. When you come

---

[3] See the story of the 'Seven Beggars', one of Rabbi Nachman's Stories, found in the book *Sipurei Ma'asiot*.

to the Rebbe, you can start being like a seven-year-old child and when you come to the *Tzaddik*, and give charity to the *Tzaddik*, then you can merit the breath which has no sin.

TETZAVEH

IDENTIFYING THE REAL HAMAN

Everyone knows that we are obliged to wipe out Amalek - we have to kill Amalek and annihilate him. But, who is Amalek?

Amalek is us. Amalek is to be found inside each and every person. As long as Amalek is inside us, nothing will help. Even if we kill Haman, we'll just get a Sisera, a Titus, a Vespasian or a Hitler in his place. As long as a person doesn't pull himself out of *p'gam habris* (blemishes related to sexuality) and from arrogance, then Haman is still alive. The *Satan* will just take another form and appear in another person. When Haman was killed, that generation was saved, but with each new generation new Hamans arise.

Haman is created from sins. Every sin gives birth to a Haman, a terrorist, a Nazi. When a Nazi comes to kill a Jew, a person should say, 'I created that Nazi!', 'I created that terrorist!' If I make *teshuva*, that terrorist will be burned up; he'll disappear.

So who is Haman? Who is Amalek? - I am Amalek. As long as I am still in this world, as long as I am still alive, there will be no redemption until I turn myself around, until I change. Nothing else will help. This is the '*nahafoch hu*' of Purim - each person needs to turn himself around from one extreme to the other.

On Purim, the sweetness of the river that flows out of Eden is revealed. On Purim, everyone goes up to Gan Eden. Everything that a person eats or drinks is the aspect of '*the guarded wine*', '*the wild ox*', and '*the Leviathan*'. They are all from Gan Eden. The *Leviathan* is from Gan Eden. The '*wild ox*' is from Gan Eden. The Kedushas Yom Tov says that through the light of Purim, it is revealed who a person truly is. On

Purim, it's specifically revealed to a person where he is truly holding. He merits seeing all his flaws, all his sins, and he then sees that, really, he is Haman.

The Kedushas Levi says that the moment a person sees his own lowliness-- where he is really holding-- he can fall into utter despair. And, specifically on Purim, he's in terrible danger because it is all revealed to him. He sees all his flaws, his forbidden gazing, how far he is from true faith, and he can fall into utter despair because of this. So, a person must drink wine on Purim, as it is written, *"Give strong drink to the woebegone and wine to those of embittered soul"* (Mishlei 31:6) to lift up his mind so that he can sing and be happy.

After a person comes to the realization that he is Haman, that he is the biggest sinner there is, he can become very distressed. Therefore, Chazal made it an obligation to drink wine on Purim, because through wine he will be able to *'nahafoch hu'* - to turn everything around. Then he can see that really it's exactly the opposite: 'Even a Haman like me, a wicked one like me, can pray, can go and hear the Megillah being read. I even went to the *mikvah*. I even put on *tefillin*. I merited such wondrous *mitzvos*.' There's no greater *kiddush Hashem* than this. The farther away a person is, the greater the *kiddush Hashem* and the greater the happiness, because *"Cursed is Haman"* becomes *"Blessed is Mordechai."* Only someone who knows he is Haman can merit becoming *"Blessed is Mordechai."*

The holy Arizal said that every Purim we are enlightened with the level of *'Yesod of Abba'*, which does not occur at any other time. The *Yesod of Abba* is always concealed, always hidden. When we read the Megillah, a revelation takes place and the *Yesod of Abba* is revealed. Such great lights descend that at that time anyone can return in real *teshuva*.

Mordechai, who is the *Yesod of Abba*, is revealed in all his glory on Purim, because the revelation of Mordechai - the revelation of the *Yesod of Abba--* draws down miracles and wonders for us. This revelation is the faith that *'there is nothing but Hashem' - 'Ein Od Milvado'.* There can be an Achashverosh and a Haman, and they can make terrible decrees, but they really don't exist. They're only an illusion. And all of these things exist only to awaken us to *teshuva.*

The main point of Purim is to make *teshuva.* Purim is not for messing around. It's not for setting off firecrackers. It's not about breaking things, about throwing up or about causing damage to anyone. Purim is about making real *teshuva.* Just as we saw on Purim over the generations, Breslovers would cry rivers of tears during the Megillah reading and they would shed rivers of tears during the dancing. This is the meaning of *"a person is obligated to drink wine on Purim"* (Megillah 7b). This drinking doesn't mean becoming completely drunk; rather one has a red face from excitement and from *deveikus* (attachment to Hashem).

Rav Natan says that on Purim a person needs to restrain himself even more than on Yom Kippur. On Yom Kippur, we are in shul 24 hours, stuck to our seats, but on Purim we need to drink wine and to sing and dance and be happy and at the same time to retain our senses and attachment to Hashem. The whole reason for drinking wine is to come to *deveikus* and to see Hashem face to face.

The Shulchan Aruch says that a person must not become so drunk that he can't say *Birkas HaMazon* or pray *Ma'ariv,* or not pray with appropriate intention. The drinking is not in order to become light-headed. The drinking is only on condition that he does not take even a single blessing or custom lightly. The essence of the *mitzvah* is to be happy: *"Wine gladdens a person's heart."* Wine has the power to stimulate the blood and when a person's blood is flowing, it's easier for him to dance, to be happy and to sing. It makes it easier to be happy and elevates the joy.

Purim is an indicator for the whole year, because a person needs to be happy all year long. A person needs to be happy all the time, but in a way that doesn't deviate from the norm. He needs to remain rational with his senses intact, not go out of his mind in any way. The mind defines a person's reality and keeps him in line. However, wine breaks down one's mental controls. That's why Rabbenu warned us that that all year long we should not drink any wine or intoxicating beverages, but on Purim we want to do the opposite, to burn away all our mental barriers.

This is the special power of Purim. On Purim, the wine doesn't damage a person, if he drinks properly. We say on Purim, *"the wine goes in and the secrets come out"*. Then a person's love for Hashem and his fear of Hashem is revealed, because if a person is filled with love of Hashem and attachment to Hashem all year long, then on Purim it all comes out and he merits dancing from love and *deveikus* to Hashem. But if the opposite is true, if he is far from *deveikus* and he's stuck in his bad character traits, in arguing with other people and in speaking lashon hara, then on Purim, when he gets light-headed, he attacks other people--because on Purim his mental barriers are removed by the wine.

On Purim, we want to burn away the barriers of the mind through wine and to truly reveal our love of Hashem and not a love for other things. A person who all year long is burning with love for Hashem has no other time to show it. So, when Purim comes around, now he can fully express his love for Hashem for a full 24 hours.

KI TISA

HASHEM'S DECREES

Am Yisrael was not fit to perform the sin of worshiping the Golden Calf. However, they felt so much haughtiness and reached such a high level of arrogance, because they had seen Hashem face to face, so there was no choice, *Am Yisrael* had to fall and perform the awful sin of the Golden Calf.

Rashi says this, that the sin of the Golden Calf was *"Hashem's decree"*, since *"Am Yisrael were all warriors that ruled over their bad impulses, so their evil inclination was not fitting to overcome them at all"*. Therefore, the whole episode of the Golden Calf was not fitting for *Am Yisrael* since their physical impurities had already been removed, but their arrogance remained. After seeing Hashem face to face, *Am Yisrael* grew in arrogance. And it was therefore *"Hashem's decree"* to throw them into such a lowly thing like the Golden Calf. The Golden Calf ruled over them *"to give an opening for Jews to return to Hashem in repentance"*. In truth, all of a person's disgraceful behaviors are *"Hashem's decree"*.

From the sin of the Golden Calf we learn that, after every time a person falls, if each time he wants to repent and serve Hashem, if he wakes up and is shocked at his own sin and his disgraceful behavior, this is a sign that all of his sins and disgraceful behaviors are simply *"Hashem's decree"*.

But, if a person feels good about his disgraceful behavior, may Hashem have mercy on his soul. This person is in bad shape. However, if every time he wakes up and is shocked at his own sins and disgraceful behavior and asks himself, 'How could I fall this low; what's going on with me? Why do I keep falling? Why can't I hold onto my Judaism?'

Then he should know that his downfalls are only to break his arrogance and they are all *"Hashem's decree".*

By all the *Tzaddikim* and also by us, if every time we sin or behave disgracefully, we wake up, and are shocked at our downfall, and we cry about our downfall; if we run to the field and scream to Hashem about the pain of sinning and behaving disgracefully, or we run to the *Kotel* and scream out to Hashem to save us from our evil inclination, then this is the sign that all our sins and disgraceful behaviors are *"Hashem's decree".*

This means that there is a condition in order for one's sins and disgraceful behaviors to be called *"Hashem's decrees".* The condition is that one wakes up and is shocked at his sins and disgraceful behavior and he repents and returns to Hashem from love.

By this process of waking up and being shocked at one's disgraceful behavior, a person receives more humility and lowliness and his heart gets more broken. Through waking up and being shocked at one's disgraceful behavior, one's willful transgressions turn around and become merits. That's why it's written that, *in the place where a ba'al teshuva stands, even Tzaddikim are not able to stand.*

THE PRAISE OF A WOMAN

"A woman who fears Hashem, she is to be praised" (Mishlei 31:30). A woman has fear of Hashem. A woman has more fear of Hashem than a man has.

As we saw, the women didn't participate in the sin of the Golden Calf, and neither did they participate in the sin of the spies. The reason for this is that, the moment the women accepted upon themselves the

10 Commandments, the moment that they accepted the yoke of Torah and *mitzvos*, nothing in the world could move them. Nothing could discourage them-- no argument, no persuading.

The faith of women is much stronger than the faith of men. The holy Zohar says of the sin of the Golden Calf that Yonius and Yombros, the sons of the evil Bilaam, convinced *Am Yisrael* that Moshe would never return. If he went up to heaven and hasn't returned yet, then they would need to make a calf, and do a new coronation with magic and sorcery. They said that with this calf they could conquer nations, and this is how they would conquer the Land of Israel.

They went to Aharon HaKohen and said to him, "Come. Let's make a calf". What did Aharon do? How did he take care of them? He said, "Go to the women. Bring me their nose rings. Tell them that Aharon commanded us to make a calf." Aharon knew that the women would never agree to make a calf-- he understood what a woman was! If she heard, *"You shall have no other gods before Me"* (Shemos 20:3) just once, nothing could influence her otherwise. No one could make her budge on this. This is the nature of a woman; once she's heard a particular precept, a commandment of the Torah, then nothing in the world can influence her otherwise.

When they came to the women, every man shouted at his wife, 'What? You don't believe in what Aharon HaKohen said? Don't you have any faith in *Tzaddikim*? You don't believe in the *Tzaddik*? The *Tzaddik* said to make a calf. Where's your faith?' Every woman answered her husband, "Come, let's go to Aharon HaKohen. Let's argue with Aharon. What do you mean, 'He said to make a calf?!' After hearing such a commandment, *"You will have no other gods..."* from one end of the world to the other, in 70 languages, not even a bird chirped, or a cow mooed while this command was being given. What do you mean 'Aharon told me!?' Do you think that Aharon can change one of the commandments!?'

The holy Zohar says about "*The entire nation removed their gold rings...*"-
what does it mean 'they removed'? The women weren't going to take off
their nose rings or earrings under any circumstances! So, they grabbed
the women's noses, and then it says, "*and they removed*". This is similar to
"*smashing mountains and breaking rocks*" (Kings I 19:11). So too, a person
can be smashed-- they broke their noses, they ripped their ears. They
ripped off the jewelry, because when men get some crazy idea into their
heads, *G-d forbid*, and they want to make a calf... Hashem have mercy.

But the women remained firm in their simplicity, in their modesty
and righteousness, and nothing can budge them in their faith,
nothing in the whole world. The Tanna D'vei Eliahu says that there's
no difference between a man and a woman, no difference. A woman
can be a prophetess-- she can be Devora the prophetess, Miriam the
prophetess. The Tanna D'vei Eliahu says, 'I swear by heaven and earth
that anyone can merit to see the holy Shechina, whether a man or a
woman, without exception.'

The holy Zohar says that there are palaces in heaven, some of which
merited to be named after righteous women. There is a palace called 'Batya
bat Pharaoh'. Thousands of women rejoice there and give over Torah
chiddushim every day. There's a palace of Serach bat Asher who entered
Gan Eden with her body, a palace of Yocheved, a palace of Devora the
prophetess. All the generation's righteous women go up to these palaces.
Each woman goes to the appropriate palace, according to her deeds.

And there are innumerable palaces, from a great many righteous
women from every generation. Each woman builds a palace above, with
her yearnings and longings for *mitzvos*. Like Devora the prophetess
whose longings and intentions were solely for the sake of promoting
and glorifying Torah. Devora made torches, large candles, so that Torah
scholars would be able to sit through the whole night studying Torah
without having the candle go out in the middle of the night. She didn't
use inferior wicks, wax or oil; rather she made everything so that the

light of the candle would be the brightest-- she used the best wax and the best oil in order that it should be the strongest light possible. So, it never once happened that the light suddenly went out in the middle of the night and they needed to shut their holy Gemaras, G-d forbid. The candles always burned until sunrise.

Hashem said to Devora, 'You intended to increase my light in Yehuda and Jerusalem, so I will increase your light in Yehuda and Jerusalem.' And He gave her prophecy. He gave her such perception and understanding that she was worthy of becoming a Judge, as the Chida says (*Rosh David, Parshat Beshalach*) that all the *chidushim* were revealed to her, all the laws of judges. All the laws were revealed to her. The Zohar says in *Parshat Mishpatim*, "*v'ta'asher Devora*." "*V'ta'asher*" is the screen of the altar. Devora merited offering herself like a sacrifice to *Hashem Yisborach*. "*And there was a screen under the cornice of the altar*." She was the aspect of the screen of the altar. The word *t'a'asher* has the same letters as the word for screen, *reshet*.

Women are the aspect of the altar. Every woman is this aspect of the altar because, in truth, they sacrifice themselves to *Hashem Yisborach*. They literally sacrifice themselves. They raise the children; they can take care of 10 children. The mothers do everything and are dedicated to their children, feeding them, giving them to drink, praising them and doing all this with such self-sacrifice. They sacrifice themselves to *Hashem Yisborach*, and this is why they can be prophetesses.

What is the meaning of the word *bayit* (home)? The *bayit* is the *Mishkan*. The initial letters of the word *Mishkan* represent '*mita, shulchan, kisei, ner*' (bed, table, chair, light). The wife cleans the home, raises the children; the house is filled with books of Torah and the children learn Torah. Her husband is able to sit and learn. She cleans the house, lights the candles, cooks and prepares the food and in this way, she builds the *Mishkan*. By fulfilling her duties and obligations she can literally achieve the level of prophecy.

"And these are the laws that you shall place before them" (Shemos 21:1). All the laws of the Torah apply equally to men and women (*Rashi*). A woman, like a man, is obligated to follow all the laws, including prohibitions like "do not steal" and "do not murder." A woman is forbidden to speak *lashon hara*. If she does all the *mitzvos* properly, eats three meals on *Shabbos* plus melava malka, doesn't speak *lashon hara*, doesn't speak nonsense, etc., then she can become a prophetess even greater than the men.

A woman is exempt from learning Gemara, but she is not exempt from attaching herself to Hashem. From this she gets no exemption. She can be attached to Hashem also when she is cleaning the house, cooking, and washing dishes, etc. The wife of Rebbe Yitzhak Derobitzer (the mother of Rebbe Michel from Zlotshov) was heard saying '*Kadosh, Kadosh, Kadosh*' while in the midst of sweeping the house. Her husband asked her, "Why are you saying '*Kadosh, Kadosh, Kadosh*?' She answered, 'I was listening to the singing of the angels. The angels are right now saying kedusha.'

When Rebbe Moshe Leib from Sasov became blind, they asked him what had caused it. He answered, 'Because of my spouse I became blind. She is always saying 'l'kavod *Shabbos*, l'kavod *Shabbos*' (*for the glory of Shabbos*). When she is kneading the dough or cooking, she says, 'l'kavod *Shabbos*.' With each time that she says 'l'kavod *Shabbos*' an angel is created. Each time 'l'kavod *Shabbos*' is said, angels are created. Then the whole house was aflame. The whole house was full of angels, and I was blinded by all the great light!'

If a woman fulfils her role as a woman, doing her job faithfully, with dedication, with joy, with awe and reverence and for the sake of Hashem, then the most menial tasks can become the gateway to nothing less than prophecy.

VAYAKHEL

A PERSON'S NAME SHAPES HIS LIFE

The holy Zohar tells us that a person's whole strength comes from his name. It's written, "*Hashem has proclaimed by name, Bezalel son of Uri son of Hur*" (Shemot 35:30). Betzalel's name is *betzal* (shelter) E-1 (of G-d). We can already see in the name that his father gave him a hint that he would be the one to build the *Mishkan*.

His father had *ruach hakodesh*, and he knew that his son would create the *Mishkan,* so he gave him this name so that he really would merit to do this. He gave him the name Betzalel so that he would make a shelter for *E-1*, G-d, that he would make a *Mishkan* for G-d. So, the Zohar tells us in its commentary on *Pekudei* that it was only thanks to his name that he was chosen to do the *Mishkan*.

At 13-14 years of age, he already built the *Mishkan* and he knew things that even Moshe Rabbenu didn't know. Moshe wanted to make the *Aron* (Ark) first and only afterwards the *Mishkan*, but Betzalel said, "First do the *Mishkan*, and then do the *Aron*." Moshe said to him, "You truly were a 'shelter for Hashem'!" So, there were things that, so to speak, Moshe didn't know and that Betzalel did.

It's written, "*He put Shemot (names) in the land*" (Tehillim 46:9). Hashem put names in the land. Hashem decreed at the creation of the world how many names of Reuven there would be, how many names of Shimon there would be, how many names of Nachman there would be and how many Natans. A person's name arouses a higher spiritual strength for a person and, with this strength, this energy, he can do wonderful things.

If you give a person the name of a *Tzaddik*, that name will also cause the child who bears it to become a *Tzaddik*. By giving a child the name of a *Tzaddik*, you are arousing the light of that *Tzaddik* that he is being named for. That light from the upper worlds is aroused, it comes down and washes over that child throughout all his life.

A person's name is not a simple matter at all. The Ba'al Shem Tov said that a person's name contains awesome secrets. A person needs to know what his name is and to consider his name deeply. He needs to know what is being hinted at, through his name, because his name is the root of his soul.

Each person has a 'soul root' that goes according to his name. A person's name hints to everything that he will go through, everything that he will experience over the course of his life – everything is hinted to in his name. It's very worthwhile for each person to know which *Tzaddik* he is named after, because a person's life will go according to his name. A person needs to live in accordance with his name. All the vitality of a person comes from his name.

This is why when a person rises up [to the upper worlds after his death] they ask him, 'What's your name? Why didn't you live according to your name!? You should have gone in the direction dictated by your name! If you'd have acted in accordance with your name, you would have achieved everything in the world!'

A person's name hints to him about everything he has to go through in this world, everything that he has to do, everything that he has to learn. Everything is alluded to in a person's name. Hashem already announced each person's name before they were created-- Betzalel will make the *Mishkan*, King Shlomo will build the Temple...

In Gematria, *Shlomo HaMelech* is 470, and *Mikdash* (Temple) is also 470. Shlomo came to the world to build Hashem's Temple. King Shaul came to kill Agag, the King of the Amalekites. *Shaul* in Gematria is 337, and *Agag Melech Amalek* (Agag king of the Amalekites) is 337.

116

So, a person's name hints to all the matters connected with him, and everything that he needs to do, and all the jobs he has to complete in this world.

The Noam Elimelech (Rabbi Elimelech of Lizhansk, z"tl) says that the names of the *Tzaddikim* are greatly limited. Hashem has a treasure trove of *Tzaddikim*, but [in this world] they are very few and far between. Who will merit to have the names of these *Tzaddikim*?

If a person wants his child to be a *Tzaddik*, first and foremost he should name him after a *Tzaddik*; this is the first thing to do. The bigger a *Tzaddik* you name him after, the more likelihood there will be that the child will become a *Tzaddik* himself. If you're going to choose a name for a child, seek out the biggest *Tzaddikim*, and then maybe, just maybe, this will guard the child. After you've given him his name, you also need to educate him and protect him and not just go to sleep on Shabbos. Rather, you need to sing Shabbos songs with him.

This is what the Noam Elimelech says, that when you give the child the name of a *Tzaddik*, that *Tzaddik* will watch over him, and guard him from bad friends and bad things. The soul of the *Tzaddik* will accompany the child every place he goes. The moment that you name someone after a *Tzaddik*, a soul spark from that *Tzaddik* attaches itself to the child.

You should have the intention that this name, that this *Tzaddik*'s soul, will be revealed within the child and will guard him, because the *Tzaddik* already sanctified this name and already served Hashem in accordance with this name. This will cause your child to also grow into a *Tzaddik*.

PEKUDEI

THE TEMPLE SACRIFICES OF TODAY

"Master of the World, when the holy Temple stood, if a person sinned, he brought a sacrifice and was forgiven, but now that there is no Temple what will be with the sinners? The Holy One answered, 'I have already established for them all of the korbanot (sacrifice) prayers; whenever a person says them I consider it as if they brought a sacrifice before me and I will forgive them for their sins'." (Tractate Megilla 31b).

When a person recites the *korbanot* prayers they should imagine the *Beis HaMikdash* right before their eyes, as though it were there in reality. It is there! It was never burned down! It wasn't destroyed! The *Beis HaMikdash* is right in front of our eyes! Nothing has been burnt, nothing! The burning of the *Beis HaMikdash* was only an illusion. It was staged purely for the sake of the nations!

It says in *Asarah Maamaros*, that at the time of the destruction of the *Beis Hamikdash, Ruchot and Sheidim* (spirits and demons) came and brought stones with them! The text says, "Burnt *avnei Sid*" (stones of *sid* (*plaster*), which in Hebrew can be read *Sheid (demon)*). They brought burnt stones and planted them in the *Beis HaMikdash*, all for the sake of tricking the nations so they would be satisfied and think they had succeeded.

The Zohar Hakadosh (on *Parshat Pekudei*, 240b) says that the stones and foundation of the first and second *Beis HaMikdash* are all still there and shining, though they are hidden away. They have all simply been hidden. The *Beis HaMikdash* was not harmed in the slightest! Not even one stone was lost! Not one stone from the stones of Jerusalem has been lost; not of Jerusalem of the first *Beis HaMikdash* nor from Jerusalem of the second *Beis HaMikdash*. Everything is still in its place! *"For they will see the return of Hashem eye to eye...*" When the redemption takes place, everyone will see that the nations never destroyed even one wall! The only thing the nations destroyed were those stones brought by the *Ruchos* and *Sheidim*. Everyone will see that it was all just an illusion.

This is why the Emek Hamelech says on the Gemara (Megilla 10:1), "*I heard that korbanos are being offered even though there is no Beis Mikdash*" - he says, know this! The service of the *korbanot* continues! The *Beis HaMikdash* exists! The *korbanot* exist! The service in the *Beis HaMikdash* continues! Eliyahu Hanavi continues to sacrifice *korbanot* in the *Beis HaMikdash*! The angel Gavriel sacrifices *korbanot* in the *Beis HaMikdash*! It's told about the Baal Shem Tov that he once saw Eliyahu Hanavi buying sheep for the services in the *Beis HaMikdash*.

When we say the *Korbanot* prayers in the morning, we are giving power to Eliyahu Hanavi and the angel Michael, who are currently the *Kohanim gedolim*, to continue their service in the *Beis HaMikdash*. By saying the *Korbanot,* we are literally taking part in the service of the *Beis HaMikdash*. As soon as we begin our prayers in the morning the *Kohanim* begin their service of offering the sacrifices. The Kohanim begin their work! They bring up the *Chatas* offering and the *Tamid* offering... When we say *korbanot*, Eliyahu Hanavi and the angel Michael get their strength to continue their service with the *korbanot*.

When a person recites the *korbanot*, he should have the intention that he is saying the *korbanot* for his own misdeeds. "*Cows that are burning and goats that are burning...*" in truth, *I* deserve to burn! *I* am those burning cows! The whole point of the sacrifices is to renounce the beastliness within ourselves. We burn the animal and slaughter it. When we mention, in the *korbanot*, the part about the slaughtering and the burning, we should imagine that it is we who are being burned, it is we who are being slaughtered.

The person is being slaughtered as a result of his sins and he must accept upon himself the four types of death penalty: *skila, sreifa, hereg* and *chenek (stoning, burning, beheading and strangulation).* When he intends this to be for himself, then all his sins are forgiven.

The *Tana Dvei Eliyahu* says, "whether a Jew or whether a non-Jew recites the verse, *"and he slaughtered it on the Northern side of the Altar"* with the proper *kavanah,* all of his sins will be forgiven." When you say, *"Hapshat Nituach, klil la'ishim* (skinning and dissecting completely for the fire)" you must have in mind that everything is being said about yourself! When the *Chatas* offering is set alight and the *Tamid* offering is being skinned, this is all happening to me! I am being skinned! I am being cut into pieces! I am being burned! The *korbanot* of *Asham, Todah, Shelamim,* etc., they are all happening to me. They are burning me, cutting me and spraying my blood.

When we say the *korbanot,* all the *klipos* (the spiritual husks) crack. The shells surrounding the *World of Asiyah* crack and fall. Everything is atoned! You must therefore be sure to recite the *korbanot* slowly and with a lot of *messirus nefesh* (self-sacrifice). When the person recites the *korbanot,* he is cracking open the *klipos* he has created!

Just as in the time of the *Beis HaMikdash,* the *Tamid* offering in the morning atoned for the sins of night time and the *Tamid* offering of the afternoon service atoned for the sins done throughout the day, so too when a person recites the *korbanot* of the *Tamid* in his morning prayers, it atones for his sins of night time and when he recites the *Tamid* offering for the afternoon service, it atones for his sins of the daytime.

People sin 24 hours a day. We have countless sins. We should receive for these sins *hereg, chenek, sreifa* and *skila.* If a person doesn't try to recite the prayers with *kavanah,* he doesn't achieve anything! Hashem says, 'What are you coming to me for?! You tell me, give me this and give me that...First, do *teshuva!* First ask for forgiveness for everything you did wrong over the past 24 hours! You brought *tumah* (spiritual impurity) into the world! You had forbidden thoughts, saw forbidden sights... say the *korbanot* with *kavanah*!'

When you recite *"ba'parim hanisrafim"*, (and the burnt cow offerings...) have the intentions of, 'I am prepared to be burned, I am prepared to be stoned!' Say the *korbanot* aloud! The mere fact that you are accepting upon yourself *sreifa, hereg* and *chenek,* the fact that you admit that you have sinned makes everything become atoned and forgiven and your prayers are accepted.

The morning prayers begin with the *korbanot*. The Zohar says, 'You must not skip the *korbanot*! The *korbanot* are the highest thing! The *korbanot* come from *Atika Kadisha*, from the *risha de'lo ityada*, as it says, *"siluka dekorbana ad ein sof."* The prayers of the *korbanot* are *"ein sof"* (endless)! You must not skip even one word of *korbanot*, don't give up on even one word!

Vayikra

WRITE THE ALEF!

When Moshe wrote down the Torah, he didn't write it from memory, and he didn't write it from Divine inspiration either. Rather, Hashem said to him, "Now you're going to write the letter *bet*, for '*Bereshit*', and so he wrote the *bet*. "Now, you're going to write the letter *raish*", and so he wrote the *raish*. "Now, write the *alef*", and he wrote the *alef*. "Now the *shin*", and he wrote the *shin*. "Now, the *yud*", and he wrote the *yud*. "Now, write the *taf*", and then he wrote the *taf*.

And when he reached the word '*vayikra*' (and He called), Hashem said to him, "Now, write the *vav*", and he wrote it. "Now the *yud*", and he wrote that too. "*Kaf*", he wrote it. "*Raish*", he wrote it. "Now, write the *alef*..." But then Moshe said to Hashem, "*I can't write the alef!*"

"What do you mean you can't write it?! What's the matter with you? Write the alef! You already wrote the whole books of *Bereshit* for me, and the book of *Shemot*, and now you're suddenly telling me you can't write? Moshe, what's going on with you? Write the *alef*!"

So, Moshe replied, "I can't write the alef of *vayikra*. *Vayikra* means that *You* called me. What? Am I worthy of You speaking to me?! Who am I, that You should speak to me? I am nothing, the nothing of nothings. I'm the worst of the lot. I can't write the word *vayikra*. Let it stay as '*vayikar*' (and it happened) – without the *alef*.

"Just like it's written about Bilaam, "*And Hashem happened upon Bilaam*". Talk to me the same way that you talk to Bilaam. Maybe, I'm just the same as Bilaam?"

The Ba'al HaTurim says that Moshe only wanted to write *vayikar*.

123

So, Hashem said to Moshe, "Stop arguing, and write the *alef*!" So, Moshe said, "Ok, I'm going to write the *alef*, but super small. I'll going to write the smallest possible *alef*."

Who was Moshe Rabbenu? What was Moshe Rabbenu? Moshe Rabbenu was such a person who wasn't prepared to write the letter *alef*, because throughout his whole life, he truly held himself to be the same as Bilaam. So too, during the dispute with Korach, Moshe believed that he was really just like Korach, while Korach believed that he was just like Moshe.

Moshe went to Korach and begged his forgiveness; "I'm sorry, maybe I did something to hurt you?" He went to Datan and Aviram and said, "Maybe I didn't act nicely towards you? I came to ask your forgiveness." They said to him, "Only now, you're coming to us? Now, the whole congregation is with *us*." Moshe didn't even have a minyan of Jews left.

In truth, Moshe was permitted to believe that he was just like Bilaam, because this really was the level at which he was holding himself. But, those others, who thought that Moshe was just like Bilaam, that he was just some kind of big sorcerer-- Hashem have mercy on them. Every one of them died in the desert.

The *Midrash Rabba* (Vayikra 15) says about the verse, *"And He called to Moshe"*, that from here you can learn that a dead carcass is better than a person who studies Torah but has no *da'at* (spiritual knowledge/awareness). What is *da'at*? *Da'at* is when you have humility and lowliness.

Da'at is when you say, "I am not worthy of anything". If a person thinks that he's better than someone else, if he has some fleeting thought that he's better than someone else, then a dead carcass is better than him. Even Moshe Rabbenu, the head of all the prophets, who took Israel out of Egypt and performed the 10 plagues and countless other miracles, like splitting the sea and bringing the Torah down from

Heaven; he was in Heaven without any bread or drink for 120 days – and he said, "What have I done, really? Who am I, anyway? What, I did something? Hashem did everything! I didn't do anything!"

This was Moshe. This was the *da'at* of Moshe. When Moshe learned Torah, he knew it was a present from Heaven. He went up to Heaven and brought down the Torah and he knew that this was a present from Hashem. If a person doesn't have this *da'at*, then the Midrash Rabbah says, a dead carcass is better than him.

The 'Matok M'Dvash' says that all the *Tzaddikim* [in the generation of the Exodus] made the *Mishkan*. Yhey fixed every little detail, every limb, using the power of spiritual intentions (*kavanos*); they made spiritual unifications over every single nail, every single plinth. On every single point, they made *kavanos* and unifications!

But, when it came to join together all the pieces of the *Mishkan*, they found that not one single piece fitted with another piece. They said, "Moshe, what's going on here?" So, Moshe said to them, "There is no other option. Even if you try to raise up the *Mishkan* for the next million years, you won't manage to join even one single piece of it to another."

And this is why it's written that Moshe raised up the *Mishkan*. Only Moshe could put up the *Mishkan*. No-one else could do it. All he did was grasp hold of the parts and they all connected themselves together. The moment that it was brought under the grasp of Moshe's hand, each section inserted itself in the right place.

The *Matok M'Dvash* says that the *Tzaddik* is beyond any comprehension. This isn't just someone who prays a lot, or who prays particularly well, or who learns well, or who goes up mountains and cries out to Hashem. Although, of course, when a person does these all things, he then becomes a *Tzaddik*.

But the matter of the true *Tzaddik*, who comes from the aspect of

Moshe, is something else entirely that's impossible to grasp. It doesn't depend upon prayers or Torah learning, it's something that can't be comprehended at all. Although, of course, it is still achieved by way of Torah and prayer.

First, a person needs to know all of the Torah, and to recite all of the prayers until his very last drop of strength. He needs to faint over every word. After that, a new spring of wisdom will be opened for him. A new level, a new spiritual level that no other human being in the whole world can comprehend. And the true *Tzaddik*, who is the aspect of Moshe, merits to achieve this only by way of his humility and his lowliness. Only by way of being truly *'nothing'*.

TZAV

A FIRE BURNING CONSTANTLY

The soul comes from the upper worlds. The soul came down to this world in order to withstand tests. *"The soul that you placed within me is pure..."* The soul is higher than the angels. It was created even before the angels. In the World to Come everyone will rule over the angels. Angels cannot rise from level to level but remain as Hashem created them at the beginning of creation and will remain at that same level forever.

In order for a person to rise from level to level, he must take all the desires that are burning in him and turn them into a burning desire to serve Hashem, *"A fire burning constantly on the altar, it shall not be extinguished"* (Vayikra 6:6). A person needs to turn his desires into flaming fires for *Hashem Yisborach*. This is the reason his soul was created, and this is why it is greater than the angels.

The Rebbe says in Lesson 1:158 of *Likutey Moharan*, "Many people have related that upon occasion they have seen a fire burning in the distance, but when they came close, they saw it was nothing... There are also individuals like this. His heart occasionally burns for Hashem and he begins to serve Him. But after a while his enthusiasm dissipates and he goes back to the way he was before."

A person has enthusiasm and fire, but afterwards the enthusiasm dissipates. 'Why did the enthusiasm fly away from me? Why did my enthusiasm fade? Why did it evaporate? I came with such simplicity and with such fiery excitement for Hashem, and suddenly it disappears. It was taken from me. I didn't sin or do any crime or anything intentionally wrong.' Rabbenu says that this kind of enthusiasm in fact was really nothing. It was simply our imagination. It wasn't real enthusiasm at all. It's still a good thing, a positive indication that there is enthusiasm here, but nothing more. If a person wants to achieve genuine enthusiasm and to really be on fire for prayer and learning, it takes a lot of very intense work.

Rebbe Natan says that sometimes, all of a person's enthusiasm is just an illusion. It's certainly good that a person gets excited, at least it's better than being like a block of wood or a stone, but this will not help him at all until he achieves true inner enthusiasm, enthusiasm with *da'at* (spiritual knowledge/awareness), enthusiasm with depth, with deep intelligence.

A person should know that he needs to achieve a deep inner enthusiasm which is *"a fire burning constantly on the altar which never goes out."* The *Tamid* fire would never stop burning. A person thinks that he has enthusiasm. That's it, he's already Moshe Rabbenu. Any minute now he'll receive a visit from Eliahu HaNavi. But, if he would realize that this enthusiasm will slowly dissipate, will fly away from him, then he would start working harder on his service of Hashem.

This is what Rabbenu says, that sometimes a person feels that his heart is on fire for *Hashem Yisborach* and he starts to serve Hashem and he gets very excited and is happy and dancing. In truth, there is reason to dance and be happy. There is reason to dance for 120 years without stopping. A person makes *teshuva*, he comes from far away, leaves all his idolatry behind... *Baruch Hashem*, this is certainly a happy event. *"I rejoice over Your word like one who finds abundant spoils"* (*Tehillim* 119:162). But how long can a person dance-- for a day or two? If it's not an eternal fire, if it is not an internal fire, if he isn't working intensely on his character traits, learning Gemara in depth, if he isn't working on *"putting it into your heart"* (from the Alenu prayer), then it won't take hold on him. He's not making an opening in his heart. He is not making a place for the fire, where the fire can take hold, so that he'll have an eternal flame.

A person is on fire. Why are you on fire? Is it a true fire? Is it a true burning from the depths of the heart? If not, then it's a temporary fire. Your blood is boiling, bubbling away. But in a short while your blood will calm down. The fire will finish and then that's it. One person burns for a month, another for a year, but after this, it ends.

The Rebbe says in Lesson 21 that the flame in the heart should rise up on its own. How do we get this flame in the heart? What ignites the heart? Only the mind can ignite the heart. The movement of the mind is what motivates the heart. By learning and understanding the Gemara on an ever-deeper level, this creates movement in the mind which creates the warmth in the heart.

If a person wants to have a mind that will be a 'self-rising flame', to have a fire in his heart that will be a true burning, the first thing he needs to do is start learning Torah with fiery enthusiasm. He needs to understand that the one crucial thing Rabbenu wants from us is our minds, because only the mind can purify the heart. Only the mind can bring us to heartfelt enthusiasm and bring us purity in the heart.

If a person doesn't have intelligence, if he doesn't learn in depth, then his enthusiasm will last only for a day or two and then he can experience such a collapse that he will not believe that such a thing could happen to him! So, know that whatever a person achieves without learning Torah, all this enthusiasm will simply disappear. Only when a person learns Torah with real depth, will he merit true enthusiasm and *"a fire burning constantly on the altar, it shall not be extinguished."*

SHEMINI

WHO MAKES IT KOSHER?

The most important clarification between impure fowl and pure fowl comes through speech, since identifying which pure poultry is eaten is only according to our oral tradition. So, why did Hashem not write in the Torah which pure fowl are permissible to eat? Why do we need to ask the sages of the generation the tradition of which fowl are permissible, as opposed to just looking for signs given to us in the Torah?

The Torah writes so many stories, for example the story about Eliezer who goes to search for Rivka and how he found her. Like it's written, *"And her bucket was on her shoulder... and she filled her bucket... and she brought down her bucket into her hand."* Here, the Torah records every single movement of Eliezer's story with Rivka, not just once, but twice. So, instead of writing the story of Eliezer two times, it would surely have been better for the Torah to give us three or four pages on the complete list of which poultry are permissible to eat. Why does the Torah need to hide and conceal things? Why should there be an obligation to ask the sages about the tradition?

The sages explain like this, that the *Tzaddikim* will teach you which fowl are permissible for eating. If you eat any poultry without permission from the *Tzaddikim* then even if the fowl is pure, yet a person eats it without permission from the *Tzaddikim,* it's considered as if he ate non-kosher poultry. If a person eats poultry, without relying on the tradition-- even if Torah law cites this fowl to be pure-- if a person eats it without relying on a tradition from the *Tzaddikim,* then it's considerered as if he ate non-kosher poultry, since what a person himself chooses means nothing.

Today, he chooses this and tomorrow he chooses that. Every decision comes from his own mindset and outlook. Today, he made the proper decision but tomorrow he won't make the proper decision, but rather a huge mistake. Does a person think that he can always make the right decision when his whole being is a burning fire of vices and lusts?

This fire burns from his *blemishing the covenant,* from looking at illicit things and from haughtiness and arrogance. How can anyone with those character traits burning inside him think that he possesses the capability to make a proper decision or even to think one clear thought?

So along comes Rebbe Natan, and he reveals a huge secret! A rooster is only kosher through the permission of the *Tzaddikim,* a pigeon is only kosher through the permission of the *Tzaddikim.* A rooster that the *Tzaddikim* did not permit remains forbidden to eat, because if it is eaten, the evil will overcome the good. Meaning, that if you listen to the voice of the *Tzaddikim,* then you will be able to clarify and bring out the good from the evil.

However, if a person tries to serve Hashem without connecting to the *Tzaddikim,* even if by himself he battles with his evil inclination day and night, his evil side will stay exactly the same, since the good inside him, little by little, will get pushed down and squeezed out by the evil. A person's good always eventually gets weakened, underneath the burden of one's imprinted bad character traits.

Furthermore, even if a person overcomes his bad character traits, then his evil inside will just come back and fight back again even stronger. Therefore, everything has to be done under the guidance of *Tzaddikim.* Every movement and thought need to be connected to *Tzaddikim* because only the *Tzaddikim* possess the ability to separate good from evil.

A TIME TO BE SILENT AND A TIME TO SING

Every person should learn books of Mussar. He should know *Mesilat Yesharim*, *Sha'arei Teshuva* and *Orchot Tzaddikim*. He should read the chapter on anger in *Orchot Tzaddikim* to learn how not to get angry and how to remain happy in every situation, knowing that everything is for the best.

This is what is written about Aharon, *"And Aharon was silent."* Aharon had suffered the greatest tragedy possible, the most horrifying event in his life; his two sons Nadav and Avihu, who were considered to be on the level of *Adam HaRishon*, were killed, slaughtered before his own eyes. He did not despair but continued in his Divine service, *"And Aharon was silent."* Nothing could make him confused.

But, there's a higher level even than *"Aharon was silent"*, which is, *"In order that my soul might sing to You and not be silent"* (Tehillim 30). This level can be seen in many stories from the Holocaust when the Jews danced and sang, even in the furnaces and the gas chambers. It's told that once the Nazis put 50 Torah scholars from the Vishnitz yeshiva into one of the gas chambers on *Simchat Torah* and, instead of falling into utter despair, they started dancing and singing, *"Ki mi'Tzion tetze Torah u'dvar Hashem mi'Yerushalaim"* (from Tzion came forth Torah, and the word of Hashem from Jerusalem). They had so much joy and enthusiasm, just as if they were dancing in Jerusalem at the Western Wall, singing and dancing.

When the Nazis saw them dancing, they screamed, "What is going on here! Why are you dancing? Why are you singing? This is heresy!" They wanted to hear the Jews crying. What is this, a dance hall? What is happening here? Can it be that they're dancing in Auschwitz? The Nazis burst through the doors and screamed at them, "Stop dancing. Stop celebrating. This is not a theater! It's not a dance hall!" But the Chassidim kept on dancing happily away, *"Ki mi'Tzion tetze Torah..."*

The Nazis told them if this is how they were behaving, then they were making fun of them. 'Get out of here right now and tomorrow at 9:00 AM we are going to torture you and cut you into small pieces! It won't be a quick death with gas, but a slow painful death. Tomorrow we'll see how you dance."

And, then, the next morning, they were informed that they needed to transfer 1,000 workers immediately to another camp, and they were 50 workers short. Somebody said, "There are 50 boys in this shack who are good workers. Let's take them." So, they immediately put them on the truck, and they were out of there. In the merit of their singing and dancing they remained alive, and this is the explanation of the verse, *"on the flame of the altar, we will go out with dance."* A Jew doesn't lose his faith for a moment or even for the slightest second, but only dances and sings even in the worst possible situations.

When a person is having troubles or has a certain problem and he doesn't fall into despair or lose his faith for a minute, but rather he strengthens himself with singing and dancing and joy, then he's not simply on the level of *"Aharon was silent"*, which is acceptance with silence. Rather, he's on the higher level of, *"In order that my soul might sing to You and not be silent"*, which is singing and dancing in joy within the misfortune, within the suffering.

A Jew sings to Hashem and thanks Hashem for each and every breath. What does it matter what you're going through? Your job is to always give thanks to Hashem for each and every breath, just like it's written about King David, *"For the conductor with the melodies, a maskil by David. When the Ziphites came and said to Shaul, 'Is David not hiding among us?'"* (Tehillim 54:1-2).

Shaul was chasing after David; everyone was informing on him. The Zephites informed on him when he was in Keilah. The people of Keilah then informed on him and David was able to flee from them only because he sang and because he would get up at *chatzos* and sing until the morning. *"And the Philistines caught him in Gat."* The Philistines caught him in Gat, and he said *"Lamnatzeach"* and started to sing and play music. When Shaul came into the cave to catch him he started singing and playing music. *"They guarded the house to kill him"* (Tehillim 59:1). He saw that they were already closing in on the house. They had the house surrounded and soon it would be encircled with soldiers armed with arrows and spears. The first thing that David did was to sing and play music. Whenever David found himself in trouble he would always sing and play music. This is how he was saved from all his troubles.

A person sees that he has such terrible problems, that he is going through such terrible suffering; the first thing he needs to do is get up at dawn and sing the morning songs. Through this he will sweeten the harsh judgments. All the judgments and the troubles are sweetened though joy and song and music, as it is written, *"May they sing in joy and be glad, those who desire My vindication"* (Tehillim 35:37). David HaMelech said all of those that desired His vindication must be glad and joyful. What is this 'vindication'? These are the harsh judgments that were sweetened though song and joy.

The Zohar says in *Parshat Vayishlach* that King David would sing all night long. He would strengthen himself with songs and praises until the morning light. A person must always make Hashem happy, and one who makes Hashem happy is thereby behaving the way Hashem requires from him and then Hashem will accept his prayers and save him from all his accusers and from all tragedy.

When people don't dance or sing and aren't happy, but rather go around in a state of brokenness, they damage everything around them. When a person is broken, he destroys all his potential, all his health. 'Why are you so broken? What disaster has occurred? Sing and dance, say a *perek* of Tehillim. Say, *"Lamnatzeach b'neginot mizmor shir..."* (Psalm 67) seven times. This brings salvation, shidduchim and healing - everything. The Arizal writes that whoever says *Lamnatzeach* seven times is guaranteed salvation - children, healing, etc.

Songs and tunes are the way to sweeten all the harsh judgments. Hashem is angry when a person doesn't wake up and sing and play music. There is no way to sweeten harsh judgments other than though joy and dancing. This is the explanation of "*on the fire of the altar we shall go out dancing*". It means that a Jew doesn't lose his faith for an instant but dances and sings and is happy at all times of life and in every situation. Even in the fires of Auschwitz. It doesn't matter where; he must always sing and dance.

TAZRIA

THERE IS NO FALLING

When a person is falling in his service of Hashem, if a person sees in himself a large deterioration and that his service of Hashem is suffering badly... at that moment comes his spiritual elevation. We learn this from Rabbenu who writes, *"In this many Chassidim are mistaken, that suddenly it appears to them that they have fallen in their service of Hashem. In truth, they have not fallen at all."*

You may think that a person can fall in his service of Hashem, but there is no concept of a person falling-- in reality, a person never falls. It's a mistake and misconception to think someone is falling in his service of Hashem.

A person learns Torah and prays-- that's wonderful, what more do you want from him? A person never falls since there is no concept of falling in one's service of Hashem. The Rebbe says, falling in one's service does not exist.

What does it mean to fall and become worse in one's service of Hashem? A person falls when he decides to stop serving Hashem and he completely gives up, G-d forbid. For example, if a person leaves Yeshiva or his shul, never to return, feeling completely hopeless that he will ever be able to serve Hashem, and instead he looks for something else to do. This is called falling away. But, if a person does not leave Yeshiva, if he always stays connected to his yeshiva and to his shul in Torah learning and prayer, he never will fall, everything he does is good.

If a person sees within himself that he's capable of doing more, meaning more Torah learning, more prayer, more charity, more kind deeds-- so, he should do more. But, if a person feels he cannot do any more, that's also good since everything he does is wonderful.

The Rebbe says, "*In this many Chassidim are mistaken, that suddenly it appears to them that they have fallen in their service of Hashem. In truth, they have not fallen at all. However, it's necessary [to feel this way] as this is the only way to rise up from one level to the next. Because the evil forces wake up and fight harder against a person [who is trying to progress spiritually] with new energy. This battleground is one's lusts, confusions, illusions, negative thoughts and obstacles. Therefore, it's necessary each time to fight and to overcome [one's challenges] again and again.*"

Every time a person advances spiritually, he needs to fight and to overcome his challenges over and over again and to subdue and break the evil forces and their obstacles on every level. Therefore, Rabbenu is telling us that a person never falls. Falling does not exist! The concept of falling is something invented by a person's evil inclination, since one never really falls, he merely continues fighting over and over again.

The Torah teaches us that when a person has already become completely covered in his leprosy, when he has completely become white, then, at that moment, he is purified. Meaning every difficulty that causes each and every person to feel as if he just fell, this should actually bring him to *teshuva*. Because, if a person feels as if he fell and it then causes him to regret his actions and it brings him to a place of humility, then his 'fall' is the exact opposite of a fall. Now he is "*completely white*"-- he's completely covered in his leprosy, he's completely in a place of repentance and *teshuva*... Now, the light of Hashem is shining upon him! Now, the light of Hashem is sparkling upon him!

METZORA

HOLY UTTERANCES

The holy Zohar says that the world stands on seven '*havelim*' (breaths / utterances). King Solomon merited these seven utterances, as it is written, "'*Havel havelim,*' said Koheles, '*Havel havelim! All is havel!*' (here, meaning 'futile')" (Koheles 1:2). In the merit of these seven utterances, he built the *Beis HaMikdash*.

All the work of a person is to merit to these seven utterances in holiness, so that each word that comes out of a person's mouth will be the aspect of the holy of holies. Every sound he makes will be the Holy of Holies. You need to sanctify your '*hevel peh*' (speech) so that no false word should leave your lips, no *lashon hara*, no tale mongering, no criticism, no words of anger, no selfish words, or haughty words, G-d forbid. If a person only allows holy words to come out of his mouth, then the Kingship of Hashem is revealed in the world, and he can bring the redemption and build the *Beis HaMikdash*.

All of a person's vitality comes from his inner self. These are the seven holy utterances. The Sfat Emet says, 'how can a person take the words which come from his inner self and speak about someone else?' 'How can you dare speak disparagingly about another Jew?' 'You were given the power of speech! You were given words! You were given these things so that you could pray, say Tehillim and learn Gemara. How can you take your vitality, your inner voice, and turn it into senseless hatred, into searching for another's faults? Don't you have anything better to do? You dare speak about another Jew? You have the *chutzpah*, the audacity, to speak about another Jew? Even if he is the biggest evil-doer. Is he bothering you? Is he going to steal your store away from you? What do you care about him? How can you speak against another Jew, G-d forbid? Is it so hard for you not to gossip about others? Go eat a piece of cake, go get a drink of something - just don't speak *lashon hara* about someone else.'

A person's speech comes from his breath which is the life force of a person. He takes his holy breathing, whatever he inhales in each moment and in each place, and he turns it into prayers and words of Torah and love of his fellow. A person speaks *lashon hara* for hours on end yet doesn't feel that he is wasting his inner essence and all of his vitality on depravity dedicated to the *Sitra Achra*? The animalistic behavior of the animals involves biting, kicking and goring, but a person's animalistic behavior takes the form of speaking *lashon hara* against others. A person can't become holy unless he subdues his animal side.

The Rebbe brings in Lesson 54 from Proverbs (10), "*The slanderer is a fool.*" If a person speaks slander or *lashon hara,* he is a fool. In addition to committing the sin of *lashon hara,* he loses his intelligence too. As the Chafetz Chaim explains, whoever speaks *lashon hara* transgresses 14 positive commandments and 17 negative commandments, which come to 31 in all. With all the details involved, there are in fact an infinite number of transgressions.

However, this person also loses his intelligence, the minute he starts to speak *lashon hara* about someone. Even if what he says is true, if it serves no constructive purpose-- he thinks that maybe there is a 'need' to say this. But Hashem knows the truth and Hashem knows if this is for a constructive purpose or not. At that very instant, he completely loses all his intelligence, until he makes *teshuva*.

When a person speaks *lashon hara,* it's a sign that the power of his animalistic side has taken control of him, which means the power of jealousy, of hatred, and all the other vulgar traits. He falls from the level of a human being to that of an animal and not only does he commit all the positive and negative transgressions, but he literally becomes an animal, he can't learn and he can't pray, because he's so busy speaking about this one and speaking about that one, about other Jews.

The Rebbe of Slonim says about the verse, "*in whom there is an affliction*", that the affliction is within you - it's not outside of you. The affliction is within your soul: "*in whom there is an affliction*." The affliction is in your inner self. The *lashon hara* comes from within. Jealousy comes from within.

When a person speaks *lashon hara* about someone else, the damage he himself suffers is very deep. The damage one does to oneself is even deeper than the *lashon hara*. This comes from something distorted and crooked within the soul. These are disfigurements of the soul. The soul is completely leprous, completely rotting. When a person speaks *lashon hara* in anger, it is not only terrible that he is angry and that he speaks *lashon hara*, but it also exposes a deep flaw in his soul. He simply doesn't realize what a Jew is. He doesn't have the correct perspective on life. He doesn't see things correctly. Therefore, he needs to purify his soul, to heal his soul and to heal his voice, so that it should be a voice of a melody which will return him to the right kind of speech.

A person with *tzara'as* needs to bring two birds as an offering. The Rebbe explains, why does he have to bring two? It's because he had defective speech-- he spoke *lashon hara* and his voice was damaged. He lost his [true] voice, and so now he gets his vitality from the '*two birds of the klipa*' and he needs a *tikkun* which will give him back his voice. So, he brings two birds in order to connect him with the *birds of holiness* who give him a good voice, a soft voice, a pleasant voice of love of people, a voice of peace between men.

Thus, Rav Natan explains, he needs to bring the two birds because the birds are the aspect of making music. They make music and sing all day long. They indicate to the person with *tzara'as*, "See these two birds making music all day long. You should also start making music and singing."

Through the two birds, his ability to sing is returned to him, along with the power of melody and a pleasantness and serenity, so that he should have a pleasant voice like a bird. Then, all his speech will only be songs and praises to *Hashem Yisborach*. Songs and praises for everyone, for his family, for his friends-- only to praise and glorify them, telling them, 'You all are so wonderful. You all are so good.'

The entire work of the *Tzaddikim* is to return the voice of melody to all of *Am Yisrael*, to every Jewish home and through this we should merit to the final redemption speedily and in our days. Amen.

ACHAREI MOT

DYING AL KIDDUSH HASHEM

Rabbenu says that this is why we see now such terrible decrees being leveled against the Jewish people, such terrifying decrees. The Rebbe says that anyone who merits it can truly feel the terrible tragedies. Two Jews were killed just today. Jews are being murdered all the time. It is absolutely impossible to sleep at night when you hear that Jews are being killed.

It appears as though there might just be a decree of destruction hanging over the Jewish people, and those who are privileged to die as martyrs every single day are the ones who are mitigating the decrees hanging over us.

Precisely the holiest souls, the purest and cleanest souls that are completely giving and want nothing for themselves-- it is these very souls that are the most wonderful and are being taken from us. It is precisely those souls that are chosen to atone for us. This is what the holy Arizal explains here in the *Sha'ar HaKavanos*. The holy Arizal explains the matter of dying to sanctify G-d's Name, that a person must sacrifice himself to Hashem every single day (*Sha'ar HaKavanos, Nefilat Apayim #3*). This is the esoteric meaning of the *tachanun* prayer (*Nefilat Apayim*) after the *Shemonah Esreh*.

A person must say, "We are guilty; we have betrayed; we have robbed; we have spoken slander; we have acted wrongly to others; we have caused others to sin; we have sinned willfully; we have been violent; we have joined other sinners; we have given wrongful advice; we have lied; we have mocked; we have rebelled; we have provoked; we have turned from the right path; we have transgressed; we have openly rebelled; we have caused harm to others; we have been obstinate; we have acted wickedly; we have destroyed; we have committed abominations; we have strayed; we have led others astray."

Everyone must believe that a single *Shemonah Esreh* prayed properly could take care of all the decrees. If we will stand and pray *Shemonah Esreh* for an hour, we will certainly take care of all the decrees. When we stand to pray *Shemonah Esreh*, we have reached the world of *Atzilus*. We must stand there for an hour, for two hours, and patiently recite every letter without rushing.

There is nothing to be afraid of. All of the Jewish people must have a copy of the *Tikkun HaKlali* with them. You can travel on the buses; you can tell people that anyone who carries a copy of *Tikkun HaKlali* in their pocket has nothing to worry about. He can travel through a maelstrom of bullets, a blizzard of shells, and they will explode underneath the bus, to the side of the bus. One hundred explosions could happen, and nothing will occur.

Anyone who has a copy of *Tikkun HaKlali* must keep it in his pocket. We should print on it that it is an anti-explosive device. It is an anti-car bomb device. One can travel on the buses anywhere; one can go to work, for there is nothing to fear. Someone should make copies of *Tikkun HaKlali* condensed onto a single page and should start handing it out throughout the country. The entire country!

The Baal Shem Tov explains how one has to serve Hashem. He was shown in a vision a man climbing to the rooftop and then falling down and being smashed to pieces. This is how one has to serve Hashem! One climbs to the rooftop and falls down and gets smashed to pieces. We throw ourselves down from above, from the world of *Atzilus*, down to the bottom of the world of *Asiyah*, from the rooftop down to the ground.

And this is the esoteric meaning of *Nefilas Apayim*, which is the everyday form of Divine service. With a single *Shemonah Esreh*, you can raise up an infinite number of souls.

KEDOSHIM

A SINGLE JEW CAN STAND AGAINST
THE ENTIRE WORLD

A person's entire spiritual task is only about nullifying himself to the *Tzaddik*. This is the entirety of one's service of G-d! There is no other work at all – only nullifying oneself to the *Tzaddik*.

King Shaul had declared a revolt against the Philistines (Samuel I: 13:8-9). Who needs this revolt? The Jewish people are not a rebellious people! But, *"[Shaul] struggled at the river"* (Samuel I:15:5). When he was at the river, he said to himself, 'I don't understand Shmuel.' See Rashi's commentary there.

The Gemara in Yoma 22a explains this phrase as Shaul's struggle and failure to understand *Shmuel HaNavi* (the prophet Samuel). What does *Shmuel HaNavi* want? To murder innocent men, babies, delicate women and children? What have they done wrong? Soldiers, one could understand. But even they did nothing wrong. Amalek did nothing at all. *"And he struggled at the river."* Shaul thought that he was wiser than Shmuel. In his mind, it was clear that he was a far greater scholar than Shmuel. He didn't have any doubt about this. *"And he struggled at the river."* What is this struggle at the river, then?

When Hashem told Shaul to go and strike Amalek, from babies in arms to the elderly, children and women too, Shaul didn't understand what Hashem was saying to him. To murder children, babies? Little, sweet, cute children? Who has ever heard of such a thing? The whole world will rise up against us and destroy us! What kind of people is this who murder babies, who murder women? What kind of a cruel nation is this? All they do is murder people!

It isn't for nothing that the Nazis killed the Jews. They said that these people are a nation of murderers! The Nazis were very refined and elevated people. They couldn't bear murderers, a nation of murderers. Wherever you open up scripture, you see that they are a nation of murderers. The Nazis resolved to deal with this nation, to redeem the world and ensure that there won't be any murderers or killers left in the world, but only nice and refined people.

So Shaul was afraid. *What is going on here? To murder innocent men?? Why is Shmuel so cruel??*

When Hashem said to Shaul to go and strike Amalek, from young men to the elderly, He said that he was exacting retribution for what Amalek did to the Jewish people when they left Egypt (Samuel I:15:2). *"Now go and strike Amalek, and destroy all that is theirs utterly, and do not have pity on him; kill men and women, young children and even nursing babies."* What did the nursing babies do? What did the young children do? *"Even unto the sheep, the camels, even unto the donkeys."* How can one possibly understand this verse? The Jewish people are supposed to be enlightened?!

Rashi brings an explanation from *Chazal* on Samuel I: 13:1, that during his reign, Shaul was as pure of sin as a one-year-old. However, he lacked this self-nullification before the *Tzaddik*, the acceptance that perhaps the *Tzaddik* knows better than he does. Shmuel said to wait for seven days. Wait for seven days! The entire nation had already assembled. They had crossed the *Yarden* and had come from the Gil'ad. *"And Shmuel rose and went up from the Galgal to the hills of Binyamin, and Shaul commanded the people..."* (Samuel I:13:15).

Shaul didn't keep a large force with him. He knew that he had no need of a lance. The verse says, *"During those days, a metal plow was not to be found in all of the land of Israel, for the Philistines had said, 'lest the Hebrews make a sword or a spear from it'"* (Samuel 19). There was no metal plow. Once upon a time, there were no swords. Not like today, when there are tanks and fighter planes; what an embarrassment.

It used to be that the Jewish people would throw some dust and it would be transformed into swords. They would throw straw, and it would be transformed into arrows. But Shaul didn't have swords or spears. Shaul had three thousand men, and each held a bit of sand in his hand, and that's how they went to war, with drop of sand! They went out to war with a drop of sand! No plow, no spear, and no sword. These are all innovations that our forefathers never even heard of.

When did a Jew ever use a sword or a spear? There was never any such thing among the Jewish people. So, the *Midrash* asks, "*If there were no swords and spears, how did Shaul manage to get some?*" The *Midrash* asks, "*How, then, did Yonasan manage to have a spear?*" If he didn't have a sword...? What, was he a member of the underground? Were they making swords for him in the underground?

Yonasan studied Torah twenty-four hours a day. He learned for twenty-four hours. He would catch a quick nap for a total of four hours and learn for twenty. When did he have the time to forge a sword or a spear? "*And the Philistines descended upon all of Israel to remove each man's plow and scythe*" (Samuel I: 13:20). And, suddenly, Shaul had a sword! Where did he get this sword from?

Did he steal it from the Philistines? Is it permitted to steal? Was he a member of the underground? What, did he dig tunnels, like *Shuvu Banim* who make swords and spears in their tunnels? They learn for an hour and then spend eighteen hours forging swords and spears in their tunnels. They make machine-guns, Kalashnikovs, they have whole ammunitions factories going, nuclear weapons... They have all kinds of things hidden under the yeshiva.

But Shaul didn't have any tunnel under his yeshiva where he would manufacture swords and spears. And Yonasan didn't have any tunnel under his yeshiva either where he would make swords and spears. So, the *Midrash* at the end of *Parshat Kedoshim* points out the contradiction here. "*There was no sword or spear to be found in the hand of any of the people that were with Shaul and Yonasan.*" There wasn't. But then, "*And [weapons were found] for Shaul and Yonasan his son.*" How could Shaul have had a sword? How could Yonasan have had a spear? Who made it for him?

The *Midrash* at the end of *Parshat Kedoshim* says, "*Rav Chaggai says that an angel made it.*" And the Sages say that it was the Holy One Himself, in His glory, who made it. "*And it was on that day, and Yonasan the son of Shaul said to the lad, his arms bearer, 'Let us go and cross over to the garrison of the Philistines, on the other side'; but he said nothing to his father. And Shaul tarried at the uppermost part of Givah beneath the pomegranate tree, in Migron; and the people that were with him were nearly six hundred men. And also, Achiyah ben Achituv, the brother of Ichavod ben Pinchas ben Eli, the priest of Hashem who bore the ephod in Shilo; and the people did not know that Yonasan had left*" (Samuel I:14:1-3).

Yonasan left. "*And between the passes that Yonasan had sought to cross to reach the garrison of the Philistines, there was a rocky crag on one side, and a rocky crag on the other side; and the name of the first was Botzeitz, and the name of the other was Seneh.*" One can still see this today near Michmash; there are two huge stones there, and there is a walkway between the two stones. It is still there to this day.

"*And the point of the first projected sharply northward opposite Michmash; and the other southward, opposite Gevah. And Yonasan said to the lad, his arms bearer, 'Let us go and cross over to the encampment of these gentiles; perhaps Hashem will help us, for nothing can impede Hashem from bringing salvation, by many or by few.'*" Hashem can bring salvation through just a few people, going out to war with just a few people-- similar to what happened with Gid'on. Hashem told him to send everyone home until there were only three hundred people left.

"*Come up to us, then we will go up.*" We will fall upon them, even if there are only two of us against a million. Just as we said today in Hallel, "*All the nations surround me; in the name of Hashem I cut them down. They encircle me, also they surround me; in the name of Hashem I cut them down. They encircle me like bees, but they are extinguished like a fire of thorns; in the name of Hashem I cut them down*" (Tehillim 118).

A single Jew can stand against the entire world, against all the non-Jews. That is why King David said, "*All the nations surround me; in the name of Hashem I cut them down. They encircle me, also they surround me; in the name of Hashem I cut them down. They encircle me like bees, but they are extinguished like a fire of thorns.*" He says, "*They encircle me, also they surround me*" to allude to the four kingdoms, the four exiles, every type of exile. A single Jew who says Tehillim can stand up against the entire world, against all the nations, against all of the non-Jews.

Because the truth is that it is impossible to stand against a Jew. The whole world could rise up against a single Jew and not be able to beat him. The main thing is to sit and learn Torah. If a man sits and learns Torah, he could slay a thousand men with a single arrow. The main thing is that a person should completely nullify himself, that he should have no existence at all, no ego, until he becomes like nothing (*Ayin*). And *Ayin* is the level of *Keter*, so he becomes united with the Divine level of *Ayin* completely.

EMOR

JEWS, FIX YOUR PLACE IN THE CAMP OF ISRAEL!

There's a conflict in *Rashi*-- in *Parshat Emor*, *Rashi* writes that the episode of the blasphemer occurred together with the episode of the man who collected sticks on *Shabbos* [1]. But there's a conflict here, because *Rashi* in his commentary on *Bamidbar* (15:32) says that the episode of the man who collected the sticks happened on the second *Shabbos* after they left Egypt. If so, that would mean that the episode of the blasphemer also occurred on this same Shabbos.

But according to *Parshat Emor*, the episode of the blasphemer took place on the first of Iyar in the second year, because that was the time when they were commanded about how to arrange the formation of the camp when it travelled.

The Tribe of Dan was arguing with the blasphemer, because he wanted to place his tent amongst them, because his mother was from the Tribe of Dan [2].

Jews always argue, always.

We see that Yaakov and Esav even fought in the womb! They were arguing already, in the womb. Now, they are arguing once again, where to camp, where the tent should go; they're arguing the whole time. '*This is my place, and this is your place!*' '*Leave me alone to pitch my tent in peace!*' '*No, get out of here, you have no place here. This is not your place.*'

Why are you embarrassing him?

So, the blasphemer went to Moshe Rabbenu and asked him, '*Is it true, that I'm not allowed to put my tent here?*' No one really knew what the story was, even Moshe Rabbenu didn't know. So, he responded to him surprisingly, and said 'you aren't suitable for the Tribe of Dan, maybe the Tribe of Reuven, or Shimon, or Levi. But not Dan, you decide."

And so, he decided to start cursing.

Beforehand, he didn't actually curse; it's written that he just pronounced the ineffable name of Hashem that he heard on Mount Sinai, which contained a revelation of the *merkava,* the holy chariot. The Zohar says that the blasphemer was at the level of the Prophet Yechezkel. In that generation, even a maidservant at the sea saw more than the Prophet Yechezkel.

He saw things which Yechezkel didn't see, he was greater than the Prophet Yechezkel!

The blasphemer showed them the *merkava,* the same vision that was shown to Yechezkel. Therefore, it's written, initially, that he pronounced the name of G-d, and it's not written that he cursed.

Afterwards, it is written that he cursed-- after they disgraced him and embarrassed him. The moment they disgrace a person, that person rises up to the greatest possible spiritual heights. He rises up to the *fiftieth gate,* he merits this. They open his mind for him and all of the masks covering the mind fall away. When a person is embarrassed, then all of the masks fall.

But he shouldn't run away from this disgrace, and flee, and go and sit outside the camp of Israel. You're a Jew! So, go fight for your rights! Go fix your place inside the camp!

Maybe you won't be in the camp of Dan, but then go to the camp of Reuven! So what, if you're on the border of Dan? You're happier there! But, just don't run away. There is no need to flee.

But they kicked him out of the camp of Israel. They kicked him out of the camp.

A person needs to know that this is the test. He needs to know that every time they disgrace him, a new spiritual gate is opened for him. There are 50 gates, and each fresh embarrassment reveals a new gate; a completely new gate is opened up for him.

This is what the Rebbe said in Lesson 48 of *Likutey Moharan*, and this is what we learn from the blasphemer. We need to know that they will kick you out of the camp, they will try to tell you that you're not a Jew…

He had to go and convert another time, he had to have another bris milah, he had to convert again, he thought that maybe there's a flaw in his Jewishness, maybe there's a blemish and that's why he had to go in the mikvahh again. He went and immersed in another seven mikvahhs. He went to a stream, to a spring, to another body of water, to immerse…

"So, I'll immerse another time!"

The main thing is that he wants to be a Jew, but he can't stand up to all the humiliation.

He's prepared to immerse in a *mikvahh*, to have a *bris mila*, to go through another conversion, but when it comes to experiencing some humiliation, then he's ready to throw it all away and leave the camp of Israel.

This is the hardest test, and a person needs to know that at first, he will be brought closer, a little, but then he'll be [apparently] rejected.

The Rebbe says [3] that from the window the man sees the *Tzaddik* going in the opposite direction, and says to him: "Where are you going?" But the *Tzaddik* says to him: "No, I'm actually coming to you!"

Even though you think that he's going in the opposite direction, the Rebbe is only coming towards you. He's only coming closer to you and bringing you closer to him.

151

The blasphemer was meant to reach a high level, the level of Moshe Rabbenu, the highest spiritual level in the world. And he would have done so, if he'd accepted the humiliation and remained quiet.

[1] Rashi says (*Parshat* Emor 24:12): "They placed him [under guard] by himself, but they did not place him with the one who gathered wood on Shabbos, for both incidents occurred at the same time."

[2] *Am Yisrael* was divided up into the 12 tribes, and each tribe had their specific camping ground, and their specific place in the travelling formation. A person's father decided which tribe he belonged to. The blasphemer's father was an Egyptian, so he didn't have a tribe of his own. He tried to pitch his tent with the Tribe of Dan, because that was his mother's tribe.

[3] See Chayei Moharan, New Stories, #85.

BEHAR

WHAT WILL WE EAT?

The questions, 'What will we eat?' and 'What will we drink?' are always in the back of a person's mind. The verse says, *"And if you will say: What will we eat in the seventh year?"* You want to know what will there be to eat? Hashem said, 'You will have the best of everything. You will have abundance. You will lack nothing.' Hashem said, 'You will have the best of everything.' Hashem promised you that you would have the best of everything, and you ask, 'What will we eat?' Is this called having faith in Hashem?

The holy Zohar explains the verse in *Parshat Behar*, *"If you will say: What will we eat...?"* with a story: Rebbe Chiya and Rebbe Yosi were standing on a high mountain and they had an abundance of food with them. They had taken with them several donkeys full of food and they stood on the mountain and witnessed a horrifying scene; two people were walking in the middle of the desert and they came across a man who had become lost and who had been sitting in the same spot for two days without food.

The man was dying of heatstroke, just seconds from death, and he says to them, 'It's been two days and I haven't had anything to eat or drink.' So, one of the men gave him something to eat and drink. The other man then shouted at the first, 'What are you doing? Don't give him anything. It's forbidden! 'You should guard your souls!' It's a matter of life and death. I don't allow you to do this. Let him die! What do you care if he dies? Your life comes first!'

So, the first man answered him, 'What do you care if I give him?' And the other responded, 'If you give him all your food, in the end you will ask me to give you from mine. You will want me to give you food, but I won't give you anything at all!'

Rebbe Chiya and Rebbe Yosi witnessed this whole scene from afar. They could understand from their movements what was going on, how one man shouted at the other not to give the man any food, and how the other man kept on feeding the weakened man, giving him to drink, strengthening and reviving him, until he recovered. He ended up giving him all his water and food and he was left with nothing at all for himself, not even a drop of water.

As soon as the two men started back on their way, after only a few minutes, the one who had given away all his food and water started getting sunstroke. There they are in the middle of the desert at noon and the sun is beating down. It's 120 degrees and he collapses and passes out under a tree. His friend screams at him, 'You see! I told you that you would pass out. I told you that you would die without food and water. And now, I am going to leave you here. I couldn't care less about you. I am going to abandon you here in the middle of the desert.'

When Rebbe Chiya and Rebbe Yosi saw how he lay there under the tree too weak to move, Rebbe Chiya said to Rebbe Yosi, 'We have plenty of food. Let's give him from ours. Let's run over there quickly, we have to save him!' Rebbe Yosi answered him, 'Wait a while, let's sit and see what happens. Certainly, Hashem is going to do a miracle for him. Certainly, there will be a great miracle. We have an ongoing story here. Don't jump in in the middle of it. Don't run to give him the food. The world is not *hefker* (abandoned by Hashem)! A person gives away all his food and now he's just going to die? It's impossible! For sure, a great miracle is about to take place!'

They stood there and watched how he was lying there weakened, when suddenly a giant snake appears and starts slithering towards him, a huge snake that could swallow him whole. Rebbe Chiya said, 'That's it! He's going to die now for sure! Why does this poor man have to die such a terrible death?' Rebbe Yosi responded, 'Don't despair. He gave away all his food and water. He trusted completely in Hashem, for sure Hashem won't abandon him now. Wait and see what a great miracle is about to take place.'

Suddenly, they see an even bigger snake come slithering down the tree, much bigger than the first snake. The second snake kills and swallows the first snake, and the man remains unharmed, under the tree, fast asleep in the middle of the desert. Immediately Rebbe Chiya and Rebbe Yosi run quickly over to him, wake him up from his slumber and give him something to eat and drink. Then they tell him the story of the great miracle that had just happened to him.

A person must believe that before he comes to this world, Hashem prepares for him, for each and every person, all the help he will need - people to save him and people to strengthen him. Wherever a person goes, with each and every move, there stands a person ready to help him. Whether you are in the middle of the desert or the middle of the sea, there will always be someone there beside you. You are never lost. Hashem is found in every place, in every situation, He is there with you. Every moment, the salvation is ready for a person. He just needs to cry out to Hashem one time, one real cry, and salvation is at hand. If you will only cry out, "*Shema Yisrael Hashem Elokeinu Hashem Echad*[4]!" or "*Ana Hashem, Hoshiah Na*[5]!" or "*b'zchut Rabbenu*[6]!" then Hashem will immediately save you.

A person must have faith and trust in Hashem. He needs to sing a little, to pray with *kavanah* and not worry about where he's going to get money from. For He who created you also created money and everything else. He created you even before He created money. All the

---

[4] "Hear O Israel, Hashem is our God, Hashem is One!"

[5] "Answer Hashem, please save us!"

[6] "In the merit of Rabbenu (Rebbe Nachman of Breslov)."

money in the world is ready for you. Hashem only wants that you will learn Torah. A person transgresses, so the money doesn't come pouring into his pockets, it doesn't just descend from the ceiling.

But what are you so worried about? Everything has already been announced in Heaven! Forty days before a person is born, it is decreed in Heaven that on such and such day he will acquire a home, on such and such day he will buy a field, what a person's income will be… Everything has already been decreed in Heaven, even before he was born.

The salvation can only come when a person really trusts in Hashem. His eyes should be turned to Hashem: "*The eyes of all look expectantly to You, and You give them their food in its proper time*" (Tehillim 145:17). 'In its proper time!' Everything in its time. Everything that a person deserves comes to him at its determined time: an apartment, furniture, etc. Everything happens at its specified time.

The main point of physical existence is dependent on money but worrying about money will distance a person from his salvation, from receiving an apartment. It will push away his income. A person thinks his whole life long about money, but he doesn't realize that the moment he stops thinking about money, then the money will come to him, it will race towards him. What is income: "*parnassah*"? It is "*par*" (a cow) "*noseh*" (goes). You run after the cow, and the cow goes away, it runs away. "Noseh!" - spelt with an *ayin*! The more you run after money, the more it will run away from you!

The Rebbe said in Lesson 225 that trusting in Hashem is infinite. There is no limit to trusting. "*Trust in Hashem infinitely*" (Isaiah 26:4). Trust is an unlimited thing, there are no boundaries to faith and trust. The essence of perfect trust is when a person's mind is bound to the Torah. Trust comes from intelligence. If you don't have any intelligence, you can't have any trust or faith. If you learn Torah then you have faith, but if you don't learn Torah then you can't. The Rebbe said that if you would just learn Torah, then you would have the intelligence to know that everything is from Hashem.

BECHUKOTAI

THE JEWISH WAY TO PURSUE OUR ENEMIES

Rav Natan of Breslov, in *Likutey Halachos,* gives an explanation about the verse *"You will pursue your enemies..."* (Parshat Bechukotai, Vayikra 26:7).

Is this really the purpose of *Am Yisrael,* the holy nation, that we will *'pursue our enemies, and they will fall before you by the sword etc...'*? Is it really our purpose, to take vengeance and spill blood, G-d forbid?! After all, doesn't Hashem seek peace for His nation? Doesn't He bless his people with peace? Isn't it enough that we receive His blessing to have peace in Eretz Yisrael? Why do we really need to *"pursue our enemies"*?

It's known that, in truth, all the worlds were only created in order for their inhabitants to know and recognize *Hashem Yisborach,* as brought down in the Zohar. And, even more so, everything was only created for the sake of *Am Yisrael,* in order that they would receive G-d's Torah, which contains holy *da'at* (spiritual knowledge) which enables us to know and recognize *Hashem Yisborach.*

Therefore, greatness and rulership are truly fitting only for *Am Yisrael,* who do G-d's will and who merited to receive this *da'at.* It's only for this reason that the whole world was created. So too, it's only *Am Yisrael* who can really be called *'Adam'* (man), as our rabbis have explained. Because anyone who doesn't have this knowledge of Hashem is only an animal in the shape of a man.

That's why each person is obligated to busy himself with the *mitzvah* of 'civilizing' the world. This means that he has to share this true *da'at,* this knowledge of Hashem, with others. This is the essence of the meaning of the *mitzvah* to populate the world, as our rabbis have explained.

When Israel merits to do Hashem's will, they're obliged to use all of their strength to share this knowledge with the nations of the world, as it's written: *"Tell the nations of His glory...etc"*, and in many other verses too.

This is the holy war that Israel is commanded to fight. All of this is only in order to restore the truth and to acknowledge that Hashem – *He* is G-d! This is the true purpose, and this is the essential meaning of the verse written in the *Parsha* that we will *"pursue our enemies"*.

This 'pursuit' is the basis of true peace, because as long as people don't merit to follow the Torah, and don't do Hashem's will, G-d forbid, as long as they don't turn their backs on their sins and they continue to blemish their souls, G-d forbid, then even if it seems they have a lot of 'peace', really they have no peace at all, because G-d says there can be no peace for evildoers. For as long as a person's not doing good deeds or acting according to Hashem's will, how is it possible that he could have real peace?! He doesn't even have 'peace' within himself!

This is the meaning of *"pursue your enemies"*. Namely, that when we do the will of *Hashem Yisborach*, then it's a *mitzvah* to run after our enemies-- in order to bring them closer to the truth, which is really the essence of peace. And then, our enemies will fall before us in their ruin, by way of our prayers and requests [for them to make *teshuva*] which they call 'destruction'.

And this is what it means, *"five of you will pursue a hundred"*. Rashi explains that they will fall before you in an unnatural way. But only if you are true soldier who will be part of a holy army, that will know the truth very clearly. Because, in the end, this ultimate truth will be revealed.

And then, it will be obvious that the five people who are clinging on to this truth will have the strength to chase after a hundred-- to chase after them with true words and with requests [to make *teshuva*] and to return them to *Hashem Yisborach*. This is the aspect of their 'ruin' [meaning, their previous, G-dless life will be in ruins] and it's also the aspect of the true weapons of *Am Yisrael* [knowledge and prayer].

And then, we will conquer them, and impart to them this true *da'at*, this true knowledge and awareness of Hashem, and then after that 100 of them will chase after thousands in turn, as it's written in the Torah.

Bamidbar

THE DEPTH OF TORAH

The main thing a person needs to do is to study the Ten Commandments deeply. He needs to understand the meaning behind the Ten Commandments, because everyone knows the simple meaning-- that it's forbidden to murder and to steal and to covet. Everyone knows, *"I am Hashem your G-d."*

But, when Hashem said, *"Do not murder"*, the sons of Esav didn't understand. They said, 'What?! Don't I already know that?! Is it suddenly permitted to murder a person in America? Is it allowed to murder a person in Russia? Whoever murders is imprisoned forever - it's the death penalty!'

When the Arabs heard, *"Do not steal"* they said, 'Don't I already know that?! If a person steals in Saudi Arabia, they cut off his hands, even to this day!'

If so, then what is the meaning of *"Do not murder"* and *"Do not steal"*-- because it's already clear that these things are forbidden?

Rather, *"Do not murder"* comes to tell us that even *thinking* about murder is forbidden, and this is what the nations didn't want to accept. When a person thinks a bad thought about someone, this alone will damage that person! This is what is referred to in 'not murdering'-- because the bad thought itself 'murders' the other person. If a person doesn't love his fellow, then he murders him.

There is no middle way. Either a person loves his friend from the depths of his soul, sees his good points and gives him the benefit of the doubt or the opposite is true: he hates his friend and doesn't give

161

him the benefit of the doubt. This is how he comes to transgress the commandment of "*Do not murder*".

If a person isn't careful about the way he thinks, then he actually causes damage, G-d forbid. If a person isn't working on breaking his bad character traits and his bad thoughts, then when the time of *The Giving of the Torah* comes, the Ten Commandments won't be relevant to him at all! "*Do not murder*", "*Do not steal*" and "*Do not covet*" --a person constantly covets, he hates and he kills, and he doesn't even feel that these commandments are referring to him.

It's written that, *you are a 'ben Adam'* (a son of man). You are called *'Adam'* (a man) but the nations of the world are not called *'Adam'*. Why? What's the difference between a Jew and an Arab? Arabs also pray-- they stand there and screech out their prayers on the loudspeakers in Jerusalem. They do this kind of screaming throughout the city. So, what's the difference between you and an Arab?

You are called *'Adam'*, but the nations of the world are not called *'Adam'*. When does a person start being an *'Adam'*? When he delves into the 70 *Anpin Nehirin* (spiritual lights) of the holy Torah! When he pays attention during the Torah lessons! And when he reviews them and understands the *chiddushim* given over in the lessons! He doesn't say that he has no strength to learn or that it's difficult for him to learn, and he doesn't leave in the middle or come late and leave early or go out 10 times in the middle. If he doesn't put his head into the learning, all his 248 limbs and 365 sinews into the holy Torah, then he will never become a *Breslover Chassid*! He will never succeed.

Why doesn't a person feel good? He has aches and pains; he can't learn, and he finds it difficult to concentrate. Why does a person have all kinds of troubles and illnesses? Because he doesn't learn! Why are you tired? Because you aren't learning! Start learning and you won't be tired. Start learning and you won't have all kinds of aches and pains!

Start learning and you will be healthy. Start learning and you will also be able to concentrate.

This is what the Rebbe tells us-- the only reason that a person has problems, weaknesses and pains is because he's not learning properly. When a person learns Gemara the way he should, that's when he becomes a human being. This is what gives him his *neshama* (his higher soul). It gives him his *nefesh* (his lower soul) and it gives him his *ruach* (his intermediate soul). Learning gives him a heart. He receives *mochin* (intellect). This is what it means to be 'Adam' (a man), "You are called *'Adam'*". This comes from learning Gemara, it comes from learning in depth.

A person needs to eat in order to live. A person needs to eat bread, and more than just bread if he wants to feel strong. So, all the more so, if he wants to learn the holy Gemara, which is a person's true 'bread', because *man cannot live on bread alone*. This is the true bread!

A person needs to grab hold of all his senses, his sight and his entire mind and put them only into learning Torah in depth. This is the making of the 'man'. If you don't eat, then your body will fall apart, your flesh will fall apart. Similarly, if you don't learn Gemara, your body will fall apart. Your mind will fall apart. Your eyes will fall apart. Your mouth will fall apart. Your ears will fall apart - they anyway just hear all kinds of garbage. If everything falls apart, then the person ceases to exist at all. Thus, says the Rebbe, only through the Torah does a person have life, through learning Torah in depth. This is what builds the brain, this is what enlivens the eyes, etc.

Eliyahu the Prophet came across an unlearned Jew. He asked him, 'Why don't you learn? Why don't you go to yeshiva?' He answered, "Me? In yeshiva? I'm an *am haaretz* (an uneducated, simple Jew). I'm not intelligent. I don't understand things. I am just a simple Jewish worker. Why are you speaking to me about going to yeshiva to learn?'

So, Eliyahu responded, 'Why on earth not?' 'Because I don't have a brain!' 'Well, what do you do for a living?' 'I fix fishing nets.' 'You fix fishing nets? You have the intelligence to know how to fix fishing nets, but you don't have the intelligence to learn Torah!?'

The Jew was so shaken up by this conversation that he immediately ran to go and learn Torah. In the end he became a great Torah scholar, one of the *Amoraim*. So, if a person knows that he has the intelligence to fix nets, and he has the intelligence to know how to hammer nails into a board and to attach two boards together, so too can he attach two *sugiot* (portions of Gemara) together or connect two parts of a verse, or two teachings in the Gemara! If a person knows how to fix a net or to attach two boards together, then he also has enough intelligence to learn Torah.

But, the moment that he says, 'I don't have the intelligence', he should know that it's just his *yetzer hara* speaking, or his laziness, or his sadness. There's no such thing as not being able to learn Torah! A person needs to apply his intelligence to Torah, to put all his ability to understand into the Torah. A person, thank G-d, has the whole day in front of him. If he wants to rest, he can rest! If he wants to eat, he can eat! There are still a few hours left in which to learn Torah. He can still find a few spare hours in which to learn-- but he must do so with all of his strength! He must immerse himself in the Gemara, the *Rishonim*, the *Achronim*, and in the *chiddushim* that come up during the lessons.

When a person learns Torah in depth and he puts all his intelligence into the Torah, then he literally creates new worlds. He creates a new existence. Suddenly, there are new laws which apply to him! He now has money to pay for his trip to Uman! Suddenly, he has an influx of spirituality and an influx of material abundance! This is because he is creating new worlds. Before he started learning, he was in a world in which he didn't have much money, but now he's in a world in which he already has plenty of money! This is because through learning he creates a whole new world, because every moment a person creates new worlds.

When *Shavuos* arrives, the holiday of the *Giving of the Torah*, a person needs to decide: now I'm going to accept upon myself the yoke of the Torah. The Rebbe asks, what does it mean to take on the yoke of the Torah? If a person says, 'From now on I'm going to learn all day I'm going to hold on to this book all day long, I'll say Tehillim all day long or I'll read *Shas* all day long', then he should know that this is not enough. The Rebbe told us that *only* a person who learns in depth is called a person who has truly accepted upon himself the yoke of Torah!

Naso

REMEMBER WHO YOU ARE

In 1933, Rabbi Yitzhak Kosovsky was appointed as the Chief Rabbi of the Johannsburg Jewish community in South Africa. After a short time, it became clear to Rabbi Kosovsky that many Jews in the community were breaking Shabbos in public, eating forbidden foods and stumbling in other prohibitions in the Torah as well.

Some of them were *Kohanim*. They would come to shul on *Shabbos* and *Yom Tov* and would go up to the *bimah* to bless the worshippers at the time of the blessing of the *Kohanim*, as is commanded in the Torah.

Rav Kosovsky turned to his brother-in-law, Rav Chaim Grodsky, and asked him, 'How should one act towards those people who break Shabbos in public, who then come to shul and go up to *duchen* (make the priestly blessing) with the rest of the *Kohanim*? Is it appropriate to prevent them from blessing the congregation?'

After all, the *poskim* (halachic decisors) ruled that a *mumar* (an apostate Jew) who breaks *Shabbos* in public is considered to be like an apostate who worships idols, and he's not permitted to bless the congregation with the rest of the *Kohanim*.

But, at the same time, is it possible to be lenient here, because those who are sinning like this are doing so because they lack knowledge about how great the prohibition is? In which case, perhaps they should be considered like a *'tinok she nishba'* (a baby who is kidnapped from its parents and doesn't know its Jewish roots)?"

Rav Chaim replied to his brother-in-law, Rav Kosovsky, 'According to the letter of the law, it's clear that *Kohanim* who break *Shabbos* in public aren't fitting to go up to *duchen*, to bless the congregation of worshippers. However, I'm giving a *heter* (rabbinic permission) not to stop them doing so, because if you stop them going up to *duchen*, many of them are likely to forget that they are actually *Kohanim*. Then, G-d-forbid, they could also come also to marry women who are forbidden to *Kohanim* or come into contact with spiritual impurity as a result of attending the dead [which is also forbidden for *Kohanim*].

Rav Chaim said to his brother-in-law, Rav Kosovsky, 'When the *Kohanim* go up to bless the congregation with the *Birkas HaKohanim*, this engraves in their own heart the recognition that they are descended from the seed of *Aaron HaKohen*, and it's possible that this recognition will bring them, in the future, to make complete *teshuva*.'

IT'S FORBIDDEN TO BE AFRAID

The main reason for the creation of the world was to reveal the awe and the kingdom of Hashem, *"awe of Hashem is pure and stands forever"* (Tehillim 19:10). A person needs to know that the only thing that exists is awe of Hashem. One must be in awe of Hashem and fear Him. He shouldn't fear anyone else, no person-- not Haman, not Pharaoh, not the Nazis. He should only fear Hashem. It is completely forbidden to fear any minister or nobleman or any robber or thief or terrorist.

The entire creation is His Kingdom which reveals the kingship of Hashem in the world. The entire creation exclaims, 'Hashem is King. Hashem was King. Hashem will be King forever.' Other than Hashem, nothing exists. Terrorists don't exist. Murderers don't exist. Nothing exists.

Rabbenu says that the first thing in serving Hashem is not to have any fear. This is the number one crucial teaching of Rebbe Nachman, that we should have no fear whatsoever. The Rebbe has no use for cowards, no use for the faint-hearted. What is there to be afraid of? There's a G-d in the world. Hashem is alive and exists. There are *Tzaddikim*, like Moshe Rabbenu and Yehoshua bin Nun. They have complete control here in this world. They are in charge of everything. If a person wants to have success in serving Hashem or in anything at all, then first of all he needs to be fearless, he shouldn't have a drop of fear in him. The *Megaleh Amukot*, Rav Natan Shapira, says that fear is the biggest *tumah* that there is in the world. When a person has fear this means that he has no faith. He must uproot this at its source.

Rabbenu says in Lesson 249, "*The most important part of a person's strength is in his heart. One who is strong in his heart and has no fear of any person or any thing is able to perform wonders and acts of strength and achieve victory in all his battles, simply through the strength of his heart.*"

A person must be courageous, undaunted under any circumstances. Only this way will he be victorious in all his battles. This is the aspect of "*Who is considered a strong person? The one who conquers his evil inclination*" (Avos 4:1). The primary battle is to overcome the bad thoughts one has in his heart as well as not looking at forbidden sights in the street.

BEHA'ALOTECHA

ANOTHER PESACH?

Moshe knew the laws of Judaism and the Sages teach us that Moshe knew that there is a Second Passover (*Pesach Sheni*). What?! There's a second *Pesach*? All of a sudden, Moshe teaches us we can make another Pesach? So maybe we should also celebrate another Succos?! We should also light the *Menorah* for another *Chanukah*?! And make another Purim?! There is *Shushan Purim*, but this isn't another Purim, it's still Purim. So maybe we should we do another Purim in the month of *Nissan*, or in the month of *Iyar*?

The *Targum Yonasan* explains Moshe knew the laws of the *Pesach Sheni*. However, he had a specific reason why he wanted to ask Hashem again about *Pesach Sheni*. Moshe wanted to teach the *Sanhedrin* that it's necessary to inquire and to question every element of Jewish Law. Even if someone already knows the *Halacha* clearly, he should still inquire about it and ask others about it. A person needs to constantly review and clarify the *Halacha*, because the truth is that in every single Jewish law there is always something new, such as a new nuance or detail that causes the whole law to change. Further, these new details and modifications also depend on the individuals involved.

Pesach Sheni is the greatest wonder! Moshe tells us that we can bring another *Pesach* offering, but what kind of Rabbi says you can bring another *Pesach* offering? Would a real Rabbi say we should have another *Rosh Hashana*? That we should travel to Uman again for another *Rosh Hashana*?! Sometimes people get to Uman too late or not at all. For example, this one didn't get to the airport on time and missed his flight. So, maybe we should have another *Rosh Hashana* where anyone who didn't get to Uman on time can come to Uman in the month of *Cheshvan!*

What?! The Rebbe doesn't want us to have another *Rosh Hashana!* So, how can there be any concept of bringing a second *Pesach* offering? *Pesach* is on *Pesach*, *Succos* is on *Succos*, and the fast of *Yom Kippur* is on *Yom Kippur*. Nevertheless, there is actually a *Pesach Sheni* which is, like all other Jewish laws, constantly developing its new nuances and details.

Why is it relevant to ask the question, *"Why were we left out?"*[7] If a person is impure then he is impure, he simply cannot bring a *Pesach* offering. What were these Jews saying, that they wanted special treatment? They were asking for Moshe and the Sages to make them a new Jewish law. What can a person do? If he was impure, so he can't bring the *Pesach* offering. However, the Holy *Ohr Hachayim* comes to teach us what these Jews were really asking. It's clear that if a person is impure, he can't bring the *Pesach* offering. Why should the Sages make another *Pesach* offering? Those who were impure were under inescapable circumstances, like one that touched a dead rat or touched something impure. There's nothing that can be done, since an impure Jew is forbidden to eat the *Pesach* offering.

The *Bnei Yissachar* asks the question, why did they tell Moshe that, *"we became impure due to the soul of a person"*. What is significant about knowing that they were impure due to the soul of a person? The *Bnei Yissachar* answers that they said to Moshe, 'Nadav and Avihu are literally living. Yosef is literally living.' They saw Nadiv and Avihu living, they saw Yosef living!

They felt these *Tzaddikim* were still living. Since truly great *Tzaddikim* became part of Hashem, they become a part of the sacred

---

[7] This is what the Jews, who happened to be impure at the date of Pesach, said-- as their temporary impurity meant that they would have to miss out by not being able to participate in the Pesach sacrifice.

name of Hashem, and they enter the *World of Atzilus*. At that moment, when they asked Moshe *"Why were we left out?"* they had a greater comprehension of Judaism than Moshe and Aharon. After that moment Moshe's comprehension expanded, but at that moment when they asked the question, they had a greater comprehension than Moshe and Aharon since they understood that these *Tzaddikim* were literally living.

The *Tzaddik* is alive! People came to Moshe and said Moshe our teacher these *Tzaddikim* are not dead, these *Tzaddikim* are alive. So, their question really was, 'Do these great *Tzaddikim* that are not really dead cause impurity?' They're extremely holy and great *Tzaddikim* that continue living even after they have died. They are simply lying down as if they are dead. So, do these great *Tzaddikim* that are lying in their graves as if they are dead cause a person to be impure?

Now, *Rashi* explains that this was the beginning of a new nuance and detail in the laws of purity and impurity since these *Tzaddikim* are really alive-- they are the 'living dead'. Yet they are greater after their death than during their life, but there is a Jewish Law that a dead person causes impurity... So, the question is whether these *Tzaddikim* are considered to be like a regular dead person in Jewish law or not? So, the decision given was that if the body doesn't move it causes impurity, but it is an incredible wonder that in the merit of this question come the laws of the *Pesach Sheni*.

BRINGING PEOPLE BACK HOME

"And as the Ark set out on the journey"-- this phrase is a *Parsha* in and of itself. It is its own book, as it says in the Gemara (Shabbos 116a), *"Wisdom has built her house, she has hewn out her seven pillars [Proverbs 9:1]. These represent the seven books of the Torah."* So, really, there are seven

books in the Torah and not just five. The book of Bamidbar is divided into three separate books. The two verses, *"And as the Ark set out on the journey"* (10:35) and *"And when it rested, he would say, 'Rest...'"* (10:36) are a book in and of themselves, found in the middle of the book of Bamidbar. Truly this is an awesome wonder that such a small section of only two lines can be considered a book on its own.

The *Parsha* of *"And as the Ark set out on the journey"* is enclosed by two upside-down letter '*nun*'s. The letter *nun* [which has the numerical value of 50] hints at the 50th gate of holiness which is the most hidden. This gate can be achieved only though: *"And as the Ark set out on the journey"*, only through traveling.

This is what the Zohar says in *Parshat Beha'aloscha* (151a), *"Go and see, there is no [letter] nun in the psalm of Ashrei."* Everyone knows that in the psalm of *"Ashrei yoshvei beytecha"* there's no verse that starts with the letter *nun*[8]. So, when do we get the *nun*? When do we merit to the letter *nun*? It comes *davka* when a person is traveling! It's such a high level of holiness, it's such an awesome gate, that it's impossible to reach it other than by traveling for the sake of heaven-- to bring people back in *teshuva*.

The Rebbe says: go, go, start traveling! All over the land of Israel there are people living by themselves in *moshavim* and *kibbutzim* who don't see any rabbis and don't listen to Torah classes and don't know anything about Judaism. The *yetzer hara* is burning! How is it possible for their children not to sin?

When a person travels on the road trying to bring people back in *teshuva*, he doesn't know how many people are actually being influenced to return in *teshuva* just from having seen him. They see a man with *payos* (sidecurls) and with light in his face and their hearts open up. Their

---

[8] Although each verse of the psalm starts with the consecutive letters of the Hebrew alphabet, *nun* is missing.

hearts start burning and they wake up. Maybe, amongst all the people, there is one who laughs and makes fun, but 10,000 are awakened to *teshuva*. People look out of their windows and say, 'If only we could be like him, with a beard and *payos.*'

When they see a religious person, a holy person, their *neshama* springs to life! It comes alive and it wants to attach itself to this Jew. A person sets out with a shining face, and he goes and knocks on some darkened door and people see such an angel and immediately everyone gets up and runs to the door. There was such a story in Gush Katif in a *Meretz* (anti-Torah) *moshav* where *avreichim* went to spread Torah and when they finished and wanted to go home, everyone started running towards them, all the children in their shorts and undershirts, and shouted, 'Why are you leaving us? Help us! We don't know what to do!'

Whoever does such an important *mitzvah* as this and travels from city to city and from *moshav* to *moshav*-- all the time learning, of course? Before a person learns for eight hours, there is no reason to go out! You need to learn for eight hours and then spread Torah for eight hours, and you can also learn on the way while you are traveling. Then a person arrives full of Torah and he has a shining face, and when people see his shining face then they immediately make *teshuva*, because everyone else is walking around with sour or broken expressions on their faces. And when someone who learns Torah shows up, they see him like a G-dly angel with *payos* and a beard, with a shining face, and everyone makes *teshuva*!

The Gemara (Bava Metziah 85b) relates how Rav Chavivah Bar Surmaki wanted to see the heavenly chariot of Rebbe Chiya. He asked Eliyahu HaNavi, pleading with him, crying, "I want to see Rebbe Chiya! I want to see Rebbe Chiya! Eliyahu HaNavi said, 'Beware! Your eyes will burn out if you see it. You will be burned up by his fire!' Eliyahu HaNavi told him, "Me you can look at, but Rebbe Chiya is completely fire: a chariot of fire, fiery angels. Be careful! You're making a very dangerous request.'

But Rebbe Chavivah couldn't control himself. He didn't stand up in the test, and he looked at Rebbe Chiya's chariot. Immediately his eyes burned up. One spark from Rebbe Chiya scorched his eyes and he was blinded. He was almost completely burnt up. The next day, he went to the cave of Rebbe Chiya and cried and cried, "Rebbe Chiya, return to me the light of my eyes." And Rebbe Chiya gave him back his sight.

The Ari HaKadosh asks: Who is Rebbe Chiya? What is Rebbe Chiya? This is a *Tzaddik* that we simply have no conception of. Why? Because he went from town to town, from *moshav* to *moshav*, day and night, to spread Torah in Israel. He didn't sleep and he didn't rest for a second. The Ari says that it is not for nothing that a person merits such levels. All the *Tannaim* and *Amoraim* are raised up by angels in heaven, but Rebbe Chiya rises up on his own. No angel or *seraph* can lift him up because they can't go up that high! Rebbe Chiya rises up and up and up to a place that cannot be described, to *Atika D'Atika*.

The Zohar says, *"Fortunate is the person who brings others back in teshuva."* (Shemos 128b). A person who brings others back in *teshuva* will have no gate in heaven closed before him. Everything is open to him. They give him everything, all the King's treasures. Hashem draws him close, hugs him and dedicates time to spend with him more than all the other *Tzaddikim*, because he dedicated himself to bring people back in *teshuva*. And they give him all the keys and open all the gates for him and reveal all the Torah's secrets to him.

Reb Natan says that if a person doesn't bring people back in *teshuva*, it's said about him: *"an offering of the wicked and an abomination"* (Proverbs 21:27). Hashem has no pleasure from his Torah. Even if a person will be the wisest and the most righteous, if he doesn't travel and bring people back in *teshuva*, if he doesn't connect with people on a lower level than he is, then his prayers are not accepted.

There are no evildoers in the nation of Israel. Even if you see a totally wicked person, you must know that it is only the *klipos* that are surrounding him that you see. The Arizal says that the many *klipos* that surround the wicked are only a reflection of the great light that is hidden within them. Even the generations' most *chutzpadik* and brazen-faced people are only covered in a millimeter of *klipos* - just a millimeter of a millimeter, which can be shed in a second and then their internal light will be revealed. They have the greatest light inside, so the *klipos* are attracted to them and fight hard to hide their great light. The moment that we're able to bring them back in *teshuva*, a ray of light will shine which will enlighten the whole world and then all of Israel will return in *teshuva*.

A person is obligated to bring people back in *teshuva*, as Yehuda exclaimed, "*How can I go up to my father if the youth is not with me!*" (Bereshit 44:34). How can I go up to my father? How can I go up to Heaven and the youth is not with me? Who is this youth? This is all of *Am Yisrael*, all of the unfortunate young people who are lost and far from Hashem. How will we dare go up to Heaven and admit that we didn't at least attempt to bring them back in *teshuva*?

175

SHLACH

RUN FOR YOUR LIFE

Rabbenu explains in Lesson 12, that the moment a person learns Torah in an incorrect way, it's considered as if he learned Torah from Jewish *demon scholars*. This person receives their Torah from the demons that have a fallen Torah from the fallen '*alephs*'.

They have the Torah of the fallen *alephs*. It's written about these *aluphim* (leaders) that King Solomon would speak in 3,000 allegories and sing 5,000 songs because he merited to achieve this in holiness. But the Jewish demon scholars receive their Torah learning from the *klipos* (side of evil).

So, we see that a person is able to learn Torah via the *klipos*. He'll be a Torah scholar, a *talmid chacham*, and the Zohar says this is actually the reason why he's bothering to learn (in order to become a 'Torah scholar'). All of his words will be in way of parable and flowery speech and with wonderful reasoning, because their root is in these *aluphim*.

Regarding these Torah scholars, it's said about them: "*The least of them tire out people, and even cause Hashem to be wearied by them.*" Because they tire out people who come to listen to their lectures and their Torah.

The purpose of learning Torah is not simply to become a Torah genius. Our purpose is to feel Hashem, to come close to Hashem, to feel Hashem's love. Like King David said, "*for me, closeness to Hashem is good.*" We should merit to feel closeness to Hashem, meaning we should come to know how to serve Hashem.

But those other people, they don't achieve any benefit. These people don't achieve any benefit, because the Torah of these 'Torah scholars' doesn't have the power to guide a person on the right path. A person may learn Torah, but he also needs to change his character traits, to change his nature and to change his inclinations.

But this one [who's learning Torah for ulterior motives] doesn't change, because he stays the same in his internal reality, in his human soul. In order for the Torah to be able to change a person's inner dimension, he needs to become a true Torah scholar who is an angel of Hashem, who is called an angel of Hashem.

But, if the Torah scholar is not like this, then the Torah that he learns doesn't bring him onto a good path. He learns Torah, so he has a lot of knowledge. He could be a genius, the biggest in the world. He can be the greatest advisor in the world. It's written about Achitophel that they would ask him for advice with the same sort of awe that a person would request things from Hashem.

Achitophel reached the level of the *Urim and Turim*, but even so, he doesn't have a portion in the World to Come. He reached the level of the *Urim and Turim* because he was on that level [in terms of his Torah knowledge.] But, being a true *Tzaddik* is not connected to this, it's not relevant.

Do'eg HaAdomi was the head of the Sanhedrin and after this he fell time after time, until he forgot all his Torah learning and he killed all the people of the city of Nov, the city of the Kohanim. And all this happened because of a delusion that entered him, that King David deserved the death penalty.

But he had a personal argument against David, so therefore he was liable to the death penalty because he was rebelling against royalty. Anyone who had a connection to him [Do'eg] was also liable for the death penalty. So much so, that even Do'eg doesn't have a share in the World to Come.

So, we see that during his lifetime, a person can experience all types of different situations. Twelve men went to spy out the land, and suddenly, within the space of 10 days, they turned into complete evildoers, simply within the time it took to make the journey. Yehoshua Bin Nun was saved from their evil counsel only because he received a blessing from Moshe Rabbenu that Hashem would save him from their advice.

And Calev ben Yefunneh, who didn't receive a blessing from Moshe Rabbenu, was very worried about what would happen. So, he began to run to the graves of the *Tzaddikim*, crying out to Hashem to save him. Because, here he was, going along with 10 friends who were sent on *shlichus* (on a mission) for Moshe-- because Moshe gave them the possibility of sinning, saying 'if you want to go, so go.'

Moshe knew what could happen, but he gave them their free choice. Calev saw this too; he knew they were going on a mission for Moshe but, even so, in the middle of the way, they switched to the side of evil. Calev didn't know what to do, so he ran with great self-sacrifice to Hevron.

So much so, that the Zohar asks how did Calev run to Hevron when he was endangering his life by doing so? The place was so dangerous that it was like deliberately committing suicide. The Zohar answers by saying, a person who is under pressure doesn't look at what's going on around him. A person under pressure doesn't look at anything; he runs to a field in the middle of the night and cries out to Hashem to save him.

This was Calev ben Yefunneh, who ran to Hevron, even though it risked his life, and not on the advice of Moshe. But the main thing was to guard his *emunah*, his belief in Moshe. In order that he would maintain his *emunah* in Moshe, he ran to Hevron in the middle of the night, even though it risked his life, and without being instructed to do so by Moshe-- but he did so in order to guard his *emunah* in Moshe Rabbenu.

MOSHE DIDN'T DIE

All of *Am Yisrael* heard the prophecy of Eldad and Medad: 'Moshe will die, and Yehoshua will bring *Am Yisrael* into the land of Israel.' All of *Am Yisrael* heard this awesome prophecy, and this prophecy spread across the whole encampment. Eldad and Medad said: 'Know, Moshe is going to die! The moment that we touch the border of the Holy Land, Moshe is going to die! And Yehoshua is going to be our leader instead. He's the one who's going to bring the people into the land.'

All the people were panicking, some of them were trembling from fright, everyone was sobbing. They cried, 'If we enter the land, then Moshe will die!'

Rav Natan explains that the controversy between the spies and Yehoshua Bin Nun boiled down to this. The spies said, 'we love Moshe Rabbenu, we want Moshe Rabbenu to live, we don't want to part from him. We're together with Moshe Rabbenu, and we want him to live, and not die. We don't want to enter the Holy Land for one reason only - in order that Moshe will to continue to live and to continue to lead us. We don't care that we're going to stay in the desert; the main thing is that Moshe should live.'

The Ari HaKadosh says (in *Shaar HaPesukim, Parshat Shelach Lecha*) that this was the amazing argument between the spies and Yehoshua. The spies said to Yehoshua Bin Nun, 'Here's what's going on, you heard the prophecy that 'Moshe is going to die, and that Yehoshua will enter the land' and so you want to enter *Eretz Yisrael*, so that your *Rebbe* will die. That's simply what you want, you just want your *Rebbe* to die, because you want to inherit his position, you want to be the leader!'

This is what Yehoshua argued back: 'Moshe is alive! Moshe is *chai v'kayam* (alive and present in the world), there is no such thing as Moshe dying, Moshe cannot die!' Yehoshua Bin Nun explained to the spies that Moshe Rabbenu is going to live on forever.

Tzaddikim are eternally 'alive and present in the world'. There's no such thing as Moshe Rabbenu dying. There's no such thing as *Rashbi* (Rabbi Shimon Bar Yochai) dying. There's no such thing as the *Ari* dying. There's no such thing as the *Baal Shem Tov* dying. The *Tzaddikim* never die – Moshe Rabbenu is *chai v'kayam*. He descends and is revealed in every *Tzaddik* of the generation.

Moshe could be revealed in everyone. The more refined and holy a person is, the more they can merit to have a revelation of Moshe, the more they'll merit that the soul of Moshe will shine out of them.

The spies argued back: 'We love Moshe, and we're not going to give up on Moshe. Yehoshua just wants to be the leader… Ok, so if he wants, he should go by himself, and he can take *Am Yisrael* with him, but we're not going to leave Moshe by himself. We are staying loyal to Moshe.'

So, what really was the error the spies made? Rabbi Natan explains that the spies humiliated Moshe Rabbenu and shamed him in the worst possible way. Not only did they not heed his voice, when he told them to enter Eretz Yisrael; Rabbenu tells us that they also didn't believe in the eternalness of Moshe Rabbenu.

They didn't believe that Moshe Rabbenu was immortal, and that his words and his leadership was *chai v'kayam* – that it would last and endure for ever and ever. And that he could be revealed in each and every person at any moment. Because they wanted Moshe Rabbenu to stay alive, physically, because they wanted the 'body' of Moshe Rabbenu to stay with them, they made him corporeal. The made the whole matter of Moshe materialistic and turned Moshe Rabbenu into a body.

Rav Natan explains that it's precisely because they argued that they wanted to stay with Moshe that they revealed their opposite intention - that they were really waiting for him to die and to go away. They showed that they wanted to be parted from Moshe, already, and to get away from Moshe's difficult leadership.

Moshe was serving Hashem with all his strength. Moshe used to get up for *chatzos* and pray with the *vasikin* (sunrise) minyan. He did *hitbodedut*, he learned Torah day and night, etc. And they said, 'We'll stay with Moshe Rabbenu, we'll be in the desert another 10 years, we'll be in the desert another 20 years, until eventually we'll get away from him, and then we can get up at 10am, or 12am, and then we can have some fun.'

'Right now, there's no choice, we have to suffer a little while longer. We already fell into the trap of Moshe Rabbenu, what can we do?' But really, they knew that Yehoshua Bin Nun would continue along Moshe Rabbenu's path, and to continue leading like Moshe Rabbenu. They didn't want Yehoshua Bin Nun, they wanted Moshe. They wanted to stay with Moshe solely because they were waiting for him to pass away.

Rav Natan asks, what did Calev Ben Yefuneh do? Where was he, in all this controversy? Calev was silent. Calev didn't know who was right, whether Yehoshua was right, or whether the spies were right. The spies were arguing that they wanted Moshe Rabbenu to live, so they didn't want to enter the land, and they were calling Yehoshua Bin Nun a murderer! That Yehoshua Bin Nun wanted to enter the land and was waiting for Moshe to pass away.

Calev said to Yehoshua Bin Nun, 'Yehoshua, what are these whisperings? Look what's being said here-- you've got 10 saintly people, *Tzaddikim*, with beards down to the ground, big, bushy *payot*... Do you hear what they're telling you? How are you not scared to enter the land-- if Moshe Rabbenu is going to die as a result?'

Yehoshua said to Calev, 'I know that Moshe will live forever! Moshe is not dependent on a body; I don't even see his body. I see Moshe's *neshama,* his soul, and his neshama is immortal and can be found in every place. It can be revealed in all the princes [the tribal leaders of *Am Yisrael*], in Elidad ben Kislon, in Gadi ben Susi. In whomever the soul of Moshe Rabbenu reveals itself, I will heed his words. I'm telling you, the moment Moshe passes away, his *neshama* will be revealed in someone else, because Moshe *chai v'kayam!'*

Calev didn't know who was right, Yehoshua, or the spies? He found himself caught between a rock and a hard place. How was he going to figure out who was right? How could he clarify something like this? So, what did Calev do? He went to Hevron, to the tomb of the holy Patriarchs, and there the truth was revealed to him.

What was he shown, there? At the very moment that he prostrated himself on the graves of the Patriarchs, he saw that the Patriarchs are *chai v'kayam* – they live and endure in the world forever! He saw that Avraham was alive! That Yitzhak was alive! That Yaacov was alive!

He realized that what Yehoshua had been telling him was the truth: a *Tzaddik* never dies, he never passes away. *Rashbi* is alive, the *Ari* is alive, the *Baal Shem Tov* is alive. It was revealed to him that 400 years after he passed away, Avraham Avinu was talking to him and telling him that Yehoshua was right, and that Moshe would exist forever. Yitzhak told him, Moshe will be around forever. Yaacov told him, Moshe will be around forever.

Rav Natan tells us, this is what was revealed to Calev at the tomb of the Patriarchs – that *Tzaddi*kim are not bound by their bodies. It's not what you see with your eyes. The *Tzaddi*k is an eternal neshama that will last forever and ever.

KORACH

JEALOUS OF NOTHING

Heaven designated Korach to perform an enormous task. Hashem gave him a tremendous gift of speech. Due to the kindness of Hashem, he was a wonderful orator and he was meant to have used that gift to unite and strengthen the people, so they would return to believing in Moshe Rabbenu. Because Korach knew very well who Moshe Rabbenu was, it's just that he couldn't overcome his own feelings of jealousy and hatred.

He should have unified the people about believing in Moshe Rabbenu and included each person in the gathering together of Jewish souls. What does it mean, to '*include each person in the gathering together of Jewish souls?*' It means that I know that I'm the least of the least and that I'm less than any other Jew.

This is the level Moshe Rabbenu merited to achieve. That's why it's said of him, "*And the man, Moshe, was the humblest of all men on the face of the earth*" (Bamidbar 12:3). And so, if he would have succeeded in gathering together the whole of *Am Yisrael*, and in bringing the whole of *Am Yisrael* back to Moshe Rabbenu, then the people could have risen up to a very high spiritual level.

Because the people now didn't really have such a connection to Moshe Rabbenu. He was walking around with a veil over his face and he was hiding himself from the public. So, slowly, slowly, the people started to forget. He was out of sight and out of mind. When you don't see someone or something, you forget about him.

When a person is sunk deep in materialism and sunk deep within 'the body', then he doesn't see things. Rav Natan of Breslov says that

Korach's job was to bring the people back to having *emunah* in Moshe Rabbenu, and to get them out of their state of 'forgetting'. But Korach didn't do this, because of his pride, his inflated ego and his lust to rule.

This happened even though Korach was initially worthy of becoming the leader of *Am Yisrael,* as the *Asarah Ma'amarot.* explains. Everyone saw how Korach rose up into the air. The whole of *Am Yisrael* saw how Korach, and his family, and his brothers were all lifted up into the air, because they used to carry the Ark of the Covenant, and 'the Ark carried those who carried it.'

If Korach could float in the air, then why wasn't Moshe floating in the air? But Moshe was hiding his true level, so he walked on the ground. No one saw Moshe levitating in the air, but they saw Korach and his sons floating in the air, while the 'odd one out', Moshe Rabbenu walked along slowly, with his staff. And so, everyone ran after Korach.

If people are running after you, great, excellent – but use it for the good! Tell everyone about the true greatness of Moshe Rabbenu. That Moshe Rabbenu, who you see walking along the ground, he's really something else entirely! Moshe Rabbenu is just hiding his greatness.

If Moshe Rabbenu could arrange things so that Korach could fly in the air, then he could certainly also fly in the air himself, and that all of *Am Yisrael* would travel on the 'wings of eagles'.

Korach fell into making a big mistake. He thought that the whole thing with Moshe was just a question of innate ability and talent. He saw that Moshe was blessed with great abilities and skills. So, slowly, slowly, Korach also started learning these skills himself, and in this way, he also acquired them for himself.

As well as this first mistake, that Korach believed Moshe was only the leader because of his abilities, he also fell into another mistake. He believed that Moshe got his strength from *Am Yisrael*; he didn't understand that Moshe was actually influencing the people with his own strength. He didn't understand that Moshe was in fact equivalent to all of *Am Yisrael*, and that he was the root of all the souls of *Am Yisrael*.

He thought that the leader gets his strength from the people, and that the more *chassidim* he has, the bigger the community he has, the more popular he is, so the more strength he'll get from everybody and then he'll be able to do miracles and perform wonders and ascend to heaven.

Rav Natan says that the matter of Moshe had nothing to do with his innate talents or accomplishments. In fact, the opposite was true. He stammered with his words and he didn't have an agile tongue. He didn't know how to give a nice speech or how to persuade people. Rather, Moshe was completely 'nothing'. What was Moshe's accomplishment? He was 'nothing'.

Moshe was included in the light of *ein sof*, the infinite light-- he was totally included within Hashem and was nullified from any other reality. No other reality existed for Moshe, Hashem wasn't hidden from him, he didn't have a connection to anything else, he just did everything *leshem Shemayim*, for the sake of heaven, just for *Hashem Yitborach*.

And this is why Hashem could choose him to be the leader of *Am Yisrael* who took them out from Egypt and brought down the ten plagues on Pharaoh and the Egyptians and who brought the Clouds of Glory and who brought the Torah down from heaven-- because he was completely nothing. He didn't have any other talents or accomplishments and he didn't get his strength from *Am Yisrael*. Rather, Moshe Rabbenu's strength only came from Hashem.

Because he was nothing, it was impossible to mimic him. You can emulate being a good speaker or being a good lecturer and it's also possible to emulate being a leader, but Rav Natan tells us-- you can only reach the level of 'nothing' by nullifying yourself to Moshe.

And by believing that Moshe is something else entirely, that we can't even begin to understand. We're unable to understand it, we're unable to grasp it. It's not abilities and it's not nice speeches. It's nothing at all like that. Moshe didn't bring the Clouds of Glory down with a nice speech and he didn't take *Am Yisrael* out of Egypt because he was a good orator.

He wasn't some 'talented leader' or a leader because he had G-d-given abilities. He was the leader because he was nothing, completely nothing, *mamash* it was like he didn't even exist.

And Rav Natan tells us, this was Korach's mistake, that because of his tremendous jealousy and his arrogance, Hashem blocked his eyes from seeing who Moshe really was, because Moshe was only nothing. And no-one else can be 'nothing' except for Moshe. Throughout all the generations, no-one else can be nothing. This only comes by nullifying the self completely to Moshe. In order to truly be 'nothing', you need to receive it from Moshe himself.

EVERYTHING DEPENDS ON A PERSON'S WIFE

In truth, everything depends on a person's wife; when he has a wife who's a *Tzadddeket*, she will lead him on the right *derech* (path), and if he has a wife who is not a *Tzadddeket*, she'll pull him off the *derech*.

And this is what happened to Korach. Korach was a *Tzaddik* – a true *Tzaddik*. It's written in *Likutey Halachos*, in Yoreh Deah Part 2, *Shiloach HaKen* (4, 8), that Korach was a true *Tzaddik*, but that his wife slowly, slowly succeeded in leading him astray. Because everything that happens to a person depends on what sort of wife he has, and each person can raise his wife up to the level of being able to receive prophecy, as in *Tanna DeVei Eliyahu* (chapter 9), where it's written that Eliyahu Hanavi says, 'I take heaven and earth as my witnesses that every wife can possess *ruach hakodesh* (the spirit of prophecy)', that every wife could be a prophetess and this depends solely on the husband.

If the husband raises up his wife, she can be a prophetess, someone who possesses *ruach hakodesh*. All the spiritual levels that a wife achieves depend upon her husband. If Sarah was a greater prophet than Avraham (as brought in the Midrash Tanchuma, *Shemot, 1:1*, and also by Rashi on Bereshit, 21:12), it's because Avraham prayed with *kavanah* (intent), and when Avraham prayed with *kavanah*, the spirit of prophecy was passed along to Sarah-- even twice as much as he himself possessed.

And it's written in the *Tanna DeVey Eliyahu*, "*Devorah the prophetess, wife of Lapidot, judged Israel at that time (Shoftim 4:4). And at that time, there was Pinchas ben Elazar ben Aharon HaKohen, the Kohen HaGadol, and this was at the time that Devorah was a prophetess. At that time, the Kohen HaGadol was in Shilo, and everyone left Pinchas ben Elazar ben Aharon HaKohen, and went to Devorah, because Devorah had ruach hakodesh and used to judge by way of her words and prophesize about them. And Pinchas ben Elazar was also in those days.*"

'Moshe Rabbenu's going to cut off everyone's *payot*. You'll come home and suddenly, you won't have a beard and *payot*.' This is what the wife of Korach always used to say to him, 'You'll see! One day he'll get you to cut off your beards and *payot*! He's crazy, he's not normal. Now, he's having some sort of fit, last time it was a different sort of fit. Everything's just one big fit of madness by him!'

'Now, he's having a big, mad fit to get out of Egypt. Tomorrow, he'll have another big fit and take you back to Egypt. Now, he's having a mad fit to cut off your *payot*, tomorrow he'll be telling you to grow your *payot* back. Everything's just a mad fit! It's not like he's really just got some Divine inspiration here, everything's just madness!'

And this is how the wife of Korach used to talk to him, day and night. 'Ok, so he brought a few lice... He arranged for a few frogs to show up... But, you'll see, that's the just the sort of thing he knows how to do...'

Korach got into all sorts of terrible errors of judgment like this, and why did it all happen? Rav Natan explains that every person has constrictions and judgements, every person is full of questions, every person is full of the *yetzer hara*, every person is full of spiritually impure blood.

So, he doesn't realize that all his *kushios* are coming from his impure blood. The same happened with Eliezer, Avraham's servant, who had a million difficult questions about Avraham Avinu.

'Why doesn't he want my daughter? Why does he want the daughter of Saddam Hussein? *Dafka*, he's sending me off to Baghdad?! 'In Baghdad, go and stand next to the water, and whoever gives you a drink of water, you'll know that's your bride, that's the bride of Yitzhak.' - Pure madness! He must be completely crazy to believe something like that...'

Eliezer had a million *kushios* on Avraham Avinu. 'What? I have here a daughter who is well-bred and who was born here and who grew up in Avraham's school. After that, she went to Avraham's seminary and she listened to all of Avraham's cassettes.' But Avraham still said to him: 'No, *dafka*, you need to go to Baghdad and from there you'll bring back home the daughter of Bethuel, the biggest *rasha* (evildoer) in the world...'

How's it possible to understand this? It's really very simple, it's clearly a case of racism. Everything is pure racism. He *dafka* wants his own family, *dafka*, someone from his own race. *Dafka*, he wants his brother's niece. What's going on here?

Rabbi Natan explains that at the very moment that a person has his *da'at* (understanding) diverted away from the *Tzaddik*, in whatever way, then even though Korach was such a big *Tzaddik* and was responsible for the *aron hakodesh* (holy ark of the covenant), and could fly in the air, and had a holy angel embedded inside of him.

His error was that his greatness gave him the space to make mistakes. Because, when he diverted his *da'at* away from Moshe Rabbenu, at that very moment he provoked against himself the *attribute of judgment*, which Hashem sent against him.

It's written (in Job, 28:22), "*And it will be sent against him, and he won't be spared.*" Hashem sent everything against him. You're starting to ponder, you're starting to think badly about Moshe Rabbenu, and without having any reason to think badly about him? Was Moshe Rabbenu exploiting him? Did he fire him from some job, so now he has an unjustifiable grudge...?

Rather, Korah accompanied the *aron hakodesh* and had the job of carrying the *aron*. It was solely because he was jealous of Moshe that he lost everything. Because, when a person is jealous, he doesn't apologise or ask for forgiveness. So, Hashem isn't able to forgive him.

A jealous person won't be resurrected at the resurrection of the dead. When a person is jealous, they really have no *tikkun*. They don't have anything, because this is a heresy, this is not believing in Hashem and not believing in Hashem's Divine supervision, that all actions are decided from Heaven, that everything is from Heaven.

It doesn't matter that a person took your slice of bread, that they took your *parnassa*, that they opened another store opposite yours or whatever else is making you resent them. Really, no one did anything to you! Here, you still have a part to play, you're still flying by yourself anyway, you're still flying with the *aron hakodesh!*

What Aharon didn't merit to do, what Moshe didn't merit to do, you merited to do it! What else do you want? You've been flying with the *aron* for the last 30 days! But in the instant that Korach diverted his *da'at* away from Moshe…

Every person is still full of judgments, except for a true *Tzaddik*. A person is full of judgments, except for Aharon HaKohen who was only *chessed* (kindness), but everyone else is full of judgments. Everyone has jealousy, but a 'normal' person immediately silences it. Judgments were at the root of Korach's rebellion. He became jealous of Aharon, and immediately now that Korach allowed the jealousy to ferment inside of him, then he went against Moshe.

CHUKAT

DYING TO PRAY

In Lesson 55 of *Likutey Moharan*, Rebbe Nachman says the following, *"And this is the aspect of dust and ashes that's said about the Para Adumah (the red cow). Because the aspect of prayer also requires the aspect of dust and ashes."*

The Rebbe's innovation here is that the *tikkun* of the *Para Adumah* in our generation can be done each day, and every second, through praying with *kavanah* (concentration/intent). Praying with real intent is like being burnt-- it's *mamash* the same suffering associated with being burnt.

When it comes time to pray, we need to disconnect from all other thoughts, and all other confusions. This disconnecting from all other thoughts is the biggest torture imaginable. A person is full of thoughts, 'What's going to be, here?' 'What's going to be, there?' 'I opened up a workshop, I opened up a factory, now how am I going to pay for all this?!'

If a person really wants to perform miracles and to perform all the salvations that he needs, this is only possible if he becomes 'dust and ashes'. We only merit to become dust and ashes through praying with *kavanah*. Praying with real *kavanah* requires so much *mesirut nefesh* (self-sacrifice), it's as if it turns a person into dust and ashes.

The *tikkun* of the *Para Adumah* is praying with *kavanah*. By praying with intent, a person is turned into a pile of crumbs, he's completely burnt up. The *Para Adumah* was also burnt, and the 'burning up' today happens through praying with *kavanah*.

The moment a person really sacrifices himself to say every word and every letter properly, the moment he really burns himself up to say every single letter in the prayers properly, this is called *mesirut nefesh*. A person can exert himself to give charity and help different *gemachs* (free loan organizations) to make a bunch of loans, and this is all truly wonderful. But real *mesirut nefesh* only comes from praying with intent, slowly, slowly. This is true *mesirut nefesh*.

The Rebbe says, we have to sacrifice our soul over every single letter, every single word, and not to rush through the words. We need to enter into each word, into each letter, we need to enter into the *Shemonah Esreh* prayer, into the letters.

Each letter wants to give you all the presents in the whole world. Each letter wants to give you all the *shefa* (bounty). Each letter grabs a person, twists him around, gives him a hug and tells him, 'don't leave me! Why are you going so fast? Why are you running away? I'll give you everything you want!' With each letter he says, a person is bringing all the *shefa* in the world to his doorstep.

The Rebbe says in Lesson 80 that a person should want to die to sanctify G-d's name, to sacrifice himself for *Kiddush Hashem*. When he comes to *davening*, he needs to say to himself, 'I'm going to die now, to sanctify G-d's name.' A person should agree to kill himself over every word of prayer, and to say every word slowly and with *kavanah*.

A person needs to not care what's going to be with the next word. Like Rabbi Moshe of Kovrin wrote, in *Ohel Yesharim*, if you kill yourself over the first word, or the second, or the third – then how are going to be able to continue to pray?! He replies, you'll have a miracle, you'll experience revival of the dead!

When a person shows up to the morning prayers, he should be thinking, 'Now, I'm going to kill myself for three hours to sanctify G-d's name.' For every letter, he has to be ready to kill himself *al kiddush Hashem*. Every single second of praying should be like the throes of dying, he's dying *al Kiddush Hashem*, he's burning himself up, like it's written, *"For your sake, we are slaughtered all day long."*

With every word of prayer, you have to get rid of your foolish ideas, your arrogance, your lust for money… Don't start thinking, 'how am I meant to pray like this? What will be?' Prayer is not some ceremony you perform, it's not like trying to catch a bus. Every word should completely transform your mind.

A human being is really just a collection of desires. He wants money, he wants honor. If a person doesn't sacrifice himself in his prayers, he'll stay like this until 120. He'll stay being a collection of lust for money, of *p'gam habris* (blemished sexual desire), bad thoughts and evil cunning. And this you call 'being alive'? If a person is going to live like this, so then why be alive?

Truly, we need to sacrifice ourselves for the spiritual work of prayer and to disconnect from our thoughts. A person spends his whole day thinking about money, about his wife, about his children, about what he's meant to be doing in another hour. Where he's going next… His brain is whirring with a million thoughts a minute. How can he disconnect from these millions of thoughts?

This requires self-sacrifice, to kill ourselves *al Kiddush Hashem*. When it comes time to pray, we have to kill ourselves. At that second, we have to recognize that G-d runs the world, that He's the King of the world, and that He's doing everything. Let Him arrange things in the world, and don't try to help Him. A person thinks all his thoughts in the belief that he's somehow helping Hashem to run the world. Instead, just sit and pray quietly, and let Him run the world.

A person needs to start his prayers slowly, slowly, letter by letter, word by word, with every word to die *al Kiddush Hashem*, because even the *sinners of Israel* are prepared to die to sanctify G-d's name. Even the bigger Jewish sinners would jump into the fire rather than give up their *da'at* (faith / religion), G-d forbid.

We need to know that praying with *kavanah* is the same as jumping into the fire. If a person agrees to kill himself over every letter, to sanctify G-d's name, then suddenly a huge light will open up for him, as the *Toldos Aharon* brings down in his book. For a whole year, he prayed with tremendous *mesirut nefesh* over every single letter. He fought to say every single letter with the right *kavanah*. One day, when he got up to the *ahavas olam* section of the prayers he said, 'that's it! It's really life or death! One more letter said with *kavanah* and I'm going to die, really!' And then, such a big spiritual light opened up for him, that he went with that light for the rest of his life.

BALAK

EVEN BILA'AM DID HITBODEDUT

Bilaam used to do *hitbodedut*. Even Bilaam would walk around the mountains, as it's written, *"From Aram Balak led me, from the mountains of Kedem"*. He'd go to the mountains of Kedem and cry out to the mountains, he'd go to the hills and cry out to Hashem with all his might. Yet despite all this, he remained Bilaam. Nothing helped him at all, he stayed 'Bilaam'.

A person thinks that just because he's doing *hitbodedut*, now he's going to find a million dollars. When he's doing *hitbodedut*, he wants to see the blessings immediately. He wants to see his *shidduch* already, to see the new apartment already, he wants to see the million dollars, he wants to have saving accounts for all his kids and his grandchildren. He says, 'I did an hour of *hitbodedut*, where's Hashem?! Why isn't Hashem answering me?!'

People don't know what hitbodedut really is. He stands before G-d, and he says, *'Ribono shel olam,* Master of the World – give it to me, already! Give me! Give me this! When are you going to give it to me?' He takes a sack with him to his *hitbodedut* and, after his *hitbodedut*, he says, 'I want to see how this sack is going to get filled up!'

It's true that our eyes look to Hashem [for help], and that Hashem is happy about this – but this isn't *hitbodedut*! What is *hitbodedut*? The Rebbe told us, in Lesson 52 of *Likutey Moharan* that a person needs to reach the level of self-nullification (*bitul*), and it's impossible to get to this self-nullification except by doing *hitbodedut*. We only need to *bitul* ourselves [like this]:

"I'm not Moshe Rabbenu, I'm not Eliyahu Hanavi, I'm not Rebbe

Nachman of Breslov, I have no idea what Breslov even is, I have no concept of what Breslev really is – the opposite! I love eating, I love to drink like a non-Jew, G-d should have mercy on me..."

And then every hour of *hitbodedut* will be something else entirely. We need to do *hitbodedut* in order to reach *bitul*. *Hitbodedut* is only to know that I'm nothing, that I'm dust and ashes, because all the time, a person thinks to themselves, 'I'm THE MOST wise, THE MOST clever, THE MOST successful, THE MOST learned, THE MOST popular person...'

Twenty-four hours a day, a person thinks to themselves, 'I'm THE MOST... THE MOST... THE MOST...' Each of us has our own proof about why we're THE MOST successful, or THE MOST wise, or THE MOST smart. If it was possible to open up someone's brain, and to peer at all their internal thoughts, you'd see that they had a million thoughts every second why they were THE MOST, THE MOST...

So, now a person needs to do an hour of *hitbodedut*, an hour to calm down from all these arrogant thoughts, and to nullify themselves, to do *hitbodedut*, to relax a bit and to start to think that I'm not 'THE MOST...' in the world. There are other wise people in the world. There are other successful individuals, there are other people with deep understanding – all this takes a whole hour!

Hitbodedut, talking to Hashem, is simply an hour where we stop running after all these arrogant thoughts and we have mercy on our poor soul! Poor thing, it can't return to its spiritual root, and it doesn't want all these thoughts. The *neshama* is Divine and it doesn't want to be listening to all this nonsense, it can't bear hearing all this stupidity.

Give your soul some rest, for an hour a day! Give your *neshama* a chance to speak, and it will tell you, 'Stop with all this stupidity, with all these thoughts. You can't see what's really going on, release me, already!

Give me some breathing space! I want to nullify myself to Hashem, I want humility.' The soul is Divine, and it only wants one thing. It wants to become *ayin*, nothing, to completely nullify itself to Hashem.

PINCHAS

THE WAR WITH MIDIAN

When Moshe sent the Israelites to wage war with Midian he picked out the greatest *Tzaddikim* to send, the ones who were the most holy. As it is written, *"Arm men from amongst yourselves for a legion"* (Bamidbar 31:3). On this verse, Rashi interprets men as referring to *Tzaddikim*. These men were at the giving of the Torah and had seen Hashem face to face.

They chose people who had never opened their eyes to look at a woman in their lives. When they went out to war, they would need to enter the houses of the Midianites, and they were terribly afraid. They were afraid that they would see a forbidden sight, since they had to take captive both men and women. So, they were worried that they wouldn't be able to properly guard their eyes. Each one took with him cartons of soot and when they entered the houses, they would pour buckets full of soot on them, so that they wouldn't be able to see them at all. As it is written in the *Midrash Rabbah* (Shir HaShirim 1:3), *"When Israel went to war with Midian, they would go in pairs. One would cover the women's faces with soot, and the other would remove her nose ring."*

The whole world knows that *Am Yisrael* is the holiest nation. They just need to guard their eyes, to go with their eyes cast down. A person needs to know that the Angel of Death is to be found in each and every street. The Angel of Death is made up of eyes, as it's written in the Gemara *Avoda Zara*, *"The Angel of Death is composed of eyes."* He is a mass of eyes. All of his 248 limbs and 365 sinews are made out of eyes.

According to the forbidden gazing a person has fallen into, so will his Angel of Death be for him. If a person fell down in a million forbidden sights, his Angel of Death will have a million eyes. Every forbidden sight that a man sees, if he doesn't cry over it immediately and make *teshuva* immediately, then he builds another floor in his Angel of Death.

Rav Eliyahu Lopian said that when a person goes out from his yeshiva or his home, the Angel of Death is waiting to make him sin, to burn up his mind and his heart. Each one of us, before he goes out from the *Beis Midrash*, before he leaves his home, should know that he is now going out to war. Just like in a war, when a person knows that there is live fire outside, then he doesn't go out, but rather waits until the shooting has stopped. If he has no choice and needs to bring food and water, then he goes out crawling on the floor. If bullets fly at his head, then he crawls even lower until he is practically flat on the floor.

One needs to know how to bend down and how to crawl and how to stoop so that the bullets won't hit him. Similarly, when one goes out into the street, he has to realize that they are firing magazines at him, they are firing non-stop at him and he has to find a way not to stumble in any forbidden sights. You don't just jump into the street without thinking! A person needs to go out with presence of mind. Which is why, each person, before he goes into the street, before he leaves his home should stand still for a while, stop and think to himself, 'Now, I am going out to war'.

Rav Natan says that all a person's free choice is in his guarding his eyes. A person says, 'I'm religious. I put on *tefillin*. I get up for *vasikin*. I get up for *chatzos*.' These are all wonderful things, but they are not the essence of his free choice. The real free choice is in controlling one's eyes. The moment that a person guards his eyes, he'll achieve all the levels in the world. He won't speak *lashon hara*, he won't be intolerant of others, he won't hate anyone. King David prayed, "*Avert my eyes from seeing futility*" (Tehillim 119:37). 'Master of the World, make me blind! Take out my eyes. I don't want to see anything in the world.'

The moment that a person guards his eyes, he returns to the level of 'before the Creation'. He merits knowing that, *"There is nothing else but Him."* He merits knowing that Hashem is one and His name is one. When he doesn't see anything in this world, then he nullifies creation. He negates this world. He has no fear. There is no creation. There is no evil. There are no Nazis. There are no terrorists. They do not exist. They are completely non-existent!

Rav Natan says that even if a person has already merited closing his eyes physically, he needs to know that there is more work involved! He needs to close the eyes of his mind! Not only does he need to close his physical eyes, but he also needs to close all the types of eyes that he has. He needs to close the eyes of jealousy, the eyes of hatred and the eyes of honor, because even though he physically shut his eyes, he can still be yearning for honor. He wants honor! Because now that he is already closing his eyes, he thinks that he is a *Tzaddik*. He wants to be given honor for doing this.

The eyes of wanting to receive honor are the worst of all. So, he needs to close all the types of eyes that he has, so that no element of looking at this world will remain in him. He needs to disconnect his senses from all the vanities of this world, so that he shouldn't have any interest in any subject in the world-- only yearning for *Hashem Yisborach*. He needs to sanctify all his senses for *Hashem Yisborach* and to believe in Hashem's Divine supervision.

When a person turns off his senses then, automatically, he'll not have any feeling for anything other than Torah and prayer and clinging to *Hashem Yisborach*. He'll have no desire for anything physical. He'll have no desire for anything other than *Hashem Yisborach* in His honor alone. And, then, he will merit understanding all the wonders of the world, all the secrets of the world, as it is written, *"Unveil my eyes that I may see wonders from Your Torah"* (Tehillim 119:18).

If a person merits closing all the different aspects of his eyes, then all the secrets of the Torah are revealed to him because all the lights and all of the secrets are found in the eyes. All the secrets of creation will be revealed to him-- how to create heaven and earth and how to change nature. All of the lights and all of the secrets will be revealed to him.

A person doesn't have to travel outside Israel to search for an income. There is an infinite amount of money in Israel, an absolute abundance. It is from Israel that the influx comes down for the whole world! A person just needs to hold up a vessel to receive it in. This vessel is called holiness-- guarding one's eyes. Because, the moment a person opens his eyes he loses his income. He loses the influx and falls into debt.

The Rebbe said, "*There is one sin whose punishment is to be permanently in debt*" (Sichos HaRan 112). The moment that his eyes are opened, he becomes a debtor. If a person were to start guarding his eyes from seeing forbidden sights then he would see such miracles, such wonders, such marvels. HaKadosh Baruch Hu would do great miracles for him.

For anything in holiness there are 10 preventative *klipos*. Any movement towards holiness has 10 *klipos* fighting against it. Every effort made to guard one's eyes has many obstacles. A person closes his eyes and they spring open! He closes them again and they spring open again. In truth, this will happen to him a million times a day, until one day he'll merit keeping his eyes closed. Even if he falls a billion times, he shouldn't get discouraged because on the billionth and first time he will succeed. A person has to constantly fight for such things, 24 hours a day. And, according to how hard a person fights, so will his reward be doubled and quadrupled. It is an unending war and the reward will be infinitely great.

MATOT

AVENGING THE BLOOD OF AM YISRAEL

When Moshe was 120 years of age, Hashem said to him, 'Moshe! If you want to continue to live, if you want to have a very long life, you can! You can live for many more, long years. But, if you want to do a *mitzvah* that is even greater than living for many more years, then you should know that there is a *mitzvah* that is even greater than staying alive.'

What could be a greater *mitzvah* than staying alive? What could be a greater *mitzvah* than the life of Moshe Rabbenu? What's more of a *mitzvah* than this, that Moshe should continue to be with us, and to lead us, and to bring more Torah down for us from Heaven?

Hashem said to him, *"Take vengeance on behalf of the children of Israel against the Midianites, and afterwards you'll be gathered to your people"* *(Parshat Matot, 3:1).*

If you want to keep living, you can! If you postpone taking vengeance against the Midianites, you can continue. You can postpone it for another 10 years, and then you'll stay alive for another 10 years! You can push it off for another 100 years, and then you'll live for another 100 years!

But I'm telling you, I'm hinting to you, Moshe, that there's a *mitzvah* that's even greater than staying alive. And that's to avenge the blood of *Am Yisrael*, and to avenge the disgrace of *Am Yisrael*. Take vengeance against the nations who are abusing and killing *Am Yisrael*! This is greater than even your life!

Hashem told Moshe, know, there is something that's even greater than your life. *"A G-d of vengeance is Hashem, a G-d of vengeance will appear."* Great is the daat that is given between two names (of Hashem). This vengeance was the true *daat* (spiritual wisdom) of HaKadosh Baruch Hu. This was the true *ratzon* (will) of Hashem, for Moshe. Hashem hinted to him that taking vengeance against the enemies of *Am Yisrael* was greater than anything, and to redeem *Am Yisrael*'s spilled blood.

Moshe said to Him, 'What?!? Taking vengeance against Midian is worth more than my life?!' So, Hashem told him, 'Yes! My true *nachat ruach* (satisfaction) is for you to avenge *Am Yisrael*! This will give me more satisfaction than if you stay alive.' Then Moshe understood everything.

He said to himself, is it worth me pushing off avenging *Am Yisrael* just so I'll stay alive a few more years? And, really, all the spiritual work that Moshe would then have done over the next 100 years, or even the next 200 years, none of it would have lasted for even one second, for as long as *Am Yisrael* hadn't been avenged, he still felt the pain of *Am Yisrael*.

The Gemara relates in Tractate Brachot (33): "*Great is the daat that is given between two names (of Hashem).*" How are *daat* and vengeance related? Rebbe Nachman explains in Lesson 20 that Hashem brings down *daat* and He sends the Torah out into the world, only by way of those souls who suffer the greatest bitterness. Only by way of those souls who are killed *al Kiddush Hashem*, to sanctify G-d's name. Only in their merit, is the Torah transmitted.

Hashem sends his knowledge and his Torah into the world not by way of the rich people, and not by way of the wise ones, but only by way of those souls who endure the greatest possible grief. And there is no grief greater than being killed *al Kiddush Hashem*.

The Zohar says that when a soul is killed to sanctify G-d's name, it should enter straight into Gan Eden! But it doesn't enter Gan Eden. Instead, it sits on the gates of Gan Eden, it sits at the entrance to Gan Eden, and it says, 'I'm not going into Gan Eden until Hashem avenges my blood. I'm not going in, until Hashem destroys these murderers, and removes them from the world!'

And, for as long as these souls aren't avenged, they don't enter Gan Eden, and because of this (that they don't enter), it's impossible to send *shefa* (bounty) into the world by way of them, and it's impossible to send *daat* into the world.

So, this is how vengeance and *daat* are connected, that for as long as the souls who were killed *al Kiddush Hashem* haven't been avenged, they aren't prepared to enter Gan Eden. And then, it's impossible to send *daat* into the world by way of them. And this is the secret that was revealed to Moshe Rabbenu in the *Parsha* of 'redeeming the blood'.

So, Moshe understood that the vengeance of *Am Yisrael* had to occur, so that these souls would enter Gan Eden, and then it would be possible to send *daat* and bounty down to the world.

Taking vengeance is the first priority, even if it cuts your life short! It's written that every morning, the sun cries and shouts, and sings: "A G-d of vengeance is Hashem, a G-d of vengeance will appear." And that every morning, it isn't prepared to shine again, unless *Am Yisrael* has been avenged. It doesn't want to shine…!

The sun wants to stay in the firmament, it doesn't want to come down and illuminate the earth at all. The sun and the moon don't want to descend to the earth until arrows and lightning bolts are shot at them. Every day, they say 'we aren't coming out until *Am Yisrael* is avenged, until all their blood that was spilt is avenged!'

Why do the nations need to laud, and sing praises to Hashem? Because the whole world knows that the Torah of Israel is true! And that the G-d of Israel is the true G-d! And, when they see that *Am Yisrael* is suffering, then everyone's *emunah* falls. All the nations experience a drop in their *emunah* too! They say, 'What?! The Jews are a quiet people, they don't harm anyone. They don't do bad to anyone, why are these things happening to them?' The whole world is watching and waiting, for Hashem to avenge the blood of the Jewish people.

Oy, there's still no vengeance?! But they have the true G-d behind them?! So, when is He going to avenge them?!

But, when they hear that He takes vengeance, and they see that He avenges the blood of His servants that has been spilt, then they praise Hashem. All the nations return to their *emunah*, their faith. Everyone starts to believe that Hashem, He is the one true G-d. So, G-d needs to take vengeance for *Am Yisrael* also for the sake of the nations, so that the nations will also praise Hashem.

MASEI

GO TRAVEL!

In Sichot HaRan (85), a person asked Rabbenu about the matter of travelling to a certain place, and whether or not he should do so. Rabbenu answered him that if a person sees that he has a journey in front of him, he should immediately travel. He shouldn't be stubborn and avoid the journey just to stay at home.

Staying at home is not considered anything. Whenever a person is told to travel, he should immediately travel. Whenever the opportunity presents itself to him to travel, a person should immediately go, since journeys rectify a person more than staying at home. Because every place a person travels to, he fixes there some issue – guarding his eyes, guarding the covenant, guarding his thoughts, praying with concentration, praying with a *minyan*, praying grace after meals with concentration... He just needs to make sure to guard himself from sinning. He shouldn't look at other women or speak with other women. He can then merit to rectify all of his previous reincarnations.

After Am Yisrael sinned with *"and these are your gods, Israel..."*, the *tikkun* (rectification) for this came through *"and these are the journeys of the children of Israel..."* The *tikkun* is to travel, travel and travel, as much as possible. Because the holy sparks were scattered across the entire world. *"These are the journeys of the children of Israel..."* is the *tikkun*. Rabbenu brought this from the *Asarah Ma'amarot*.

This is the way to bring back a person's *emunah*. Because, staying at home, he has no *emunah*. At home, he eats, drinks cola. What sort of *emunah* does a person need at home? If a child gets sick, he takes him to hospital, he says some *Tehillim* and he sees miracles. But, with G-d's help, no one should be sick, and no one should need to see miracles.

When does a person see miracles? On the road, he meets people, his car breaks down and suddenly someone appears to give him a ride. He has no car, and suddenly offers him a ride. It's all miracles within miracles.

All of this comes from a blemish in a person's *emunah*. Today, there's no *emunah*. People simply have no *emunah*. Everyone lives off the money that he makes, from his salary, and he has no *emunah*. Only when he travels, it's possible to return his *emunah*, and by so doing to nullify the idol worship.

This is why Rabbenu tells us that a person shouldn't be stubborn (when a journey presents itself). On the contrary, the more he can travel, the more he's able to fix. Every place a person travels, he's certainly going to be doing something holy there. People will see him praying, people will see him eating a slice of cake or taking a drink and making a blessing with concentration. As Rabbi Yisrael Baer said, he came close to Hashem from seeing Rabbi Yisrael Karduner making a blessing with concentration, washing hands with concentration, saying '*hamotzi lechem min ha'aretz*[9]' with concentration, grace after meals… After seeing this, he decided, 'this is the Rabbi for me'.

There's no need to rush. Instead of saying the prayer for washing the hands in two seconds, so say it in ten seconds. '*Hamotzi lechem min ha'aretz*' is ten words, so say it in ten seconds. Why blast through it in three seconds? If you grab yourself another three seconds, maybe you'll live another 70 years in the merit of doing so?

The Rebbe brings that which was said about Ya'akov who should really have gone down to Egypt in iron chains but merited to go instead on chariots. If it's decreed that a person needs to go to a certain place, then they'll take him there against his will. He'll get sick and need to go to some specific hospital. Or, there'll be a war, G-d forbid, and he'll

---

[9] The blessing before eating bread.

be taken as a prisoner to that place. If he doesn't choose to go in his car, comfortable and relaxed, then eventually he'll end up being taken there in iron chains. And, perhaps only in his next reincarnation. It's possible that if he doesn't go to a specific place in this lifetime, he'll need to come back in another reincarnation in order to go to that place and he'll have no choice. So, providing a person has the strength to do so, he should travel!

Devarim

THE HOLINESS OF THE KOTEL

The *Beis HaMikdash* was destroyed twice. On two occasions, the *Sitra Achra* was able to overpower and destroy the *Beis HaMikdash*. But Hashem never abandoned the *even ha'shtiah* (the Foundation Stone). Hashem never abandoned the *Kotel*. The presence of the *Shechina* has never departed from the Western Wall.

A person should feel a yearning for the *even ha'shtiah*, a yearning to go to the *Kotel*, as it is written, "*My soul yearns, indeed it pines, for the courtyards of Hashem*" (Tehillim 84:3). If a person loves someone, then he'll make every effort to be around him. The same thing holds true for a person who loves the *Kotel* and feels that this is his root source; he'll try to go to the *Kotel* as often as possible.

Why don't people feel the holiness of the *even ha'shtiah*? Why don't people feel the holiness of the *Kotel*? There are people who, year after year, don't go to the *Kotel*. There are a half a million Jews living in Jerusalem, you hardly see them at the *Kotel*. The Chatam Sofer says that by not visiting the Western Wall, the *even ha'shtiah*, we are in fact insulting the *Kotel*! This is the place of the Shechina. This is an unforgivable offense.

When Hashem sees that we are neglecting Jerusalem and the *Kotel* and are not making the effort to get there, this awakens His anger and wrath. As it is written, "*The stone that the builders scorned has become the cornerstone*" (Tehillim 118:23). The stone that was scorned is the *even ha'shtiah*. The greater the thing, the more exalted it is, the more despised it is, the more hidden it is. The *Satan* knows what is good for a person, he knows exactly what is the very best for him. So, he works to distance him as much as he can from this thing. Everyone despised the *even ha'shtiah*.

All the *Tzaddikim* are called 'builders' (from the verse, "*The stone that the builders scorned*"), except for King David, who is the only one who merited knowing the secret of this Stone. He merited knowing that without this Stone, without its holiness, it is impossible to achieve any real spiritual advancement, no spiritual endeavor will be completely accepted. All of David's efforts were only concerning this Stone. All of his searches, all of his yearnings: "*My soul yearns, indeed it pines, for the courtyards of Hashem.*" All this was for the Foundation Stone, for the place of the *Beis HaMikdash*.

Before Hashem created the physical world (the world of *Asiyah*), He created the Foundation Stone and the Temple Mount and the *Kotel*. Reb Nasan explains that the Foundation Stone is the root of the creation. The world was created from this Stone (Yoma 54b) and it is the source of our free choice. Just from going to the *Kotel* alone, a person can overcome his evil inclinations and choose the good path. The *Kotel* is the crown of creation, the 10th level of holiness, the level of *Keter*, which is why free will is completely annulled there and the only choice is choosing good.

When a person goes to the *Kotel*, he's not standing in this world. He isn't in this world at all. The *Kotel* is the Holy of Holies-- it's another world altogether. Even if you imagine that you're still in this world, that you're here in the world, know that no matter how you got to the Temple Mount, to the *Kotel*, you are now in the world of *Atzilus*! You rose up straight to the world of *Atzilus*. It just seems to you that you are still in this world because you are in such a state of uncertainty and illusion, but really, you're in the world of *Atzilus*.

Every time you touch the *Kotel* and give it a kiss then you immediately enter the world of *Atzilus*. It's a change in nature! Even a person's body changes, everything changes. A person gets a new nature and new body. Every time a person comes to the *Kotel*, he immediately merits having all the lights of the world of *Atzilus* shining down on him.

The *Kotel* is really the Holy of Holies. It is the Foundation Stone. A person goes to the *Kotel* and he literally walks in Gan Eden, especially at night at chatzos and in the early morning, because the "river that flows out of Eden" (Bereishis 2:10) flows under the Temple Mount, under the *Kotel*, and so a person comes to the *Kotel* and literally tastes Gan Eden. He sees Gan Eden and can detect the fragrance of Gan Eden. He feels that he is now in Gan Eden, just like Adam and Chava (Eve).

Rav Natan says (*Likutei Halachos*, Hodaah 6:50), "*when they came out from Egypt with miracles and wonders and the sea split for them with a wondrous and awesome miracle, they sang, 'You will bring them and plant them at the mountain of Your inheritance' (Song of the Sea, Shemos 15:17). This is the Beis HaMikdash which is the main reason for all the miracles of the Exodus from Egypt and the Splitting of the Red Sea. The whole purpose was to bring them there, as it's written, 'And he took us out of there in order to bring us...' (Devarim 6:23).*"

We need to know that the *Kotel* is the source of all the miracles in the world. All the miracles since ancient days were drawn from the Western Wall. Avraham did miracles. Moshe did miracles. Even the miracles of the Exodus from Egypt were drawn from the *Kotel*. All of the miracles that happened in Egypt, the ten plagues, the Splitting of the Sea-- all the miracles were drawn from the Holy of Holies. Everything came from the *Kotel*. This is Rav Natan's *chiddush*. "*You will bring them and plant them at the mountain of Your inheritance.*" Moshe Rabbenu connected himself to the Holy of Holies, attached himself to the *Kotel* and the Foundation Stone, and this is how he drew down the miracles and wonders.

So how can a person not go to the *Kotel*? All the miracles come from there! The miracle of the Splitting of the Sea, the miracles of the Ten Plagues, the miracle of the clouds of Glory, the miracle of the Pillar of Fire, the miracle of flying through the air-- the *Kotel* is the source of all the miracles, the source of all the wonders, the source of all the salvations, all the healing and deliverance, all the income. Everything comes from the *Kotel*. A person comes to the *Kotel* and he can bring miracles to the world.

VA'ETCHANAN

THE SECRET OF THE SONG

All of the anger that was directed by Hashem towards Moshe was caused by *Am Yisrael*, as it's written, *"And Moshe suffered harm because of them"* (Tehillim 106:32). *Am Yisrael* were the ones responsible for the anger. *Am Yisrael* caused the terrible mistake which resulted in Hashem bringing Moshe down from his level and causing him to strike the rock and thereby not enter Eretz Yisrael.

A person needs to know that even when he is faced with the hardest situation, going without water and not having anything to drink and also having all kinds of questions on Moshe Rabbenu, he still needs to cast away all his questions and continue with simple faith and know that Moshe, who did miracles and wonders until now, will certainly continue to do miracles and wonders.

Am Yisrael cried so much for water and were so alarmed that there wasn't any to be had, they caused Moshe Rabbenu to fall from his level. Once Moshe Rabbenu fell, Hashem told him that now he had to hit the rock, just speaking to it would no longer work. And that is when *Am Yisrael* lost everything. They lost the first and second Temples too at this time, because if Moshe had entered the land of Israel, the *Beis HaMikdash* would never have been destroyed.

So, that's when Moshe initiated a new kind of service for *Am Yisrael*-- the service of prayer alone, accompanied by song and melody! It was a service of pure supplication! As it's written, *"And I implored Hashem at that time"* (Devarim 3:23). The Baal HaTurim explains that the word *"va'etchanan"* has the same numerical value as *"shira"* (song). Moshe sang before Hashem so that He would hear his prayers because a person needs to begin with songs and *zemiros ha'boker* (the songs before the morning prayer service) so that his prayers will be accepted.

This is explained in *Likutei Moharan 42*, where it says that through music the judgments are sweetened. *"Whoever sings the letters of the prayer, and the sounds of the singing are pure and clear, then he clothes the Shechina in radiant garments"*. The *Shechina* is the letters of the words of the prayers. If you said the words of prayer with song, then the *Shechina* speaks from your throat and Hashem takes note of the prayer.

This is what the Baal HaTurim is saying, and this is the foundation of all foundations, that *'va'etchanan'* is the same numerical value as 'song'. Even Moshe Rabbenu sang before his prayer, before *'va'etchanan'* (And I implored...). So that Hashem would take note of his prayer and accept it.

The *Sfas Emes* says in *Parshat Va'etchanan* that, spiritually, there are 'accusers' that arise to oppose every prayer, but when a person accompanies his prayer with song and melody and really experiences the prayer, then the prayer is accepted without any opposition. One should have the intention that through his song and his prayer he will draw down all kinds of salvations.

During *Shemoneh Esreh*, he should be careful to say the words very slowly. *"Because You are the Almighty King Who is a faithful and merciful Healer..."* (from the *Shemoneh Esreh* prayer). Hashem is a faithful Healer. Hashem is ready to heal every illness. Why do we need to go to doctors? If a person would say the *Refaeinu* prayer with *kavanah*, then he wouldn't need to go to any doctor! A person only needs to say the words very slowly and with *kavanah*, *"...because You are the Almighty King Who is a faithful and merciful Healer."*

The Sfas Emes says that the true, unique point that a person has in his life, the only moment that he is truly acting *l'shem shemayim* in his life, is when sings and expresses himself though melody to Hashem.

This occurs only when he is praising Hashem, because even when a person learns, for the most part, he is learning only for himself. Does a person really learn for Hashem's sake? He wants to be a Rosh Yeshiva, he wants to be a Dayan (Rabbinical judge), he wants to be the head Rabbi, he wants that people will say he is a great learner...

There are people who learn in sscret for 120 years and still are really only learning for themselves! They want to feel that they are learned people, intelligent people, people with wisdom and knowledge. Rabbenu said that even if a person says, *'This is to bring the Shechina out of exile'* before everything he does (which is certainly a wonderful thing to say and maybe one time we also will merit doing this). But, really, does he have any real connection with the *Shechina*? He's an earthly being! He's in the pit with snakes and scorpions which are his desires and bad character traits. What connection is there between him and the *Shechina*?

So, the Sfas Emes says the only place that's without any personal benefit, where a person doesn't get any personal honor and doesn't think to get money for it, is only song and melody. Because, only though song and melody a person comes to attach himself to *Hashem Yisborach*. Through music and song, a person can bring down all the secrets. This is why song (*shira*) has the same root as the word 'line/path' (*shura*), as in: *"My foot stands on a straight path"* (Tehillim 26:12). The minute a person sings, everything starts to straighten out.

If a person envelops his prayer in song and melody, then certainly Hashem will accept this prayer. This is the secret of why Leah gave birth to the line of Moshiach ben David whereas from Rachel descended only the line of Moshiach ben Yosef. Since Rachel only remained silent in the face of embarrassment, she was given the line of Moshiach ben Yosef. But Leah who was always giving thanks, singing and praising Hashem all the time, merited the line of Moshiach ben David, who is completely song and thanks, as it's written, *"By day Hashem will command His kindness, and at night His resting place will be with me"* (Tehillim 42:9).

King David said, I sing about everything, I make melodies about everything. *"Thank Hashem for He is good; His kindness endures forever"* (Tehillim 118:1). King David said, *"…His kindness endures forever."* Hashem's kindness will continue forever! Kindness is always being drawn down! There will always be miracles! Rebbe Levi Yitzhak from Berditchov asked, what does it mean: *"His kindness endures forever?"* It means that all the wonders and miracles and kindness that David merited having, were drawn down forever to each person throughout all the generations. We only need to know how to continue the miracles. We need to know how to draw down the kindness, because the miracles are ready and waiting for each person in every generation, every day, and every hour. And one draws down these miracles through melody and song.

Why aren't people uplifted by prayer? Why aren't they able to change their fate though prayer? Why don't people become healed through prayer? It's because they aren't enveloping their prayer in melody and song. The preferred prayer, the one that rises up without any opposition, is the one that is purely melody and song.

How can you stand and pray when you just saw a forbidden sight in the street? You defiled your eyes and now you want to stand up and pray *Shemoneh Esreh*? What kind of *Shemoneh Esreh* will this be? Because of a person's sins, he faces opposition to his prayer from being accepted. But, if you would sing and dance a little before you prayed, if you would praise Hashem and make *teshuva*, then Hashem would be ready to forgive you and receive your prayer.

This is the wondrous secret of prayer which is chosen and accepted without any opposition, and it comes specifically through melody and song. A person wants his prayer to be accepted and wants it to bring him all kinds of salvation and healing to his whole family and to all of *Am Yisrael* and to whoever needs it. But this comes only though enveloping the prayer in melody and song. This is how we'll merit the final redemption, speedily and in our days, Amen.

EIKEV

DIAMONDS IN HASHEM'S CROWN

The verse says, *"And you shall cleave to Him"* (Devarim 11:22). But, Rashi says, 'surely is He not an all consuming fire; how is it possible to cleave to Him?' But rather, Rashi explains, what it really means is to cleave to the scholars and sages, and I will consider it as if you were cleaving to Him.

Rabbenu says that first of all, a person needs to believe in all the *Tzaddikim* and all the *Admorim* and all the *Roshei Yeshivas*. He needs to cleave to all of them! He should believe in all of them, hold by all of them, and love all of them. Each and every Jew has a point of *yiras shamayim* (fear of Heaven) that his friend doesn't have. One prays better. Another is holier. One does more acts of kindness. Another is more learned and understands things more deeply. When you believe in all of them, cleave to all of them and admire all of them, that is when you are doing the positive *mitzvah* of "cleaving to Him."

One must appreciate the unlimited virtues of all those who are great in Torah learning and of all the Gedolim in all the generations. In particular, in this generation one must be attached at all times to the *Tzaddikim* of the generation. They all are worthy, and they all keep guard over the modesty and holiness of *Am Yisrael*. The Rebbe wants us to love them with a deep, profound love-- all the Admorim, all the Rabbis that have established *kehillas*, that bring people back in *teshuva*, and that guard the purity of our educational system. Hashem loves them all! The *Tzaddikim* of today are extremely precious! They keep guard over the precepts of the religion, the boundaries of Torah, and we need to love them and connect ourselves with them because they are Hashem's emissaries.

If you spoke against a group of Jews or about some individual Jew, then that's it! You lost everything! You lost all holiness, everything. If you believe that Hashem exists, then how can you speak against someone whom Hashem loves? Hashem loves all the *Tzaddikim*. Hashem loves all of *Am Yisrael*! Do you think that *Am Yisrael* is composed of just the 10 people you like? Hashem loves everyone! You need to learn out from the fact that, just as Hashem loves everyone, similarly, you also are supposed to love everyone.

The Rebbe explains in Lesson 17 of *Likutey Moharan* that it's possible to crown Hashem every day. *"Every single Jew is a diamond in the crown of Hashem."* But when we find fault in a Jew and speak out against him, even in the slightest way, we diminish the crown of Hashem. We decrease the diamonds that are in Hashem's crown. We belittle Hashem's crown.

But when we look for the goodness in every Jew and reveal his good points, we build Hashem's crown anew, because each and every Jew is a diamond in the crown of Hashem. With every virtue or good point that that you find in a Jew, you are building the crown of Hashem, because every Jew is a diamond in the crown of Hashem. With each diamond and each good point, with each and every virtue that you find in any Jew, you are setting another precious gem in the crown of Hashem.

The No'am Elimelech says (*Parshat Devarim*) that there is a spiritual world called '*All of Israel*'. Each Jew needs to be included in this place, because there is no person who doesn't sin or fail to guard his eyes or his hands, etc. But if he is included in '*All of Israel*' with every Jew and especially with all of the *Tzaddikim* of *Am Yisrael*, then all of his sins are forgiven.

You need make yourself part of *Am Yisrael* and to love everyone. You need to love each Jew and shouldn't have any complaints about any Jew. It is forbidden to think badly of any Jew or harbor any ill will against him, even if he oppresses you or embarrasses you. Then, if you connect yourself with each and every Jew, you rise to the place called *'All of Israel'* and at that moment all your sins are forgiven!

RE'EH

THE REASON WE CAME INTO THE WORLD

Am Yisrael is a holy nation! *Am Yisrael* is looking to serve G-d only through purity and holiness! They're not looking to reach 'prophecy' or 'heights', which is what most of the world is after. The mistake of Bilaam and the nations of the world is that for them the main thing is to be a big person! An important person! Someone famous! But *Am Yisrael* is looking for one thing only-- how to serve Hashem through holiness and purity, which is the opposite of all the methods and all the teachings of the world, who don't know what is holiness. They have no idea what the concept of holiness is!

The Holy Nation of Israel is not satisfied with words. With us, we first start working on holiness, guarding the eyes, the holiness of the covenant-- we fight for these things! We fight to be saved from the negative commandment of *"do not follow after your heart and after your eyes"*, even when it's very hard and a person doesn't see almost any way in which he can be saved from it. But he knows that he has to fight it, he has no choice-- he was brought into the world for this.

It is written in *Even Shlomo* from the *Vilna Gaon* that man comes into the world just to conquer this inclination. A person comes into this world only for this, not for anything else. Everything else just comes to help a person in holiness. People think that holiness is a side issue, that there are 613 *mitzvos* and there's also the negative commandment of *"do not follow after your eyes..."*

The Rambam says, *"Twenty-four things hold back repentance... and one is, when a person doesn't realize how looking [at forbidden sights] is a great sin, for it motivates a person to actually take part in illicit relations as implied by, "Do not follow after your heart and after your eyes"* [Numbers 15:39] (Rambam, *Laws of Teshuva*, Chapter 4).

The Rambam says it's a mistake for anyone to think that it's possible to skip the "*do not*" of "*do not follow...*"-- to put it in parentheses, to put it on the side, and say, 'There are 613 *mitzvos*; so what if I'm not careful about only one *mitzvah*! Not everyone is meticulous about every single *mitzvah*! I'm meticulous about being a Torah genius, about being famous, about being a master of *ruach hakodesh*, but being meticulous about the "*do not*" of "*do not follow...*"-- there's no time for it. It's not possible; I'm a busy person, I drive a car, I need to get around; how can I guard my eyes?'

Really, the world is making a mistake! Of course, a person can guard his eyes! Even a person who drives can guard his eyes. He can ask *Hashem* that He guard his eyes! Because through prayer a person can reach everything. *Avraham Avinu* went through the whole world in holiness and didn't see a thing! Likewise, so did the children of *Ya'akov Avinu*; they went all the way from Israel to Egypt and didn't open their eyes the whole way! The *Midrash* says that they didn't see anything on the way. A person can travel the whole world guarding his eyes. It's certainly possible to guard one's eyes on the way. The Rambam says that someone who looks at women forbidden to him, rationalizing it as inconsequential, that person damages his eyes. He claims, 'What did I do?! What sin did I commit?! It doesn't affect me badly...' He should know that it's a lie!

There's a story about the *Beis Yisrael* who once met with some professors. They asked him, "Why are the *charedim* so afraid of every sight, of every glance, and for us professors these things don't have any effect on us and don't bother us at all?" So, he told them the following allegory of the Bedouins and Europeans. "The Bedouin walks every day on stones, thorns, and thistles. From the day he was born he's been walking on the sharpest stones, and it doesn't bother him at all. He doesn't feel any pain because he got used to it. On the other hand, as soon as a small pebble enters the shoe of a European, as soon as a little sand comes in, now he can't walk! His foot hurts him! He suffers a lot from it. The comparison is that you professors are like the Bedouins; you have sullied yourselves so much, in endless impurity, so one small stone, one small sin, sneaking a peek, an illicit glance, it doesn't affect you anymore! But a person who is refined and upright of heart, every little small thing, every small sin, every forbidden glance, every forbidden sight bothers him! It hurts him! It stabs him like a stabbing sword!"

The entire man comes from the eyes! The moment someone guards his eyes, he will reach all the levels in the world. He won't speak *lashon hara*, he won't criticize, he won't hate, he'll keep *Shabbos* and put on *tefillin*. And, it's not just the physical eyes that need to be guarded; also the mind's eyes need to be protected. A person can guard his physical eyes, but he still has endless eyes. He has eyes of jealousy, eyes of hate, eyes of pride... He has to watch every kind of eye that he has! He has to detach from every sense in this world! He shouldn't have eyes at all for this world, for any matter in this world! All the senses, all the desires, they should only be for G-d Almighty-- for His honor. When he guards his eyes then he'll merit to fulfil the verse, "*Uncover my eyes and I will see the hidden things in Your Torah*" (*Tehillim* 119:18). The secrets of the Torah are revealed to him, the secrets of creation and all the wonders of the yoke of Heaven.

SHOFTIM

THE GATES OF WISDOM

Rabbenu, Rebbe Nachman, says in Lesson 286 of *Likutey Moharan*, *"The main delight of the Garden of Eden is the perception of Divine wisdom – both the upper wisdom and the lower wisdom, which correspond to the Garden of Eden. However, the only way to merit this is by virtue of the gates – for there are gates, the gates of the Garden of Eden, by virtue of which one merits entering the Garden of Eden, that is, the perception of the upper wisdom and the lower wisdom – and these gates are buried and hidden in the earth, as in: 'Her gates sunk into the earth'* (Lamentations 2:9).

"Furthermore, extracting, lifting and setting up these gates that have sunken into the earth require the 'master of the earth' – someone who can rule over the earth. But know, by studying Torah rulings, one merits becoming a king and ruler of the earth. Then one is able to lift up and set up the gates that have sunken into the earth."

When we get to the *Parsha* of *Shoftim*, judges and police officers, we can merit to enter Gan Eden. The main delight of *Gan Eden* is the perception of Divine wisdom, it's to see Hashem face-to-face, and to know that *ein od milvado* – there is only G-d.

And it's impossible to get to any perception of the Divine any other way, except by studying the *poskim*, i.e. Torah rulings, and studying the *halachos*. The Rebbe explains in Lesson 286 that we need to be persistent about studying the *poskim*. If we want these sunken gates to be revealed to us, if we want the merit of attaining a perception of Divine wisdom, and of entering into Gan Eden, then we need to consistently learn Torah rulings.

"Her gates are sunk into the earth" – we need to raise up the gates of

halacha. We need to be experts on the in-depth laws. By way of studying the *poskim*, we will merit to become 'rulers of the earth', we'll merit to become 'judges and police officers'. This is why it's written: *"Judges and police officers you will appoint in all your **gates**."*

You need to build the gates! You need to know all the gates of *halacha*, you need to build these gates for yourselves, because there are gates that lead to *Gan Eden*, where you can enter into *Gan Eden*, and enter into Divine wisdom.

After the destruction of the Temple, these gates were hidden and interred in the ground. So, how do we raise them up? Raising these gates only happens by way of learning *halacha* in-depth, and learning the *poskim*-- learning the *Rambam*, the *Tur*, the *Beis Yosef*, and all the other commentators.

The Rebbe says in Lesson 62, that when a person has no *kavanah* (proper intention) in his prayers, this is a sign that he has no *emunah*. It's heresy, every word that a man rushes through without *kavanah*, it's heresy.

When a person really knows in his heart that the whole world is full of *Hashem*'s glory, when he really feels Hashem and really feels that Hashem is standing over him and watching him during his prayers, this is called having *emunah*. Then, he'll pray in a relaxed way and he'll say each letter slowly.

If a person says even just one word in his *Shemoneh Esreh* prayer with *kavanah*, if he says it slowly, in a relaxed way, then he's *mamash* called a *Tzaddik* and he deserves all the presents in the world.

But Rabbenu says, the fact that you had the proper *kavanah* for a single word is great, it's wonderful that you had the right *kavanah*! But you still shouldn't think that you are now a Jew with complete *emunah*. To have *kavanah* is amazing, it's wonderful, but it still isn't called real *emunah. Emunah* is when you have the right *kavanah* during every single word of prayer. *Emunah* is when you can talk to Hashem in no less a way than you speak to your good friend.

A person can hate the *apikorsim* (heretics), he can want to throw stones at them and be prepared to fight against them with sword and with spear, through fire and through water – but Rabbenu is showing us in Lesson 62 that all the work to be done is really within ourselves. With the heretic that hides in our own heart.

Because, if a person doesn't pray with *kavanah*, this is called being a heretic! We have enough of our own heresy to deal with, we don't need to try to rectify other people's heresy, to try to fix the secular people. If we start by rectifying our own heresy, then there won't be any more secular people in the whole world, and everyone will make *teshuva*.

KI TEITZEI

WHERE'S THE MERCY?

The world needs great mercy! Spiritually and physically, everyone needs mercy (see *Likutey Moharan* 105). Everyone needs salvation, miracles, *shidduchim* and healing for their families and children. Everyone needs mercy.

Everyone is asking for mercy, but they don't know where the mercy is. They ask, 'Why don't I have any money? Why aren't we healthy? Why is this one sick and that one sick? Where is the mercy?' But people don't even know how to ask for this great mercy. In truth, Rebbe Nachman says, the mercy is within our reach, it is not far away. The mercy is nearby. It's there for all to see, as it's written (Devarim 30:11), "*It is not far away from you, it is not in the heavens...*"

Everyone asks for mercy, but they don't know where the mercy is. The Rebbe reveals that mercy is something everyone can see; it's right in front of your eyes! Hashem wants to have mercy on you. Hashem wants to help you, to have mercy on you. Hashem loves you. Hashem wants to give you all the mercy in the world-- to give you a good income, miracles, children, healing, Torah. He wants to give you everything!

Why did Hashem create you? He didn't create you to suffer. He wants to give you everything! Just be a 'good boy', listen to your Father. Hashem isn't so far away from you.

There are two types of mercy. One is simple mercy (*rachamim p'shutim* of *Zeir Anpin*), and the other is the great hidden mercy (*rachamim gedolim* of *Atika Stima'ah*). As it's written, "*With great mercy I will gather you*" (from the Haftora, Yeshaya 54).

In truth, we desperately need Hashem to have mercy on us. However,

227

in this generation, because of our many sins, there is no one who is able to pray in such a way as to draw down the mercy. In fact, Hashem Himself has to pray about this.

And what is it that is going to cause Him to pray? The Torah. The Rebbe says that we need to awaken the mercy in the world, the great mercy of *Atika Stima'ah*, as it is written, *"With great mercy I will gather you."* And there isn't anyone who prays so well that he can draw down this great mercy, because no one knows how great Hashem is, or how infinite He is, or how good Hashem is, due to our distress and suffering. Hashem Himself needs to pray about this.

The best thing for us is that Hashem Himself should pray and draw down the great mercy, because how well are we really able to pray? And even if we go to the *Kotel* and pray there, even if we say the whole book of Tehillim, it's certainly wonderful, but it's not yet true, complete prayer. We need Hashem Himself to pray! But how can we cause Hashem to pray for us? It is only by studying Torah.

The Rebbe is saying here a wondrous idea. If we will only learn Torah, then Hashem Himself will pray for us, and take upon Himself to worry about us, and He Himself will give us everything-- income, healing, children, miracles, and salvation. If we want to awaken Hashem to pray for us and to draw upon us great mercy, then we must learn Torah, for who is able to sweeten the harsh judgments other than Hashem Himself!

Hashem wants to give us everything. Hashem only asks that we help him to pray. Hashem wants us to give Him the strength to pray, so to speak, as in *"I will gladden them in My house of prayer"* (Yeshaya 56:7). Hashem says, *'I also pray! Help Me to pray!'* The moment that a person takes upon himself to learn Torah, then he will already receive mercy. Hashem Himself will pray for him. A person thinks that he can run the world without learning Torah, that's impossible! People just don't have any idea; they don't really believe that by learning Torah they will draw down mercy.

The Rebbe says that the world needs great mercy, but one cannot awaken the mercy other than by studying Torah and learning in depth. Even if a person cries out and prays, if he doesn't learn Torah then he can't awaken Hashem's mercy, because Hashem asks, 'What are you shouting about? Why are you praying? Do you want to live? What are you living for? To eat even more cholent, even more kugel, even more pizza? Is this the reason you are alive?'

You need to live to study Hashem's Torah, so that you can activate your mind. A person builds himself by learning Torah. Without Torah, there is no 'person', you don't have a *Tzelem Elokim* (image of G-d). You can only build yourself up through the letters of the Torah, through another word and another Rashi, and another Gemara, another *Ritva*. This is how you build yourself bit by bit. This is how you build your mind. You are actually creating yourself through the letters of the Torah. Until you have all of *Shas* in your head, you are not called a human being at all.

The Rebbe says in Lesson 105 that *teshuva* is learning Gemara. If you want to do *teshuva*, then start learning Gemara. A person is full of resentment and bad thoughts, but if he learns Gemara he won't have any resentment or bad thoughts. Hold a Gemara in your hand and everything will work out. Your thoughts will fix themselves. Everything will work out fine! A person is scatterbrained, his mind flies in every direction. That's why he needs to bind the parts of his mind together, which, according to the Rebbe, can only happen by learning Torah.

When a person learns Torah in depth, he puts his mind into the Torah. This is how he creates new worlds. Then he creates a new reality! Suddenly a different set of laws applies to him! He has wealth, he has health! Suddenly, he has spiritual and material bounty! This is because he created a new world. Previously, he was in a world in which he didn't have money and, now, he's in a world where he does have money! Now, he is in a completely new world, because every moment a person builds new worlds. If a person learns Torah in depth, then he creates new worlds every second.

WIPING OUT THE MEMORY OF AMALEK

By way of *simcha*, happiness, we'll surely be saved from all our transgressions! By being happy, we'll merit to have every type of healing! By way of *simcha*, we'll merit to have every miracle. By way of *simcha*, we can wipe out Amalek. We can erase all the sins! By being happy, we can escape from all the transgressions in the world.

We need to take great care about being happy, always. Because the moment that there is even just a drop of sadness, maybe on account of a sin that we've done, or because we have money worries, then a person is made in such a way that he'll then fall into an even bigger sin. Because of his sadness and his worry, a person falls into doing even greater sins!

There are people whose greatest pleasure lies in being sad – they wallow in sadness all their lives. If you try to cheer them up even a little bit, you simply irritate them. They've never tasted a drop of *simcha*, happiness, their whole life long.

"And the rule is, that we need to make every effort, and use all our strength, to be only happy always, because the nature of man is to be drawn to bitter depression and sadness, on account of the difficulties and circumstances of the time; and every person is full of suffering. So, we need to force ourselves, with tremendous strength, to be happy, always" (*Likutey Moharan* 2:24).

A person falls into sadness because of the force of all the suffering he's experiencing. The suffering is what causes him to enter that sort of bitter, black depression. It puts his brain to sleep and disconnects him from his senses.

Depression is really an anesthetizing drug. Depression is a narcotic that gives a person some 'quiet' and some 'calmness' – but it's all just imaginary.

In truth, the opposite is happening-- the depression only amplifies the suffering; it only makes it greater. So, the person's main spiritual work is the battle against feelings of depression – which is something that requires a lot of *mesirut nefesh* (self-sacrifice).

Rav Natan of Breslov says that in order to fight against *yeoush*, despair, you need *mesirut nefesh*. Happiness doesn't just appear by itself. Being happy is the hardest thing of all. The biggest obstacles of all surround *simcha*, happiness. Everything that the *Satan* is fighting about, it's just to prevent people from being happy! This is what he's fighting about. The whole battle is just to stop you from being happy. This is the work of the Satan - that you shouldn't be happy, that you shouldn't dance, that you shouldn't rejoice.

Each and every one of us experiences insults and humiliations, each of us goes through challenges with our body and soul. There are a million reasons why you could be unhappy. The nature of a person is to be depressed and sad. But happiness can readjust everything. If a person sings to Hashem, and dances, then all the goodness will be sent to him.

So, there is no reason to be depressed. Everyone has a sharp intellect, everyone can attain all the things that exist in the world, but only if they leave their sadness and depression behind. With *simcha*, you can merit to turn your 'downs' into 'ups', and to sweeten all the harsh judgments, and turn them into salvations.

Rav Natan says that the main thrust of Haman, the Amalekite's, accusations and challenges was to do with happiness. He couldn't stand when *Am Yisrael* was happy, when they were dancing, full of joy, and singing on their festivals and Shabboss, etc.

Shabbos is coming. Shabbos is *simcha* and dancing. For six days, you got some food, *Baruch Hashem*, you aren't sick – so start dancing and rejoicing! Your wife is healthy? Start dancing and rejoicing! You have children? Start dancing and rejoicing! You don't yet have children? In the merit of all your dancing and happiness, you'll have offspring!

You still don't have a *shidduch*? In the merit of your rejoicing, you'll find a *shidduch!* When Shabbos comes, you need to sit with your children and make them feel happy, and to sing with them enthusiastically. Don't just say, 'Poor me, I'm depressed, it's hard for me to be happy, what do I have to be joyful about?!' It's difficult for everyone to maintain their happiness. You need a lot of *mesirut nefesh* to stay happy. But, by way of *simcha,* a person can subdue all the *klipos* (side of evil) and can become purified from all the *tumah* (spiritual impurity).

A person sees that he's stumbling, that his body is getting the better of him, that Amalek is beating him, and wants to flip him into sadness, and bitter, black depression – but even so, it's still forbidden for him to lose his concentration! He needs to immediately go and look for some friends to dance with, to cheer himself up, to say some *tehillim* with, and to search out all different types of strategies to continue to stay happy.

A person needs to know that his soul isn't at all connected to transgressions. The soul is always a *Tzaddik* (a holy person), it's always pure, it's always holy. Whenever a person falls into sins, it's only because he isn't happy enough. So, it's forbidden to lose your concentration, don't let anything pull you down, no sin, no problem, not even if you stumbled into some transgression.

Just make *teshuva* and start to be happy again! Sing, hum a melody, recite some *Tehillim* – the main point is just not to fall into depression! Because this is the war between Amalek and the soul. This is the main war you're fighting against the *yetzer hara*-- which just wants to drag you down into sadness.

Ki Tavo

ONE TRUE CRY

A person must discover the deep advice through which he will be able to escape the deepest pits of hell, as it is written, *"Counsel is like deep water in the heart of man"* (Proverbs 20:5).

The most important thing is that a person cries out to Hashem day and night. Every hour, he should cry out to Hashem, to draw down the advice he needs by crying out. *"And they cried out to Hashem in their distress"* (Tehillim 107:6), because all advice is revealed though crying out to Hashem.

Baruch Hashem, we're eating well and sleeping well. We're drinking and we're happy. Everything is great-- it should last 120 years - a million years! But the question is where will all this eating and drinking get us? If we don't cry out to Hashem, where will it bring us? When we're eating and drinking and sleeping well, then automatically we lose our orientation, our sense of direction! Breslov is all about shouting out to Hashem. Everyone shouts out to Hashem to get out of his own personal hell, to escape from his forbidden gazing and his forbidden thoughts. Everyone needs to cry out to Hashem to reveal the advice of Rabbenu. "Counsel is like deep water in the heart of man." A person needs to reveal the *'nachal novea'* (the flowing river).

Rabbenu is the flowing river, a gushing spring of advice, but a person has to dig a little-- at least a few centimeters! If a person will give one true cry, then whole geysers of good counsel will emerge, there will be rivers full of advice. All the advice will be revealed to him on how to escape from his own personal hell.

When a person is in public, he can cry out a silent cry. *"From the depths I cried out to You, Hashem.*" This is the heart's cry from the depths. All advice is drawn though the 'voices'. There are seven voices: "*the voice of Hashem on the water, the voice of Hashem hewing out flames of fire, the voice of Hashem making the desert tremble...the voice of Hashem causing hinds to calve and stripping the forest bare*" (Tehillim 29). These are such powerful voices, voices that strip the forests bare, that uproot trees. There are such cries, cries that can uproot trees-- these are the kinds of cries that we need to cry out to Hashem!

When Hashem gave the Torah, he gave it with such a voice that the entire world was shaking. All the mountains were uprooted from their places. We need to awaken the seven voices of the Giving of the Torah at every moment. Hashem can give you such voices, such screams that all the mountains would be uprooted from their places. All our foreign ideas, all of our bad habits and desires-- all the bad that you inherited though your genes, it all will be uprooted from its place.

Reb Shmuel Shapira, one of the great Breslover *Chassidim*, would shout from *Ma'ariv* until the morning until he would be throwing up blood. His veins would be bursting from his throat and literally spilling blood, and still he would cry to Hashem. In this merit he had such holy and pure children, grandchildren and great grandchildren.

We need to return to the Breslov of old, to cry out to Hashem and shout out until the advice is revealed. The advice is revealed though the voice of Hashem, because Hashem is speaking to us every moment and every second. Hashem is shouting to us all the time. When a person cries out to Hashem, he awakens the upper voice and all the deep advice on how to get out of the hell he is going through. So, even though a person has long *payot* and a long beard-- that's all wonderful, he has wonderful appearance, but if he doesn't cry out to Hashem, then he will be stuck in hell with his *payot* and his beard.

If you merited becoming a *ba'al teshuva*, then prove that you're a real *ba'al teshuva*-- prove it! Cry out to Hashem. Don't leave your Gemara. Don't leave the *Likutey Halachos* or your siddur. Cry out to Hashem, 'I don't want to fall any further! I don't want to go to places that I once went to, and I don't want my children to go what I went through!'

Now, you're a captive, you're in the pit of hell. Esav hunted and captured you. The *klipos* captured you. Cry out to Hashem, 'I implore You, Hashem, please deliver me!' 'Hashem save me!' You weren't born a *Tzaddik*. You are already 20 years old and only just now starting to learn, and it is a million times harder to start learning at this age. A million times. But the reward will also be a million times greater. The harder it is, the greater the reward. If you just cry out to Hashem, this will build the world-- wars will be cancelled. If you just cry out to Hashem, you'll bring back a thousand people in *teshuva*.

To achieve anything in holiness, you need to cry out and shout to the heart of the heavens. Obviously, you have no desire to learn. Obviously, you have no desire to pray. Can a person change in an instant? He's the same as he used to be, just in a different form. He hasn't changed inside, he just put on a *shtreimel* and a long coat. A person says, well if that's all there is, then what did I make *teshuva* for? But in truth, you became a *ba'al teshuva* so that you would cry out to Hashem, so that you would shout to Hashem. And this is the advantage of being a *ba'al teshuva*: that it's hard for him to learn Gemara. It's hard for him to pray. It's hard for him to sing the Shabbos songs. It's hard for him to stay in yeshiva for so many hours. So, that's why he has to shout and shout. And through this he merits to rise up to the very highest places, says the Zohar. He goes up to the *Sefira* of *Binah*, where the secret of the redemption is found.

But, a person from Meah Shearim who was born a *Tzaddik*, what does he have to shout about? He sings the Shabbos songs out loud; he prays, he sits calmly in yeshiva. He doesn't feel that he needs to cry out to Hashem. He is simply doing what comes naturally to him. So, the Zohar says, he can go up only as high as the *Sefira* of *Yesod*. But, in truth, even a person who was born in Meah Shearim can achieve the aspect of being a *ba'al teshuva*. He can also scream out to Hashem just like a *ba'al teshuva*, but this can happen only if he merits feeling that he is truly deficient, that he is also still far away from Hashem.

A person must believe that Hashem wants to do miracles and wonders for him at every moment, as it's written, *"and for his wonders to the children of man"* (Tehillim 107:8). Hashem wants to do the most wondrous things for us. *"In You our fathers trusted... to You they cried out and were delivered"* (Tehillim 22:5-6). The wonders and miracles are according to one's cries and shouts, because the salvation of a person is ready and waiting to take place, every minute and every second. No matter what kind of trouble he is in, no matter what place he is in-- even in the heart of the sea or in the middle of the desert, Hashem has arranged everything to assist him. His salvation is already prepared and waiting for him! He just needs to really cry out to Hashem, just one true cry.

NITZAVIM

LOVE YOUR NEIGHBOR

Our main mission is to fill ourselves with love for our fellow man. Only through loving others can a person receive the light of the Torah and the light of the Rebbe. Loving others is the first condition for having one's prayers answered. First, a person has to love others with all his heart and soul. Everyone should be willing to give his life for another, to give everything that he has to another, to give his soul, his body, his money, his time, his energy and his mind to his friend. Only then will a person merit having a holy mind and heart.

If there is any kind of separation between one person and another, then right away one's prayers are not accepted. This is what Haman said to Achashverosh, *"There is a certain nation, divided and dispersed among the nations"* (Esther 3:8). They are completely divided! Even if they will call out and pray, their prayers will not be accepted. This is why Esther said to Mordechai, *"Go and gather together all the Jews"*-- you need to assemble them and unify them; they must stand together!

If a person feels unity with each and every Jew, if he is prepared to nullify himself before everyone, if he feels love for everyone and believes that each and every Jew is more of a *Tzaddik* than he is, then he will merit having all his sins forgiven. As the *Yehudi HaKadosh* said, when two people are sitting and drinking a cup of tea and each one believes that the other is better than he is, and he feels embarrassed in front of the other person, and he feels awe for the other person, then immediately all his sins are forgiven.

How does a person come to love others? Only through submission. Only if each person gives in to the other, only then can he love the other person. The Land of Israel is also called "the land of Cana'an" which comes from the world "*hachna'ah*", which means submission. It is a land which fosters the trait of submission. Just as the Rebbe says in *Shivchei HaRan*, the land of Cana'an facilitates submission. In order to have his prayers accepted, a person needs to always give in to others. If people don't submit to one another, then their prayers are not accepted.

There is nothing worse than senseless hatred. The *Beis HaMikdash* was destroyed because of the sin of senseless hatred, despite the fact that the people learned Torah and behaved correctly in every other way. Therefore, we are duty bound to be continually increasing our unconditional love for everyone. This means that a person shouldn't offend anyone, yell at anyone or slander anyone and he should always feel subservient to every Jew.

It's written in the *Igeret HaRamban*, that when a person speaks with someone, he needs to feel ashamed in front of him, to be in awe of him and to feel embarrassment and fear from each and every person, from each and every Jew. What is this fear? He should fear that he might insult him or offend him-- perhaps I will say something that will insult him.

A person's main test is in loving others, and most of a person's prayers need to be about loving others-- that he should love his friends, and also each and every person he meets, with all his heart and soul, with self-sacrifice. Loving other people is a matter of self-sacrifice-- it's not easy! Everyone has mishaps and misunderstandings with others. He needs to know that it's all nonsense-- the other person is not really guilty of anything.

When people knock him down or offend him or make him suffer, he should respond by loving the person who did this to him, loving him in his heart and not holding anything against him. Just the opposite! He should have mercy on his friend and appreciate that he is just in a bad mood, that some foolishness has taken hold of him and his heart will then burst with mercy for this friend. He really is full of mercy for him. This is called *achavas chaverim* (loving others).

This was the case with David and Shaul. Shaul was pursuing David and wanted to kill him, to murder him, but David acted in the exact opposite way-- he couldn't love him enough! He loved him with a deep and profound love, because King David knew that it was just that a kind of craziness had taken hold of Shaul, some stupidity had gotten into him.

The main test is that when someone is opposing you, you have to keep on loving him with a deep and profound love. After all, this person still prays and puts on *tefillin* and goes to Uman. He learns Torah and he gets up for *chatzos*. He has a limitless number of pearls and diamonds inside him. So, on account of a bit of stupidity, I should reject him, G-d forbid?

There are 600,000 letters in the Torah relating to the 600,000 Jewish souls. Every letter in the Torah is associated with a soul. If there is no brotherly love, and a person doesn't love each and every Jew with his heart and soul, then he can't receive the Torah.

The moment that we love one another, each person awakens the other. He is becomes awakened by the other person's good point. One person gives a lot of charity, another prays for a long time. Every Jew has a good point. There's no Jew that's not a *Tzaddik* inside, in the depths of his soul. Everyone has a spark of holiness. We need to connect ourselves to all these sparks in every Jew, just as the *Ben Ish Chai* says, 'there is no person that doesn't have his hour'. Even the biggest evildoer has real thoughts of *teshuva*. The moment that a person speaks negatively against another, then he can no longer receive from that person's good point.

Everybody is always screaming, "*Love your neighbor as yourself!*" Everybody is always screaming out, "*I love everybody!*" The truth is, the more that a person says that he loves everyone, the more he actually hates everyone. The more he speaks about loving others, the more he shows that he is full of hatred for others, because the further a person is from the *mitzvah* of *"Loving your brother as yourself"*, the more he talks about it. This *mitzvah* is the hardest *mitzvah* to fulfill, because a person is an egotist-- he wants to have the best food prepared for him, he wants people to speak nicely to him at home, that everyone should honor him and bow down to him; everyone should kiss the dust of his feet...

VAYELECH

WE HEARD MUSIC

In the Zohar in *Parshas Vayelech*, in the commentary of the Sulam, we find an explanation of this verse from Isaiah, *"From the end of the earth we hear melodies-- glory to the righteous."* When the Jewish people entered the Land, everywhere they walked they heard music and praise of G-d bursting forth from every stone, from every corner.

If a person was worthy of having a pure ear, then he would hear it. It had to be an ear that was truly pure. As it says, *"The praise of Moshe [was heard] at that time."* What are the melodies? *"From the end of the earth we heard melodies-- glory to the righteous."*

Who brings all couples together? Who brings the grooms and the brides together? The seven beggars (from Rabbi Nachman's story of the Seven Beggars). As we see in the story, the moment when a person longs for them, they come right away. These seven beggars are incorporated within the true *Tzaddik*-- Rabbi Nachman of Breslov. He is the *Tzaddik*, there isn't anyone else! There is no other! There is no one who comes close to him!

The verse says, *"And all your people are Tzaddikim, all are beloved, all are pure, all are holy."* Yet only Rabbi Nachman is the *Tzaddik*, only him! He is the one who uplifts all the souls and he arranges all of the couples. When you connect yourselves to him in truth, then this is the true match. This is the match that was ordained during the first six days of creation that the Divine echo announced. According to Shmuel, the Divine echo announces the match every single day.

"And they heard a voice." They heard that everything is the *Tzaddik*, that there is a *Tzaddik* who does everything. He takes care of everything and he arranges everything. They heard a voice that said, *"This is the Torah that Moshe placed before the children of Israel"* (Devarim 4:44).

242

HAAZINU

DANCE AWAY YOUR SINS

Even though during all of the Jewish Holidays there is a mitzvah to rejoice, on the Holiday of *Succot* it is a mitzvah of its own! The verse "And you shall rejoice in your festivals" is said about *Succot*. On *Succot* in the Bet Hamikdash there was unusual Joy. The Sages established extra Joy for the Holiday of *Succot*, multiplied Joy! The entire Holiday was set aside for non-stop dancing and rejoicing!

Certainly one must study Torah as well, for if a person doesn't have Torah he lacks the ability to dance [from holiness and purity], as Rebbe Nachman explains (LM2 31): "Through melody it can be recognized on a person if they accepted upon themselves the yoke of Torah, and the sign is "on their shoulders they will *yisa'u* (lift it)" (Bamidmar 4) as our Sages expound (Arachin 11) "There is no mention of the word *yisa'u* in the Torah without reference to song, as it says '*sa'u zimra* – raise up song', and this verse was said in regard to the sons of Kehat whose jobs were to lift up the Holy Ark on their shoulders, which refers to accepting upon themselves the yoke of Torah."

One who accepts upon himself the Yoke of Torah can sing, dance and make music.

In the Bet Hamikdash there was extraordinary joy as the Torah itself says, "And you shall rejoice before Hashem your G-d seven days". It's a *mitzvah d'oraisa*, a Biblical Commandment! This commandment is not said on Pesach, not on *Shavuos*; it is said only by *Succot*. It is a biblical commandment to rejoice constantly for seven days! The Torah commanded us to rejoice and dance non-stop, day and night, for 7 days!

How would they do this?

They would bring every musical instrument, they would play with violin, harps, and cymbals, etc. Each and every person would play with the instrument he's familiar with. But the dancing? The strongest, stormiest dancing? The dancing while juggling? This only the greatest *Tzaddikim* would do! The moment the dancing began only the greatest loftiest holiest *Tzaddikim* would dance; they would do flips, cartwheels, somersaults etc., like it says about King David. Only esteemed men who toiled all day in Torah and *Mitzvos* and faithfully took care of the needs of the community, who didn't sleep all night and day, who sacrificed their entire beings for G-d and His People – only they were the ones who would be dancing, flipping and spinning in the Holy Temple.

Nowadays, it is incumbent on every Jew to dance and rejoice during these holy days, and to know that this happiness and dancing is a great and awesome rectification for the soul. A person does not know which kind of harsh spiritual judgements are waiting for him in the coming year. The Rebbe says *(Likutey Moharan* 206), A person sins and harms his soul; at first things continue to go well for him, Hashem then begins to send him slight hints; if he still doesn't get it Hashem calls to him louder, until the person starts getting kicked and pounded with suffering.

You sinned? Do teshuva! The same Torah that told you it's a sin tells you about teshuva! But if you don't do teshuva then maybe after some suffering something will start to sink in; you will begin to do teshuva, begin to sob over your spiritual blemishes, get shaken up a drop! If not, then G-d forbid, a spouse will get sick; if not a spouse then the children G-d forbid!

The Rebbe promised that he will fix everything, but the question is how will he fix? How much suffering must prevail over a person to receive his fixing? Sometimes it hurts to go to a doctor, and if someone is really sick the surgery can be painful. We are Jews! Nothing is rectified for free! By the Christians nothing is needed to be done; just go to the

Priest and confess to him once a year and he says 'forgiven forgiven'; afterwards everyone continues as before. By Jews there is no such thing! For sins a person must pay! On every transgression he must pay! If a person doesn't do teshuva, and doesn't wake up, then he starts getting hit with suffering as it says "There is no suffering without sin".

There are 22 days from Rosh Hashana until Simchat Torah to fix everything. Kabalistically, from Rosh Hashana until Yom Kippur the Judgements are sweetened; we sweetened our yetzer harah that it shouldn't control us. Now from Yom Kippur until Simchat Torah there are 12 days for forgiveness of sins; we are now building the New Year. Until now we got the Ktiva and Chatima. writing and sealing of the decree. Rosh Hashana is the sealing for the complete *Tzadd*ikim, Yom Kippur for the beinonim, regular people. Now is the time to build! The building is on *Succ*ot! With joy! Dance! Song! Fervorous prayer! And according to how much a person sings and dances during these days, that is how he builds the coming year.

Through dancing and singing all of a person sins are forgiven. What is the Hebrew word for dance? *Machol. Machol* means to be forgiven! All of a person's sins are forgiven! Through the *macholot* - dancing - not one sin remains! No sins! No Judgements! The Arizal says that in addition to the joy which we are commanded on Simchat Torah, whoever rejoices and dances on the night after Simchat Torah, dances until dawn, he merits that all his sins will be completely nullified!

The dancing and joy build the coming year. Through dancing one imbues the coming year with healing; through dancing one imbues the coming year with salvation and all of one's needs, the spiritual consciousness of the coming year, the heart of the coming year.

With the help of Hashem we will merit this year, through joy, singing and dancing – forgiveness of sins and sweetening of judgements, and the complete redemption speedily in our days, Amen!

V'ZOT HABERACHAH

NO MAN KNEW HIS BURIAL PLACE

Moshe is mentioned seven hundred and seventy times. Count and you'll find that in all of Tanach, Moshe is mentioned exactly seven hundred and seventy times. That is twice the numerical value of "*Shechinah*" (385). Moshe is the upper *Shechinah* and the lower *Shechinah*. "*Shechinah*" is equal to three hundred and eighty five, multiplied by two is seven hundred and seventy. Moshe Rabbenu merited that the Torah mentioned his name seven hundred and seventy times, two times the word "*Shechinah*." The upper *Shechinah* and the lower *Shechinah* parallel Rachel and Leah.

The *Imrei Yosef* says here that Rachel and Leah are the upper and lower *Shechinah*. That is why Leah was buried in *Ma'aras HaMachpelah*. What is *Ma'aras HaMachpelah*? The Sefer HaTemunah (III:60b), says that the hidden light of the seven days of creation is hidden away inside *Ma'aras HaMachpelah*.

That is where the light of Gan Eden is. Adam HaRishon went for a walk and he saw a light bursting forth from the ground. He went walking in *Eretz Yisrael*, in the fields. Hashem had banished him from Gan Eden, so he went walking in *Eretz Yisrael*. He went for a walk in some field in Chevron, and suddenly he saw a light bursting out of the ground. The Zohar teaches that there was a light bursting out of the ground, and Adam realized that he had found *Ma'aras HaMachpelah*. He immediately wanted to be buried there. He didn't reveal the site to anyone, only to Chanoch before he died, and Chanoch was the one to bury him there.

This is what King David said, "*I will walk before Hashem in the lands of life.*" The Sefer HaTemunah says that all of King David's desire and

246

all of his prayers were devoted to this-- to being buried in *Ma'aras HaMachpelah*. "*I will walk before Hashem in the lands of life.*" That is called "*the lands of life.*" The word "*lands*" is plural because the light of the *Ma'aras HaMachpelah* is a light that is manifold.

The *Sefer HaTemunah* says that, in truth, five couples are buried there - ten people altogether. There are Adam and Chava and the three Patriarchs together with the three Matriarchs. So, who is the fifth couple? The fifth couple is Moshe and Tzippora. Heavenly angels came and carried Moshe Rabbenu from Mount Nevo to *Ma'aras HaMachpelah*.

This is the meaning of the verse that we read in *Parshat VeZot HaBerachah*, "*And no man knew his burial place.*" No man knew-- not even Moshe Rabbenu himself! Moshe himself didn't know where they would bury him. So, Moshe Rabbenu also merited to be buried in *Ma'aras HaMachpelah*. The Sefer HaTemunah says that angels came and took him and Tzippora and removed them from their graves. That is the meaning of the phrase, "*And no man knew his burial place*". Even Moshe did not know where he was to be buried. Moshe had no idea where Hashem wanted to bury him. Ultimately, though, the angels came and took him to *Ma'aras HaMachpelah*.

These ten who are buried in Ma'aras HaMachpelah parallel the ten *sefirot*. Adam is the sefirah of *Keter*, Chava is the sefirah of *Da'at*. Avraham is the sefirah of *Chochmah*, and Sarah is the sefirah of *Binah*. Yitzchak is *Gevurah* and Rivkah is *Chessed*. Then, Yaakov is *Netzach*, and Leah is *Hod*.

GLOSSARY

Achashverosh	The King of Persia at the time of the Purim story.
Achavas Chaverim	To love our fellow Jew (literally, to love our friends).
Achdus	Unity.
Adam HaRishon	Adam the first man.
Admor	A Rebbe in a Chassidic court.
Ahavas Olam	The prayer before the Shema, in the morning services.
Al Kiddush Hashem	In order to sanctify God's name.
Alenu	The closing prayer of the daily prayer services.
Aliyah	Literally, 'going up' - both to the Torah, and to the land of Israel.
Aluphim	Leaders.
Am Yisrael	the nation, or people, of Israel.
Am Ha'aretz	An unlearned man; a boor.
Amoraim	The latter Talmudic sages.
AN"SH	Abbreviation of *Anshei Shelomeinu*, or 'our people', used in reference to other Breslov chassidim.
Anpin Nehirin	Kabbalist concept, *literally:* shining face.
Apikorsim	Heretics.
Ari / Arizal	Rabbi Yitzhak Isaac Luria Ashkenazi.

Aron	Ark of the Covenant.
Asarah Ma'amarot	A holy book written by Rabbi Arzariah of Fano.
Asher Yatzar	The blessing recited after using the bathroom.
Asiyah	The world of action – one of the four kabbalistic worlds.
Atik Yoman	A kabbalistic term referring to higher worlds.
Atika D'Atika	A kabbalistic term which means *the Ancient of Ancients*.
Atzilus	*The highest of the four kabbalistic worlds.*
Aufruf	A celebration held by the groom on the Shabbos before his wedding.
Aveira (pl: aveiros)	Sin, wrong-doing.
Avodah Zara	Idol worship.
Avodas Hashem	Literally, 'Hashem's work' - refers to any holy endeavours, prayers or mitzvot, etc.
Avodas HaTefillah	Literally, 'the work of praying' - refers to praying.
Avos	*Literally:* The fathers.
Avreich	A married student who's serious about learning Torah, often full-time.
Ayin	*Literally:* nothing.
Ayin Hara	The evil eye.
B'Iyun	In depth.
Baal HaTurim	A work authored by Rabbi Yaakov ben Asher.
Ba'al Teshuvah	(plural: *ba'alei teshuva*) A person who returns to God (repents).
Baal Toke'iah	The one who blows the Shofar in synagogue on the High Holidays.

Baalei Batim	Householders who work instead of learning Torah full-time.
Bachur (pl: bachorim)	An unmarried student who's learning Torah in a Yeshiva.
Baki	Knowledgeable.
Baraisa	Tannaic statements that are found in the Gemara, but that have a lesser status than mishnayot.
Baruch Hashem	*Literally*: Bless God. *Colloquially*: Thank God.
Bat Kol	A voice from heaven.
Bein Hazmanim	Literally, 'between times' - refers to the period between the 9th of Av and the first of Elul, when Torah institutions are closed for the Summer.
Beinonim	The people who are considered to be neither righteous, nor wicked.
Beis Din	A religious, Jewish court of law.
Beis HaMikdash	The Temple in Jerusalem.
Beis Midrash	*Literally:* The house of learning. Colloquially, the yeshiva's main study hall.
Beis Yosef	Rabbi Yosef Karo.
Ben Adam	Human being.
Ben Ish Chai	A work authored by Rabbi Yosef Hayyim.
Bentch	To bless - usually refers to reciting the grace after meals.
B'ezras Hashem	With God's help.
Bimah	Dais in the synagogue.
Binah	Understanding.
Birkas HaMazon	The blessing after meals.
Birkas HaKohanim	The blessing made by the Kohanim.

Birkas HaShachar	The blessings recited in the morning, from the prayer book.
Bitachon	Trust (usually refers to trust in Hashem).
Bitul	Self-nullification.
Biyas HaMoshiach	Hebrew for: The coming of the Moshiach.
Bnei Torah	*Literally:* Sons of Torah. Refers to Torah observant Jews.
Bnei Yissachar	An Chassidic work authored by Rabbi Zvi Elimelech Shapiro of Dynov.
Brachah (pl: brachot)	A blessing.
Briah	The world of creation – our world, one of the four kabbalistic worlds.
Bris Mila	The circumcision ceremony typically held eight days after a Jewish boy is born.
Chadar (pl: chadarim)	Religious pre-school.
Chaburah	A Torah study group.
Chai V'kayam	A biblical expression usually used to refer to a dead Tzaddik, as being still 'alive' spiritually, and present and acting in the world.
Chalakah	A celebration where a three year old Jewish boy has his first haircut.
Chalban	The Milkman. Referring to the kabbalist, Rav Chaim Cohen, z'tl.
Chanukah	The Festival of Lights celebrating the Maccabean victory over the Greeks.
Chas v'shalom	*Colloquially:* God forbid.
Chassid (pl: chassidim)	A group of religious, orthodox Jews who usually follow their own 'Rebbe'
Chassidei Breslov	(or '*Chassidim*') Devout students or followers of Rabbi Nachman of Breslov.

Chassidus	The spiritual path originated by the Ba'al Shem Tov, and followed by his students, including Rabbi Nachman. A sect of Judaism which emphasises joy in its practice and teaches that every Jew, no matter his level, can get close to Hashem.
Chatam Sofer	A work authored by Rabbi Moshe Schreiber.
Chatima	To be sealed for the good, after Rosh Hashanah.
Chatzos	The time of halachic midnight.
Chavrusa	A one-on-one study partner, when learning Torah.
Chayei Moharan	A biography of Rabbi Nachman of Breslov, written by his student Rabbi Natan Sternhartz.
Chazal	The initial letters of the following expression in Hebrew: **Ch**achmanu **Z**ichronam **L**'vracha. *Literally:* "Our Sages, may their memory be for a blessing."
Cheshbon Nefesh	taking a self-reckoning or personal accounting of our own deeds.
Chessed	Kindness.
Chevrah Kaddisha	The organization responsible for preparing a Jewish body according to halachahh, before burial.
Chida	Rabbi Chaim Yosef David Azulai.
Chiddush	A novel idea or insight, especially within
(pl: chiddushim)	Torah learning.
Chizuk	Strengthening, spiritual encouragement.
Chochmah	Wisdom.

Chol HaMoed	Refers to the intermediate days between the first day (or days) of Yom Tov, and the last day (or days) of Yom Tov, of either Succos or Pesach.
Chuppah	The marriage canopy used in Jewish weddings.
Chutz L'aretz	*Literally:* Outside the land. Refers to anywhere outside of Israel.
Chutzpah, Chutzpadik	Brazen, shameless, cheeky.
D'Oraisa	Refers to a commandment or mitzvah that's derived directly from the written Torah, as opposed to the Oral Torah.
Daas	Godly awareness, knowledge or wisdom.
Daf Yomi	The daily study of a specific, set page of the Gemara.
Dam (pl: damim)	*Literally:* blood, or bloods. Refers to 'blood money'.
Darshan	Someone who gives over a Torah class or lesson in public.
Dati Leumi	*Literally:* National-religious. Describes a group of more modern orthodox Jews in Israel.
Davka	On purpose, specifically.
Dayan	A judge.
Derech	Path.
Derech Eretz	Good manners. '*Derech Eretz kadma le Torah*' literally means that you have to put practical considerations before learning Torah.
Deveikus	Closeness or clinging to Hashem.
Duchen	To make the priestly blessing.
Ein Od Milvado	*Literally:* There is only Him (i.e. God).

Ein Sof	The infinite.
Eis Ratzon	A favorable time.
Emunah	Trust, faith and belief in Hashem. *Emunas Tzaddikim:* believing in the words of our Tzaddikim.
Ephod	The breastplate worn by the Kohen HaGadol.
Eretz Canaan	The land of Canaan.
Eretz Yisrael	The land of Israel.
Erev	*Literally:* The eve of. *Erev Shabbos* refers to the time before candle-lighting on Friday.
Even ha'shtiah	The foundation stone that the world was created from.
Gabbai	Responsible for managing the services within synagogue, and / or attending a rabbi or Rebbe, in a capacity similar to a private secretary.
Gadol HaDor	*Literally:* Great one of the generation. Refers to the senior, leading figure in the Torah world.
Galus	Exile.
Gan Eden	The Garden of Eden, paradise.
Gaon	Torah genius.
Gashmiyus	Materialism, materiality.
Gedolim	*Literally:* Great ones. Refers to the leading Torah personalities of a generation.
Gehinnom	Purgatory.
Gemilus Chassadim	Acts of kindness, good deeds.
Gemach	A free loan fund for money or other items.
Geula	Redemption.
Gevurah	Strictness.

Gog and Magog	The last war that's meant to occur at the end of days, ushering in the time of Moshiach.
Hachna'ah	Submission.
Hachnassas Orchim	The mitvah of hosting guests.
HaKadosh Baruch Hu	*Literally:* The Holy One, blessed be He. Another term for God.
Hakafot Shniyos	Referring to the custom to dance with the Torah all night long on the night after Shemini Atzeres.
Hakaras HaTov	Gratitude.
Halachah (pl: halachos)	Jewish law. *Halachic:* Deriving from Jewish law.
Hallel	Prayers of thanksgiving said on Rosh Chodesh and Jewish festivals.
HaMelech	The King.
HaNavi	The Prophet.
Hashem	G-d.
Hashem Yitbarach	G-d, may He be blessed.
Havdalah	*Literally:* separation. The service performed at the conclusion of Shabbos, before returning to the mundane activities of the rest of the week.
Hefker	Abandoned by Hashem.
Heter	Rabbinic permission, or leniency.
Hilulah	Anniversary of a person (usually a Tzaddik's) passing.
Hishtadlus	One's own personal or physical effort.
Hisbodedus	Personal prayer to G-d in one's own words.
Hod	Glory.
Hodaah	Thanks.

Ibburim	Refers to containing sparks of a particular soul, or souls.
Igeret HaRamban	The letter Nachmanides wrote to his son.
Ikker	The main thing.
Kabbalas Shabbos	Welcoming the Shabbos.
Kadosh	*Literally:* holy.
Kadosh Kadoshim	Holy of Holies; the innermost sanctuary of the Temple.
Kal ve'chomer	All the more so.
Kaparah	*Literally:* Atonement. Often refers to a financial or material loss that occurs instead of something worse happening.
Kavanah (pl: kavanos)	Intention.
Kedushah	Holiness.
Kedushas Levi	A work authored by Rabbi Levi Yitzchok of Berditchev.
Kedushas Yom Tov	Rabbi Chanayah Yom Tov Lipa Teitelbaum, the Grand Rebbe of Siget
Kehillah (pl: kehillas)	Community.
Keitz	The end, usually specifically referring to the end of days.
Kesubah	Marriage contract.
Keter	*Literally:* crown. The highest of the ten sephirot.
Kiddush Hashem	Something that sanctifies God's name.
Kiddush Levanah	The monthly blessing recited over the sighting of the new moon.
Kibbutz	Often secular agricultural settlement in Israel founded on socialist principles. *Kibbutznik:* Member of a kibbutz.
Kippah	Skull-cap.

Kisei HaKavod	*Literally:* The holy throne. Refers allegorically to God's throne in the Heavens.
Kivrei Tzaddikim	Plural of *kever Tzaddik*, or the grave of a holy, righteous person.
Klipa (pl:klipos)	The husks of evil.
Kloiz	The main synagogue in Uman, originally built by Rabbi Natan.
Kohen HaGadol	The High Priest.
Koheles	Ecclesiastes.
Kollel	A place where married men learn Torah.
Korbanos	*Literally:* The Temple sacrifices. Here, it means the recitation of the sacrificial service in the morning prayers, in lieu of actually performing the sacrifices in the Temple.
Kotel	The wailing or Western wall of the destroyed Temple, that still stands in Jerusalem.
Kushios	A difficulty or question about something within the Torah.
Kriyah	The Jewish custom of tearing the clothing upon being told of the death of a close relative, as a sign of deep mourning.
Ktiva	To be written in the book of life (during Rosh Hashanah)
Kvitlach	A note requesting a blessing that's sent to a Tzaddik.
K'vod HaRav	*Literally:* The honor of the Rav. A respectful greeting offered to rabbinic figures.
L'kavod Shabbos	*Literally:* In the honor of Shabbos

Lamnatzeach	The opening word of a number of Psalms, *literally:* for the conductor.
Lashon Hara	Evil speech, gossip.
Likutei Halachos	The main work of Rabbi Natan Sternhartz, Rebbe Nachman's principal student.
Likutei Moharan	The main work of Rebbe Nachman of Breslov.
Limud Torah	*Literally:* Torah learning.
Lishmah	For its own sake, or for God's sake, without any other ulterior motives.
Lulav (pl:lulavim)	The palm shoot used as part of the four species required for Succos.
Maariv	The evening prayers.
Machlokes	Strife, trouble-making, discord.
Machol (pl: macholot)	Dances.
Maggid of Mezeritch	The leading disciple of the Baal Shem Tov, the founder of Chassidut.
Malach	Angel.
Mamzer	A child born of forbidden relations, according to Jewish law.
Maseches	Tractate - usually referring to the Gemara.
Masmid	Someone who is constantly engaged in learning Torah.
Masorti	Traditionally religious.
Matan Torah	The giving of the Torah.
Mechitzah	The barrier between the men and women's section of a hall or synagogue.
Megillah	Scroll.
Mamash	A Hebrew expression of emphasis, akin to 'truly', or 'really'.
Maskil	Used to begin a number of Psalms.

Melevah Malka	*Literally:* The queen's meal. Refers to the meal that occurs after the end of Shabbos, to bid farewell to the Shabbos Queen.
Menahel	Head teacher.
Menorah	The candelabra in the Temple; the candelabra lit on the festival of Chanukah.
Meraglim	Spies.
Meshugga, Meshugganer	Yiddish terms for craziness, a crazy person.
Mesilas Yesharim	A work on Jewish ethics written by Rabbi Moshe Chaim Luzzatto.
Mesirus Nefesh	Self-sacrifice.
Midda Keneged Midda	A measure for a measure.
Middos	Character traits.
Midrash	Stories and explanations from the Gemara and other holy books.
Mikvah	A pool of ritually pure water that cleanses a person from their spiritual impurity.
Milah Deshtusa	*Literally:* Foolish words.
Milchama (pl: milchamos)	War, wars.
Minchah	The afternoon prayers.
Minyan	A quorum of at least 10 men required for Jewish communal prayers.
Mishlei	The Book of Proverbs.
Mishnayos	Plural of *Mishna*. Refers to the Tannaic statements that are part of the Oral Torah.
Mitzvah	(plural: *mitzvos*) Commandment(s), good deeds.
Moach	Mind, intellect.
Moranu	*Literally:* Our teacher.
Moshav (pl: Moshavim)	Often secular, collective farms in Israel.
Moshiach	The Messiah, Jewish redeemer.

Motzoei Shabbos	The night after Shabbos has ended, Saturday night after nightfall.
Mumar	An apostate Jew.
Mussar	Jewish ethics; the practice of improving character traits through self-discipline.
Nachat Ruach	A pleasantness of spirit.
Nahafoch hu	*Literally:* It was overturned / turned around for the good.
Navi	Prophet.
Ne'ilah	The final prayer service on Yom Kippur.
Neshamah	The Divine soul.
Netz	Sunrise.
Netzach	Eternity.
Noam Elimelech	Rabbi Elimelech of Lizhensk.
Nukva	The female side (a kabbalistic term).
Ohr HaChayim	A work authored by Rabbi Chayim ben Moshe ben Attar.
Orchot Tzaddikim	An anonymously-authored work on Jewish ethics.
Ovdei Hashem (also *'ovdim*)	*Literally:* Hashem's workers, people who are continually engaged in mitzvos, prayer and learning Torah.
P'gam HaBris	*Literally:* A blemish in the covenant. Refers to physical immorality.
Para Adumah	The red cow that was burnt in order to purify the Jewish people.
Parshah	Refers to the Torah portion for each week.
Parnassah	Livelihood.
Pashut	Simple, in all simplicity.
Pasul	Halachically invalid / not kosher.
Payos	Side-curls.
Perek	Chapter.

Pidyon HaKlali	The general redemption payment which sweetens all the judgments over a person. *Pidyon HaKollel:*
Pidyon Nefesh	A redemption of the soul (a payment made to a Tzaddik that is used to redeem the person's soul from where it is trapped).
Pirkei Avos	Ethics of our Fathers - a collection of aphorisms from Chazal.
Poskim	Halachic decisors. A *psak* is a halachic decision or ruling.
Protekzia	Influence, nepotism (often a by-product of endemic corruption).
Prutah	A coin of very low value.
Rabbenu	Rabbi Nachman of Breslov (but also means 'our teacher' when used in reference to other Rabbis).
Rambam	Rabbi Moshe ben Maimon (aka Maimonides).
Rasha	Evil-doer.
Rashbi	Rabbi Shimon Bar Yochai.
Rashi	*Rabbi Shlomo Yitzhaki.*
Ratzon	Will or desire.
Refaeinu	The fourth blessing in the Shemoneh Esreh prayer, said for healing.
Refuah sheleimah	*Literally:* A complete recovery, or healing.
Ribono Shel Olam	*Literally:* Master of the World. Another term for God.
Rishonim	The early Torah commentators.
Ritva	Rabbi Yom Tov ben Avraham Asevilli.
Rosh Yeshiva	The head Rabbi of a yeshiva.
Ruach Hakodesh	Divine intuition.
Ruchniyus	Spirituality, spiritual matters.

Samech Mem	Refers to the head of the forces of evil.
Sandak	An honorable position given at a bris, refers to the person who holds the baby.
Sanhedrin	The highest Jewish court of 71 rabbis (which hasn't operated since the Temple was destroyed.)
Seder HaYom	A work authored by Rabbi Moshe Ben Yehuda Makhir.
Sefer HaMiddos	The Book of Traits, authored by Rebbe Nachman of Breslov.
Sefer HaTemunah	A kabbalistic text written in the 13–14th century.
Sefira (pl: sefirot)	A kabbalistic world.
Seforim	Holy Jewish books.
Segulah	A practice which results in a spiritual or material benefit, which is not logically derived.
Seichel	Wisdom, intellect, brains.
Seraph	A type of angel.
Seudah shlishis	The third Shabbos meal.
Sfas Emes	A work authored by Rabbi Yehudah Aryeh Leib Alter.
Sha'ar HaKavanos	A work authored by the Arizal.
Sha'arei Teshuva	A work authored by Rabenu Yonah of Gerondi.
Shabbos	The day of rest of the Jews, beginning Friday night and lasting all day Saturday.
Shacharis	The morning prayers.
Shalom Bayis	*Literally:* Peace in the home. Marital peace.
Shamash	Attendant.
Shamayim	Heaven.
Shavuos	The Feast of Weeks.

Shechinah	The Divine Presence in this world.
Shefa	Bounty.
Sheker	Lies, untruths.
Shemittah	The seventh year of a seven year cycle, in which the land is left unworked.
Shemoneh Esrei	The central prayer, consisting of 19 blessings, that is said three times a day.
Sheva Brachos	The seven blessings that are recited for a newly-married Jewish couple on each of the first seven days after their wedding.
Shidduch (pl: shidduchim)	Marital match, a date with a view to getting married.
Shira	Song.
Shiur	Torah class or lesson.
Shivchei HaRan	Another biography of Rebbe Nachman of Breslov.
Shliach Tzibbur	The one leading the prayer service.
Shlichus	Going out to do outreach, some other mitzvah.
Shlita	An honorific term appended to the name of holy men during their lifetime.
Shmiras Einayim	*Literally:* Guarding the eyes. Refers to the mitzvah of not looking at immoral, spiritually damaging things.
Shtreimel	A round fur hat typically worn by chassidim on Shabbos, festivals and to other communal celebrations.
Shulchan Aruch	The Code of Jewish Law, elucidated by Rabbi Yosef Caro.
Shushan Purim	The day Purim is celebrated in 'walled cities', on the 15th of Adar.
Sichos HaRan	Conversations of Rebbe Nachman.

Siddur	A Jewish prayer book.
Simchah (pl: simchas)	Happiness. Also used to refer to a happy occasion like a wedding, for example.
Simchas Torah	Jewish festival celebrating the giving of the Torah.
Sinas Chinam	Baseless hatred.
Sipurei Ma'asiot	Rebbe Nachman's Stories, a collection of highly mystical kabbalistic tales.
Sitra Achra	*Literally:* 'The other side'. The dark side or source of negative spiritual forces, also an aspect of the yetzer hara.
Siyatta dishmaya	Heavenly help, Divine providence.
Smicha	The process of conferring rabbinic status on an individual.
Sofer Stam	The practice of writing mezuzahs, sefer Torahs and other holy texts. (Also called 'safrus'.)
Succos	The Festival of Tabernacles.
Sugya (pl: sugyos)	The section of Torah being learnt, usually refers to Gemara.
Sulam	A kabbalistic work by Rabbi Yehuda Ashlag.
Tachanun	Supplicatory prayers said after the Shemoneh Esrei service.
Tallis	Four-cornered prayer shawl.
Talmid Chacham	A wise Torah student.
Tanach	The acronym of **T**orah, **N**evi'im and **K**tuvim, i.e. Torah, Prophets and the Writings.
Tannaim	The early Torah sages from the time of the Talmud.

Targum Yonasan	The official Babylonian, Aramaic translation to the Prophets.
Techiyas HaMeisim	The revival of the dead, that will happen in the times of Moshiach.
Tefach (pl: tefachim)	A biblical unit of measurement, approximately 8-10 centimeters.
Tefillin	Black boxes containing holy texts that are worn on the arm and the forehead.
Tehillim	Psalms.
Teshuva	Repentance.
Teshuvos	Responses to halachic questions.
Tikkun	(plural: tikkunim) Spiritual rectification. *Tikkun Olam* – rectification of the world. *Tikkun Chatzos* – Midnight prayer, said to rectify / lament the destruction of the Temple.
Tikkun HaKlali	*Literally:* The General Rectification. The Ten Psalms (numbers: 16, 32, 41, 42, 59, 77, 90, 105, 137, 150) prescribed by Rebbe Nachman as a powerful spiritual remedy.
Tinok she nishba	A baby who is kidnapped from its parents and doesn't know its Jewish roots.
Tisha b'av	The ninth of Av, the date on which we remember the destruction of the Beit HaMikdash.
Tohu v'vohu	*Literally:* Chaos and emptiness.
Toivel	To immerse in a mikvah.
Toldos Aharon	A work authored by Rabbi Aharon of Zhitomir.
Tosafos	One of the more famous groups of commentators on the Gemara, dating from approximately the 12th century.

Tumah	Spiritual impurity.
Tur	See: Baal HaTurim.
Tzaddik	(plural: *Tzaddikim*, feminine: *Tzaddekes*), The righteous one.
Tzaddik Yesod Olam	*Literally:* The Tzaddik, the foundation of the world.
Tzar'as	Sorrow, sufferings.
Tzedakah	Charity.
Tzelem Elokim	The image of G-d
Tzitzis	A four cornered garment normally worn by Jewish men under their clothes, with fringes / strings at each corner.
Tziyun	The grave of a Tzaddik, e.g. Rebbe Nachman's grave.
Uman	City in the Ukraine where Rebbe Nachman of Breslov is buried.
Urim and Turim	The stones on the High Priest's breastplate that lit up to answer questions.
Vasikin	Dawn minyan.
Vilna Gaon	Rabbi Eliyahu ben Shlomo Zalman of Vilna.
Yam Suf	The Sea of Reeds.
Yarden	The River Jordan.
Yehudi HaKadosh	Rabbi Yaakov Yitzchak of Pesicha, aka 'the Holy Jew'.
Yeoush	Despair.
Yeshiva	Religious Jewish institution for learning Torah.
Yesod	Foundation.
Yetzer Hara	The evil inclination.
Yetzira	The world of formation – one of the four kabbalistic worlds.

Yichus	Genealogy, especially referring to notable or famous ancestors.
Yirah; Yiras Shemayim	Fear of Heaven.
Yishuv HaDaas	A settled mind.
Yom HaAtzmaut	Israel's Independence Day.
Yom Kippur	Annual day of fasting and atonement.
Yom Tov	Jewish festival day.
Yoreh Deah	One of the four orders of the Shulchan Aruch.
Zechus (also Zocheh)	Merit, to merit.
Zemiros	Jewish songs, usually containing biblical verses, that are typically sung on Shabbos, and on other Jewish festivals and happy occasions.
Zer Anpin	One of the kabbalistic *partzufim*.
Zman	Period of time.
Zt"l	Stands for: **Z**ichron **H**a**T**zaddik **L**evracha: *Literally:* May the tzaddik's memory be for a blessing.

ADDITIONAL RESOURCES

If you would like to learn more about Rabbi Eliezer Berland, you can read **One in a Generation Volumes I and II,** which contain hundreds of hours of interviews, stories and first-hand sources about who he really is.

There are many additional books available in both Hebrew and English, including collections of Rabbi Berland's Torah lessons, miraculous stories of the people he's helped and compendiums of his advice and prayers. A good place to start is the **www.ravberland.com** bookstore, which you can access here:

https://ravberland.com/product-category/english-books/

LEARN MORE ABOUT RAV ELIEZER BERLAND AND SHUVU BANIM

For the latest news and updates in English about Rabbi Eliezer Berland and Shuvu Banim, please visit our website at:

www.ravberland.com

You can also listen to real-time updates, announcements, and stories in Hebrew by calling the Shuvu Banim hotline.

THE SHUVU BANIM HOTLINE:

In Israel, please call:	*9148 or 02-800-8800
In the USA, please call:	845-640-0007
In the UK and Europe, please call:	+44-203-807-3333

If you would like to send a name for a blessing from Rav Berland, or for any general information or queries please contact us at: <u>ravberland.com/contact</u>

To make a *pidyon nefesh* please visit: <u>ravberland.com/pidyon-nefesh</u>

Made in the USA
Middletown, DE
15 February 2021